Married to Africa

A Love Story

G. PASCAL ZACHARY

SCRIBNER

NEW YORK   LONDON   TORONTO   SYDNEY

SCRIBNER
A Division of Simon & Schuster, Inc.
1230 Avenue of the Americas
New York, NY 10020

First Scribner hardcover edition January 2009

SCRIBNER and design are registered trademarks of The Gale Group, Inc.,
used under license by Simon & Schuster, Inc., the publisher of this work.

For information about special discounts for bulk purchases,
please contact Simon & Schuster Special Sales at
1-800-456-6798 or business@simonandschuster.com.

Designed by Kyoko Watanabe

Manufactured in the United States of America

1 3 5 7 9 10 8 6 4 2

Library of Congress Control Number: 2008010607

ISBN-13: 978-1-4165-3463-1
ISBN-10: 1-4165-3463-6

In memory of Michael Zachary (1928–2004)

I was drawn to the heart of Africa by a song.

—Louis Sarno

Contents

CONTENTS

PART ONE

Lake Tahoe, San Luis Obispo, Berkeley, Portland

2003–2004

As we walked up the steps of City Hall in San Francisco to apply for our marriage license, Chizo asked me, "Is it only when whites and blacks marry that the government makes you get a license?"

We were married in November 2003 on a rooftop in San Francisco, surrounded by fifteen friends. The day was clear and the sky was blue. We were in the Haight-Ashbury neighborhood, and a breeze blew in from the ocean, making hats hard to keep on. Chizo had arrived in America only three weeks before and everyone was a stranger to her, except for the two Africans, both of whom she had met in Africa. Chizo's mother and father, as well as her siblings, were home in Nigeria, unable to obtain travel visas to America. She was marrying for the first time, I for the second. My two children from my first marriage joined us, my son, Liam, as my best man. Chizo was given away by a prominent Nigerian journalist from her home city of Port Harcourt.

A close friend of mine got a quickie minister's credential and presided over a secular ceremony. He remarked on Chizo's quiet dignity. We each wore white Nigerian lace: long flowing robes that made us look like angels. Chizo wore a pink head scarf, puffed into the shape of a crown, and long braids dangled alongside her face.

There was a glitch. I'd forgotten Chizo's new pink shoes. They were still at our house, across the bay, in Berkeley. Chizo refused to begin the ceremony without the shoes. When I asked if we could marry barefoot, *offering to remove my own shoes, she grew impatient. "I have no family here, and you want me to go without my shoes?" I withdrew my suggestion, and our guests waited while a friend drove over the East Bay bridge to collect the shoes.*

After the ceremony, along with the wedding cake, Chizo served bowls of pepper soup and plates of pounded yam, staples from her Igbo heritage of spicy foods. I led a champagne toast and, afterward, introduced everyone to Osita Osadebe, a Nigerian bandleader and singer whose highlife music was a kind of sound track to our love affair. Chizo broke into a special dance and for a time I danced near her, until my daughter, Oona, pulled me away and then we watched Chizo dance alone.

We didn't take a honeymoon because our honeymoon happened in West Africa, where we met, fell in love, kept a house, held various jobs, traveled and hatched a plan to come to America. In the United States we made a new life, confronted challenges, improvised solutions. In time we came to realize that no matter what happened in America, we could never leave Africa behind.

We are married to Africa, each in our own way. This is our story.

Chapter One

Winter Loves Her

Listening to my tales of youthful winters in New York did not prepare Chizo for her first encounter with intense cold. We are in the Sierra Nevada, walking on the edge of Lake Tahoe, the south end, on the border of California and Nevada, with all those tacky hotels and casinos. It is January and the snow is heavy. Chizo wears a pair of brown sheepskin boots and thick socks. Her feet are still cold. Her eyes peek out of a furry hood, her petite body encased in a wool sweater, a down jacket and an ankle-length coat. We are holding hands, as well as two people wearing thick gloves can.

I lead her out onto the frozen lake, explaining that there is water underneath this ice, telling her that in spring the lake thaws and becomes flowing water again. I tell her how, as a boy, I skated on a frozen lake. I tell her how people fish on frozen lakes, cutting holes into the ice, sending down their hooks. I tell her how the surface of a frozen lake can sometimes crack without warning, swallowing up anyone standing on the surface. I tell her we need not be worried now because it is too cold for the ice to crack.

We move farther onto the hard ice, farther from the safety of the shore.

My wife does not believe there is water underneath the ice, and I cannot convince her. I am accustomed to her skepticism after more than a year in America together. In West Africa, where we met and fell in love, our life together seemed solid. When I faced something

I didn't understand, she was there to help guide me. I owe her. For a long time in West Africa, she was my talking dictionary, a walking omnibus of cultural knowledge, my own personal Africa encyclopedia. She was not bashful either, often intervening to stop me from making a grievous mistake in my dealings with Africans. Chizo's cultural knowledge was part of her appeal to me because, without a trusted guide in a foreign land, a visitor can be lost. In exchange for her help, I felt an obligation to comprehend the ways of her people, as best I could, treating what I didn't understand with respect and sympathy, at least at first.

Chizo does not always display a similar tolerant attitude toward others, not in America anyway. Here I am not her talking dictionary. I am not her encyclopedia of America. When my country bewilders her, her first reaction is to question the sanity of Americans, just as she now questions whether we actually are walking on a sheet of ice or I am playing a trick on her.

"There is no lake here," she insists. "Don't lie to me. We walk on land, you trickish devil."

I do not lightly listen to Chizo invoke the devil. I answer by retreating from the ice, moving us back onto the lakeside, where there is solid ground beneath the hard snow. The sound of snow crunching under our feet makes Chizo smile. Her eyes light up. Her full lips are red and wet. Her dark skin is luminous even in the cold.

I reach down for a handful of snow, retreating from Chizo until I reach a suitable firing distance of about fifteen feet. Then I throw a snowball at her. I strike her leg and throw again, barely missing her head. The next one hits her in the chest. She bends down and tosses a ball of snow at me, the first snowball of her life. She misses me. I bend, grab snow and throw back, hitting her. Keeping my distance, I toss again, only now Chizo charges at me, on the attack, hitting me with snow, high and low, coming closer, until she is right on top of me and the snow is flying.

I am frozen in place, my feet sunk deep into the snow. I am defenseless. I cry for mercy and she ignores me, laughing. "This is your snow," she says. "I have mastered it more than you."

From a few feet away, she throws snowballs into my face. I am close enough to see the thrill in her eyes. The snowballs batter me and I sink to the cold ground, surrendering. Now I regret ever starting this snowball fight. To protect my face, I curl up in the fetal position. The snow rains on my back. Chizo is triumphant. "I am master of your American snow," she cries.

I laugh out even though I am angry over the pummeling I've received. Chizo is too fast, too powerful for me. I have learned not to roughhouse with her, but on this snow-covered ground, in the middle of winter, I felt emboldened to challenge her. She proved me to be foolish. I rise to my feet and snap a picture of her, standing tall, an African in winter, her first time seeing snow and already the queen of it.

She brushes the snow from my face and beard. I start to complain and she kisses me. "You made good on your promise," she says, reminding me how in Africa I promised to show her snow someday.

I am reminded now why I risked spoiling our love affair by bringing her to America: why we decided to endure the inevitable misunderstandings and cultural collisions that occur between two people who grew up in completely different places and who remain, no matter the intensity of our shared feelings, such strangers to one another that marriage is at times one long cultural trip wire that we keep setting off.

I decided to endure all of this so she could experience snow.

We walk up the hill to where people are sledding. The hill crests at about two hundred feet and slopes down to the lakeside, making a perfect spot for sledding. The air is still, the sky is clear. We can see for miles across the lake and to the mountains in the distance. Below us people are sledding. We watch them for some time until Chizo decides to borrow a plastic sled from another visitor. The sled is circular, the size of a garbage-pail top. Chizo sits inside the top and steadies herself. She looks down the slope and out onto the frozen lake. I hold the edge of her sled, steadying her. About a dozen people are sledding now, stretched out across some fifty yards. She waits for the people on either side of her to launch and then finish their rides. Then she says she is ready and I gently push her sled and she flies off, screaming as she barrels down the slope.

Midway to the bottom, she steers past a rock, then soars into the air, coming down hard. She's still in the sled, still hurtling downhill. I'm relieved and let out a breath. I try to capture her with my camera but she is too far away even for my zoom. I can see only the bundle of her clothing. She glides another thirty feet, slowing, slowing, then stops.

When she gets to her feet she waves to me. She returns to the top of the hill and sleds down again. She avoids the rocks once more, reaching the bottom still on the sled, her journey drawing to a close. After three more trips, she returns the sled to its owner and waits to borrow another. The next sled is as long as her body and has a short rope with which to steer. She looks like she's in a bathtub and her ride this time is more impressive. Cutting sharply over the snow, she spills from the sled halfway down and climbs back to the top, wanting to try again. The next time, she gets all the way down the slope, riding like an experienced sledder. Watching her performance, I am proud of her. She is a natural, a marvel, a force of nature. When she returns to the top, she says, "I love winter."

And winter loves her.

We retreat to our motel room, gaining relief from the cold. Outside our door, long icicles hang from the roof, and I go out and crack off two of them and return to the room. I hold the icicles like daggers while Chizo stands next to the wall heater, naked, warming herself. I run one of the icicles along the hollow of her back and then down her leg. She jumps and grabs one of the daggers. As I kiss the back of her elegant neck, she pretends to plunge the icicle into my side. We have a series of brief icicle fights, the ending always the same: Chizo stabs me.

I hand her my icicle, flip on the TV and begin to watch an NFL playoff game. Chizo can't stop talking about sledding, and I mute the TV and listen to her.

"It's scary," she says. "Oh god. It's scary, horrible. Unless you are a man with a heart, like people who go to war. They don't care about death and life. That's how it looks to me. Oh god. It looks like I'm facing dead. Talk less of when you are seeing those holes. Your mind is flying. It's like seeing a big accident face-to-face. You're dying in that moment."

She pauses, turning away from the heater, warming her back while staring at me. "I screamed to help me strong my heart," she says. "I can't be quiet, because I feel I'm facing my dying. I feel a giant of ice is ready to swallow me."

When she's finished describing her experience sledding, she pronounces the name "Tahoe" with her Nigerian accent, turning one word into two, as if she is saying "Ta" and "Hoe." I am always unconsciously translating her brand of English into my brand of English; the task is second nature to me now, so that I'm usually surprised when people tell me they struggle at first to understand Chizo's English. I no longer do. Her words have a certain poetry to me and I take delight in listening to her speak.

She asks me to get more icicles and I find even longer ones this time, so long that Chizo asks how they are formed. Having not lived in wintry climates for many years, I am fuzzy on the details. "Icicles are a mystery to me," I say. "Just enjoy them."

I go back to watching the football game. I lie in bed, facing the TV. She lies down next to me, curling up against my body. We are both under the covers now. She has yet to figure out the rules of football; though the game makes no sense to her, she doesn't object to me watching. The TV is turned down low, and she whispers in my ear, "You are my everything and I am your everything." She draws me closer. "What you want is what I want," she says. "What I want is what you want."

These last two sentences, simple yet seductive, are Chizo's romantic mantra, as much of a philosophy of marriage as she ever expresses. Since we fell in love in Africa, she's repeated these lines as if they represent an ontological position. An incantation, these words are a love potion. I am smitten all over again.

I tell Chizo I am surprised how natural she is on a sled and how much she enjoys the cold weather. "I am master of your winter," she says, "even more than you." I watch a long pass play and shout as the ball is nearly intercepted. Then I jump up. Chizo has placed one of the icicles between my legs. I push away the icicle and sigh.

"You are my king," she whispers.

Her words warm me. Flush from her triumph on the sledding track, holding her curious icicles, Chizo is spreading her joy.

I switch the TV to another channel. It is two days before Martin Luther King's holiday and I toggle between the football game and a documentary on King's life. I am always trying to expose Chizo to the history of the civil rights movement, which she barely knows about because she was born in Africa, not America, and in 1971 (three years after King's death). I want her to learn more about the struggle by African-Americans for justice and what we white Americans call race relations. She does not always draw the expected conclusions from these lessons. We are watching King deliver his famous "I Have a Dream" speech. He speaks of a future America where people will be judged not by the color of their skin but by the content of their character. Tears are coming to my eyes. I think King's dream is wonderful and I say so.

Chizo then tells me her dream. "My dream," she declares, "is someday blacks will take over. Then whites will be begging blacks for everything."

I am stunned, breathless. Our eyes meet. I pull her body closer, then release her, breathing again. I find a certain logic in Chizo's dream. This is not the first time I have heard her speak of her desire for blacks to take revenge on whites. I can understand why some blacks resent whites and want to keep to themselves. I can even understand why they might want to punish whites. Yet I am an advocate of integration, and I remind Chizo that Martin Luther King, Jr., helped make it possible for her and me to live together safely in America—to live together, walk the streets and travel the nation—without fear of arrest, violence or even blatant discrimination.

I ask her if she favors King's vision of integration, of unrestricted mingling between blacks and whites.

"I do, but white people don't want it," she says. "We blacks want it. But whites don't."

"I want it," I say.

I am an exception. She says that whites cannot imagine the experience of blacks under slavery (in America) and colonialism (in Africa) and that integration will be possible only after whites themselves suffer in a similar way. "Someday blacks will rule the way whites rule today," she says. "After that blacks and whites will rule together."

I am silent now, thinking of what to say, wondering whether, at least on a personal level, Chizo and I are ruling together, or whether I am ruling her or she is ruling me. Which phase are we in? I hear King talking again, in his marvelous voice. His words bring more tears to my eyes.

"Stop crying," Chizo insists. "Since the creation of the world, white people have ruled. God gave whites the power."

Her words deliver me from my reverie. I stop crying. I ask her why God would favor one race over another.

"Because God is white."

"God is not white," I say. "If there is a God," and I emphasize the word "if," "he can't have a race. He must be beyond racial category, neither black nor white nor any other skin color."

My words fill the room because I am now shouting. King is gone from the screen, the football game is back and I strain to hear Chizo say, "From the time I was born, I thought God was white."

"Did the priests tell you that?"

"No one told me God is white. I got the idea on my own. What else could God be?"

Chizo was raised Catholic in Nigeria and her own African priests were trained by white priests, mainly from Ireland.

* * *

I tell Chizo that God might not be white after all. He might be black. Then I say I hope God is black because whites can learn something from worshiping a black God.

Chizo looks unhappy. She isn't ready to accept the idea of a black God.

I watch the football game. My team is winning. I am happy for the diversion.

Chizo gets out of bed, lingers in front of the heater, then steps away and stands in front of the TV. Imitating me talking, she says, "I am an atheist, I don't believe in God."

Then she switches into her Nigerian voice and says, "By force, I will make my husband believe in God."

The next morning we are back sledding near the lake. Now we have our own sled, a round black hard-plastic bowl that we bought the night before. Chizo flies down the hill, many times. I am tempted to do the same. I am older than Chizo, and my body is not as elastic as hers. I am afraid of hurting my back on the way down.

Chizo insists I must sled down the hill.

I do what she says.

She holds the sled while I prepare myself. The snow is packed hard on the hill, so that the surface is like a sheet of ice, which is why the sleds are moving so fast. The speed of the sled makes collision with the rocks, partly submerged downhill, dangerous. I want to avoid the rocks. I want to avoid flipping. I want to avoid embarrassing myself.

"Don't be afraid," Chizo says. "Don't rush. Go slow."

She is always telling me to slow down. When we first met, she called me "the rushing man." For weeks I thought she was calling me "Russian man." I kept reminding her that I'm an American, not Russian. She knew this and yet the nickname persisted. Then one day she got so frustrated with my impatience that she clearly pronounced the words "rushing man" and I understood my nick-name for the first time. Now I always think of the importance of slowing down, though at this moment I don't understand how I can go slow while sledding downhill. Before I puzzle out an approach, she pushes my sled from the landing and down I go.

I am hurtling toward the lake now. I keep my head up, look-ing out, watching for rocks, the glare penetrating my cheap sun-glasses, making it hard to see. I take a breath, steer past a big rock, then glide past another. I let out a breath, starting to relax. My sled slows, then stops, and I believe for the first time that I am out of danger. Lying on my back in the hard snow, I look up the hill and see Chizo cheering for me. I wave. I've completed the first sledding voyage of my life and I want to try again.

I make two more trips—without hurting myself—then give the sled back to Chizo. I watch her sled again. As she prepares for her final run, a man cries out halfway down the hill. I watched him hit a rock and tumble onto the ground and scream. I thought he was joking. Now he is still screaming. He speaks with an Indian accent and I think he's a tourist, maybe someone who has never played on ice before.

He can't move. I fear he is paralyzed or has a broken back.

Chizo's path is clear and she takes her last run down the hill. Another good run for her. By the time she climbs back up the hill, an ambulance has arrived. Two men with a stretcher and another guy are tending to the injured man. He still isn't moving. Chizo grabs my hand. She takes us closer to the injured man, so close that before I realize what she's done we are peering over the shoulders of the emergency workers. Surely we are violating the etiquette covering emergencies.

I grab Chizo's arm and tell her we must keep our distance and let the professionals handle the situation. She gets angry with me, accuses me of callousness. "You Americans and your rules," she says. "You are cruel."

I explain that her involvement could worsen the situation, even pose risks for the injured man, but she's left me by then, moving past the emergency workers and out of my sight, probably getting close to the injured man, maybe touching him or telling him something.

I cannot see her now and feel afraid. Suddenly, I see her running. One of the emergency workers is chasing her up the hill, toward me, shouting, "Keep out of our way! Stay back!"

I approach Chizo and she looks stricken. "I told him to pray, that's all," she says. Then she starts complaining about American rules, her voice loud, attracting the notice of the gathering crowd. I am embarrassed and I wonder, Do I claim her now, in front of all of these people?

I go over to her, draping my arm around her shoulders. We move carefully up the icy hill, the lake at our backs now, and the onlookers too. At times like this, I wonder how I ended up marrying an African, even one as compelling as Chizo.

We return to our car and I am ready to drive away, back to the motel and then on to Berkeley, where we live. "Go back," Chizo says. "Follow the ambulance. I want to find out what happens to him."

I refuse. I tell her we will only get in the way. I tell her that the injured man's family will surely be waiting for him, rooting for the best. I tell her that in America we let the professionals do their jobs. "We're not needed," I say, "and it's time for us to go."

On the long ride home, Chizo does not speak for hours and I think next time I will follow the ambulance.

Chapter Two

Crazy for Crabs

"Drive faster!"

I hit the accelerator harder, Chizo sitting next to me, smiling, her head cocked sideways so she can see the speedometer.

"Faster! Faster!" she says.

Her voice is urgent and seductive, as if she is singing a love poem into my ear. Oh, how I want to please her! I push the pedal again, loving her with the accelerator. Gripping the wheel, I take the car past seventy-five miles per hour and, in the pounding rain, hold hard to the road. My worn-out wipers blurring the windshield, I can barely see through the darkness and fog and wind and rain.

We are heading south on Highway 101, slicing through the coast of central California, on our way to Avila Beach, a small town with a pretty harbor, a cute boardwalk and the state's only nuclear power plant. We are taking our first romantic weekend getaway since we arrived in America. Chizo wears an Adidas workout suit, a light blue one that clings to her skin and shows off her petite figure. She chews on honey-roasted peanuts, her eyes shifting back and forth from the road to the speedometer. She slides a tape into the player and the voice of Daddy Lumba, a pop star from Ghana, comes on. He's singing his hit song "Dangerous."

"Too slow," she says over the music. "Follow the Lexus. Fast!"

I kick the pedal again, trying to follow the SUV that's just blown by me.

"He's going eighty," I say. "Too fast for me."

Chizo chews peanuts and lowers the volume on the Daddy Lumba tape.

"Chase him," she says. "Are you not a human being? Is not the driver of the Lexus a human being? If he can go faster, you can too."

I tell Chizo that driving above the speed limit, late at night, in the pounding rain, in the face of a blinding fog, is unsafe, danger-ous, dumb and reckless. I tell her the other driver has a stronger car than I do. I tell her I have never driven so fast, so far in my life, and that includes driving in lengthy periods of perfect weather. I tell her to please, please, please, permit me to drive slower.

She won't let me. "You talk too much," she says and boosts the volume on Daddy Lumba.

I listen to Lumba, Ghana's king of highlife, instead of fighting. He is singing about dangerous girls and dangerous boys, young Africans taking risks, conquering fears or simply never feeling fear in the first place. How appropriate is this song. I feel fear now, wondering whether I am driving too fast on this winding, slick road, drenched in darkness and fog. I strain to see the lights of the Lexus racing in front of me. I cannot see the body of the car, only the lights. I try to keep pace with these lights, then I see nothing as the road bends to the left. I ease into the curve, tapping the brake, slowing my car, the speedometer arrow dipping momentar-ily below sixty, a speed smack in my comfort zone.

Not Chizo's zone. She pokes me in the shoulder. "Be a man!" she says. "Go faster. You drive like old person. Are you trying to funny me?"

I laugh. I take delight in Chizo's English. She and I are still not accustomed to sitting together in the front seat of a car. In Africa, I never drove. I always hired a driver or caught a taxi. Chizo and I sat in the backseat. She never saw me behind a wheel. Not even once. I am not an enthusiastic driver anyway and, honestly, I don't enjoy driving. I prefer being driven around. In Africa, when I hired a taxi or a driver for a day or a week or even a month, I never missed driving. I wish I had a driver in America. I'd be able to enjoy the ride, think about what I'm doing next and not worry about how I'll get where I'm going.

There were other benefits too. In Africa, we would sit in the backseat of a car, hold hands, kiss and cuddle one another. At times, we would find common ground by complaining about the driver or the conditions of the road or the car or both. In Accra, Chizo knew the streets, many of which are unmarked, better than most drivers, so she often commanded the driver. "Take by your right," she would say. "Now take by your left." She had a store-house of shortcuts that would give pride to any professional driver. Even our regular driver, a genial, intelligent man named Stephen Kobina, appreciated Chizo's road know-how and cool under duress. He came to adore her so much that he called her "Auntie," a term of endearment in Ghana.

In America, there is no Stephen, there is only me. I drive out of necessity, and often badly, in Chizo's view. I make wrong turns, miss obvious parking spaces and know no shortcuts. Worse, I fail to pro-vide a vehicle that is commensurate with my wife's sense of self. I drive a 1993 Volvo station wagon. Chizo calls this ten-year-old vehi-cle my "crap car" and repeatedly asks when we will buy a new one.

I owned the car before I met Chizo in Africa, and when we came to Berkeley, the old Volvo was waiting for us. Volvos are popular in Berkeley, even old ones. In Berkeley, there are actually more Volvos per capita than anywhere else in the United States. Mine is a safe, sensible family car and, while aged, runs fine. Even in dry weather, in the brightness of the day, however, the Volvo handles poorly. To compensate, I tend to take curves slowly, staying off the brake, letting the car, with its puny four-cylinder engine, benefit from my restraint. Impatient with my caution, Chizo has decided that tonight, no matter how hard the rain or dense the fog, she will show me the advantage of keeping pace with the speeders.

Chizo doesn't drive herself. In Africa, only the wealthy or the well connected know how to operate a car, and Chizo qualifies as neither. Most people don't have cars in Africa anyway, so a driver's license is considered either a novelty or gratuitous. And a license is even more rare among women than among men. In cities, women take taxis or a variety of buses or they simply walk. In America, Chizo wants to drive. She is studying the California's driver handbook so she can pass the written test and get behind the wheel, at least accompanied by a legal driver. The test is rigorous. If she gets more than six wrong answers, out of twenty-five questions, she fails.

Chizo actually didn't study at all before she took the test for the first time. She was under the impression (she told me later, when the whole story came out) that she didn't need to. She went to the test with a fifty-dollar bill and when she finished guessing at the answers, she handed in the two-sided test paper to the woman in charge. Then she gave the woman the fifty-dollar bill.

Chizo stood quietly and waited for the woman, seated behind a counter, to give her a learner's permit, which would allow her to practice behind the wheel of a car.

"What's the fifty for?" the woman asked.

"For my learner's permit," Chizo said.

"You can't buy it," the woman snapped.

"Are you sure?" Chizo asked. "Other people do."

"We wouldn't call it a test if you could pass by paying."

"That's why I am giving you bribe," Chizo replied. "You don't take bribe?"

The woman stood up from her chair and came out from behind her desk. "You see that camera?" she asked, pointing at a corner of the ceiling. "You're being filmed right now."

"You are spying on me. You are filming me. Oh, American people. They are trickish."

"Say what?" the woman asked.

Chizo pointed at the ceiling. "That little black something is a camera?" she asked. "Are you sure?"

She is pleading, yet certain the woman is teasing her.

"No joke," the woman says. The little black thing is a camera.

"Can't you erase the pictures? No one will know you've taken the money."

"I'm not grading your test," the woman huffed. Then she tore Chizo's test into tiny pieces, dropping them in a garbage pail.

Chizo later told me she wanted to grab the pieces and paste them back together.

"Go home and study the book," the woman told her.

"You canceled my test."

"You failed," the woman said. "You're lucky I'm letting you take the test again."

Chizo didn't consider herself lucky. "You canceled my test," she repeated. "I've been canceled."

The woman motioned to a security man. An older black man came over to Chizo and gently took her arm. He told her she was indeed lucky. Chizo let him walk her out of the testing room and into the main lobby of the DMV building.

She felt ashamed. He picked up a driving manual and gave it to her.

"I have one," she said.

"Take another one anyway," he told her. "They're free."

She took one and left.

Chizo kept the experience a secret. About a month later, she told me the story.

"Did I do terrible?" she asked.

"You made a mistake. You don't bribe people in America," I said. "Please, don't try again."

She agreed, then cried out, "Are there no fast-fast ways of getting what you want in America?"

Driving eighty miles per hour, I'm burning gas faster than I expect. At the King City exit, I pull off the highway and stop at a gas station. Chizo runs inside the shop for a bottle of water while I fill up the Volvo. Only when I'm back on the entrance ramp to the highway do I realize I've left the gas cap at the station. I pull the car to the shoulder of the road, put on the flashing lights, set the parking brake and tell Chizo I need to return for the gas cap.

She comes with me. The rain is slowing now. I hold her close to me. We walk along the side of the highway, down the entrance ramp, cross a road and stop at the pump I used. The cap is on the pump. I don't know why I put it there.

"You happy," she says.

I am. Volvo gas caps are expensive. There's a fresh spring in my step and I don't mind the howling of the cars on the highway. There is no rain now, and the fog is lifting. We move up the entrance ramp, then onto the shoulder of the highway. I see the lights of my Volvo flashing ahead. I put on the gas cap, and get behind the wheel again and take off. I bring my speed to seventy-five quickly, comfortable that I can see far ahead of me now.

Chizo stays busy next to me, working the Africa tapes, playing the deejay for a West African music station that exists only in our private world. She plays Oumou Sangare, Kojo Antwi, Osadebe, the Oriental Brothers, Papa Shee, Franco, Tabu Ley, Toumani Diabate, Brenda Fassie, Commander Obey, Fela. There are dozens of tapes in the plastic bag at her feet. The music comes from all corners of Africa: Ghanaian highlife, Congolese *soukous,* the *mapouka* of Ivory Coast, Senegalese swing, Malian blues, Nigerian gospel and Afrobeat, Reggae from South Africa.

Each tape brings back memories, the music magically transporting us to Africa. I feel far away, the darkness of the road annihilating one reality and creating another. In an instant, I am seeing Chizo dancing for the first time, at the club Chester's in Accra, Ghana. Then we are together on Labadi Beach, riding horses south of Accra, the sea wind at our backs, the vast Atlantic stretching out all the way to New York. Suddenly, my memory visits another country, where a civil war is raging. I am in central Africa with a few local journalists in a van, and small children line the dirt road shouting how there are no land mines on the dirt road ahead. Then I recall our small house in Ghana. A whitewashed bungalow a mile from the ocean that Chizo called "our love palace." When the government agency made the electricity go off and the piped water stop flowing, Chizo would place candles around the house and silently visit the reservoir in our compound, returning with a full bucket of water on her head. She would dump the water into an even larger bucket in our kitchen. And later, she would heat the water so I could have a hot shower before going to bed. Sometimes, she would spoon the steaming water onto my body, creating the illusion that we had a house with a proper bathroom.

Alone with my memories of Africa, the time passes and I grow comfortable with driving fast. I am quiet, intent on driving, unaware of Chizo, until she selects a Brenda Fassie tape that ends my solitude. Brenda is singing "The Lord Is My Shepherd." I am mad for this song, even though I never worship the Lord and would sooner admit that Chizo herself is my shepherd. In Accra, Chizo often listened to this song in the mornings while she cooked break-fast, prepared the water for my shower, got herself dressed. Com-ing over the car stereo, "The Lord Is My Shepherd" is like an old friend visiting me after a long absence. Brenda's voice is strong and confident, and her beats are irresistible. I hear Chizo's voice singing along and I flash onto an image of her swirling around our house in Accra, the house on Kuku Hill. She's dancing with our Fante maid, gyrating elegantly while I tap on my computer keyboard.

I first heard Brenda, South Africa's supreme diva, sing in the middle of a civil war in Burundi. I was reporting on efforts by peace-makers to reduce strife between the country's two main ethnic groups. In Bujumbura, Burundi's nerve-racking capital, Brenda's hit song "Sum' Bulala" was playing everywhere, providing relief to those weary of war. Traveling into the bush in a small truck with some local journalists, I heard the song and couldn't forget it. We drove in the mountains that ring the city, looking for the headquar-ters of the army commander in charge of fighting the Hutu rebels. "Sum' Bulala" opens with the snapping of fingers, the strumming of a guitar and then Brenda's soaring, mesmerizing voice. Some men scat behind her as she repeats the title of the song, harmonizing to her melodies. I had no idea of the meaning of her words but her singing calmed my jangled nerves. The driver kept checking for land mines, calling out his window to children lining the road. The kids kept waving us on, saying, "No mines, no mines." I asked one of the reporters why they listen to the children. "They are more honest than the adults," she told me.

Most, if not all, of Brenda's tapes are bootleg copies. In African cities, her tapes—indeed, everybody's tapes—sell for about a dollar from street vendors. Even in the age of the iPod, tapes remain the most popular way for musicians to spread their work, because relatively few people have CD players. Chizo and I bought plenty of tapes, played them on the boom box in our house or on a small portable tape player that we took to the United States with us, a keepsake, since we never play the tapes except in the car.

Brenda is gone now, dead from AIDS and her hard-living ways. Peering out into the night, I cradle the steering wheel to the beat of Felix Liberty singing "Mandela." Liberty is a Nigerian singer whose voice is at once sweet and mournful. I sing along, urgently, clipping my words to match Liberty's distinctive accent.

"Nigeria, the giant of Africa," Chizo exults. "We are the Super Eagles." Her pride in her home country is always close to the surface. I watch Chizo imitate me shaking my head. I stop shaking my head and laugh nervously, unsure whether she is laughing with me or at me. Her imitations of my movements are startling in their authenticity, which depresses me. Do I really look this ridiculous when I move? I think I have plenty of rhythm (for a white person), but watching Chizo imitate me, I realize anew that I move to music like a man receiving a large jolt of electricity every few seconds.

Chizo won't stop imitating me and I find her movements painful to watch. "Where is Felix Liberty?" I ask, trying to get her to stop. "Is he still alive?"

She doesn't know.

"I wish we had a Felix Liberty CD," she says, petting my head.

So do I. The tape is disintegrating. We probably got a bad one. Or maybe all of the Liberty tapes are bad. Chizo bought another copy once in Lagos and that was bad too. Now we have two bad copies, both filled with pops and skips and other strange sounds. Liberty sounds great anyway, his voice proud and clear and certain.

We arrive around midnight. Chizo exults over how quickly we got here. I admit I am impressed too. We're staying at a small, precious hotel on a pier jutting into the Pacific just south of the university town of San Luis Obispo. I pull the car onto the pier, joining a half dozen cars on one side of the hotel.

The rain is coming down hard again and the sea air stops me like a wall. I run inside the hotel, without waiting for Chizo. I am, after all, "the rushing man," in Chizo's words. She is accustomed to me charging ahead, impatient. I find a young man at the check-in desk. He pulls up my reservation on the computer. All is well. He has a room for me. I slide him my Visa card and he glances at Chizo sauntering into the lobby, stepping lightly in her black-and-white Bebe shoes, looking like she owns the place. She is carrying a backpack and dragging a small rolling suitcase, making her grace seem effortless. She looks pretty too, her dreadlocks tied behind her head in a small bun, exposing her elegant neck. I resist the impulse to rush and kiss her.

The desk clerk looks past me and eyes Chizo suspiciously. "What do you want?" he asks her sharply. "We're sold out. No rooms left."

I curse to myself and regret not rushing over to her. The clerk is waiting for an answer. "She's with me," I say.

My words tumble out so fast they run into each other, and the clerk asks, "Are you together?"

I want to claim Chizo—to make it clear to this clerk that the black woman in the lobby is my wife—but I'm tired and I want my room key now. I don't like this guy either. I decide he doesn't deserve an explanation.

"She's with me," I repeat, slowly this time.

He looks at me, then at Chizo. She doesn't smile at him. She turns to me and says, loud enough for the clerk to hear, "I got soaking wet coming in from the car. What kind of rain is this? Is God angry at America?"

No rain the next morning. The sky is cloudless. We rise late, eat breakfast, stroll on the beach, then depart from the harbor on the afternoon whale-watching boat. I have a long history of fears around boats, linked to my father's Captain Ahab imitations. My dad loved boats, but he didn't know much about them. At sea, he kept crashing, running aground, having engine trouble, generally turning even calm waters into a menace. As a child, I considered a routine boating trip to include a rescue by the Coast Guard. Only years later did I realize that my father, a native of Brooklyn and a landlubber his entire life, purchased his first boat on impulse. My first boating trip was also his first trip. He bought a boat moored somewhere on the Hudson River north of New York City and, without any training whatsoever, he boarded the boat, turned on the engine and drove off. No wonder we actually came close to colliding with the Statue of Liberty on that maiden voyage. Had I not been preoccupied with marathon vomiting, I might have been frightened. My dad, of course, never showed any worries over his boating mishaps, invariably acting as if every botched voyage had gone completely as planned.

Chizo and I have been on a boat together before. In Togo, a tiny West African nation with expertise in the field of voodoo, I once hired a small motorboat to transport us to an island in a large lake. The people living on the island are known for their intense attachment to various juju practices. Chizo sat stiffly as if ready to do battle with any sea monster that might attack our craft. We reached the island safely, saw some live chickens slaughtered against stone altars and met a priestess who wouldn't talk to Chizo but spoke to me after Chizo walked away. The priestess sold me a talisman called a "traveling fetish." I held the small wood sculpture in my hand so Chizo would not see it. After my consultation with the priestess, Chizo excoriated me in rough language anyway, saying, "Never you joke with juju."

I defended myself, telling her I considered juju a way of understanding the world and juju fetishes a form of art.

"You whites play with powers you don't understand," she replied angrily. "You will pay for your foolishness."

On the boat back, Chizo again erupted, insisting our visit to the juju island posed risks to both of us. When I turned my head to admire the small retreating island, she pushed me out of the boat. I sank under the water, started to panic—and then found myself standing straight up, my feet firmly on the bottom of the lake and my head well above the waterline. I was only about a hundred yards from the shore and, breathing easily, I walked in. In my left hand I held fast to the small wooden juju charm given me by the priestess.

As we board the whale-watching boat, I hope I do nothing that prompts Chizo to throw me overboard. The Pacific is much deeper, and less forgiving, than any Togolese lake. The whale-watching boat carries about twenty-five people, and a crew of three. Mindful of my experiences at sea with my father, I put on a life jacket. Chizo does the same. We stand in the front of the boat, with a dozen others, leaning against a rail, peering out into the ocean.

The boat clips along at a good speed, the wind smashing our faces, the roar of the motor swallowing our voices. We forgot to bring binoculars, so we are searching the distance for whales with our naked eyes. I am impatient. Chizo is determined. "Let's keep on spying with our eyes," she says. Neither of us has ever seen whales at sea. Indeed, Chizo was never on a boat in her life until our Togolese juju ride. She learned to swim as a child in the rivers and streams of Nigeria's Delta region, but the ocean is alien to her. With her left hand, she grips the railing, her right arm wrapped around my waist.

She sees the whales first, five or six of them, spouting and leaping. She points to them, and I search the horizon and finally see them. What a thrill. I've never seen so large a sea animal and neither has Chizo.

The captain keeps a respectful distance from the whales. "Why don't we get closer?" Chizo asks.

"Whales can be dangerous," I say.

"Liar," Chizo answers. "Liar, liar, liar."

I imagine she has never read *Moby-Dick.* I begin to tell her about Ahab and the Great White Whale. She catches only snatches of my words over the noise of the sea and the engine. Finally, she gets me. "The whale smashing the boat," she says. "Eating the American people?"

"Happened," I say. "Could happen again."

The chance of a violent encounter with the whales excites Chizo. "In olden times, I wonder how American people caught whales," she says. Another passenger, a man with a teenage son, tells her that boats would come close enough to the whales for sailors to throw harpoons at them and drag those killed onto the ship. Chizo pretends to throw a harpoon, and the man corrects her technique. Her harpoon throws seem to improve under his tutelage.

She turns to me and says, "Darling, this friendly man is teaching me how to throw harpoons." I thank him and he gives me a firm handshake.

Chizo tells me to throw an imaginary harpoon, and I do, but badly, she says.

"Hold the harpoon high above your head."

I do what she says, and she tells me to raise my throwing arm higher.

"Now throw," she says. "Throw."

I rear back my arm and toss my harpoon into the air, using so much force that my momentum carries me into the railing.

Chizo follows my harpoon with her eyes and jumps up and down, screaming. "You've hit the whale!"

I smile broadly and Chizo grabs me. "My hero, my king, my superman," she shouts.

The man with the teenage boy is edging away now, and other people stare at us. I look into Chizo's eyes and tell her that I know her harpoons hit the whale. Mine missed, I say.

Chizo kisses me on the lips. "You speak the truth, my king," she says. "I throw a powerful harpoon. I kill many whales." She invites me to toss more harpoons.

I am tired and suddenly bored with watching the whales and pretending to harpoon them. I wonder why I am not getting seasick. I am strangely serene, my head clear and stomach calm. Perhaps the whale-watching boat is going so fast or maybe the ocean waters are easy today. As the boat turns back toward the harbor, we say a cheerful farewell to these glorious sea creatures and I look forward to the steadiness of terra firma.

When we dock, I thank the captain for a smooth ride and he credits the weather. I am grateful I escaped the voyage without getting sick. I am hungry and want fresh seafood from one of the restaurants on the pier.

In Ghana, we ate fish straight from the sea. Chizo and I would drive to the port at Tema and watch the fishing boats arrive and unload their catch. She enjoyed dickering over the price of the day's catch. She favored the local tilapia and would sometimes buy the "smallish" shrimp that fishermen caught, because I like shrimp. The highlight of our visits to Cape Coast, a gorgeous fishing village about seventy-five miles west of Accra, came when we stood on the beach in the late morning with the wives and children of the Fante fishermen and watched their husbands and fathers arrive onshore in narrow, long wooden boats from which they threw nylon nets into the ocean. As the boats approached land, the fishermen would jump into the water and the kids on land would rush to meet them. Together they pulled the boats ashore, dragging them along the sand, then letting them rest not far from the coconut trees. Then the wives would collect the catch of the day in small plastic bowls, somehow apportioning the fish among themselves. Chizo and I stood by them, inspecting their fish, inquiring about prices, bargaining without much energy and finally choosing our fish. Then we would walk to the beachfront restaurant nearest our bungalow and ask the chef to clean and grill our meal.

Memories of beach dining in Africa distract me from the choices available on the Avila pier. Lost in thought, I find myself standing in front of a crowd of yelping sea lions. Chizo is gone. I creep along the pier, hoping to surprise her. I pass the seafood shack that serves meals outside on benches overlooking the sea lions. I go to the back of the shack and hear Chizo's voice, then I see her. She is standing near an enormous tank of Dungeness crabs, watching them push and shove one another.

"These crabs are huge, they are giants compared to our crabs in Africa," she says.

A man is helping her choose a crab for lunch. She wants a big one. He shows her a few, and she refuses them, until he picks one that is nearly three pounds, a giant among giant crabs, a crab with menacing claws.

"Everything is so big in America, even your crabs," Chizo says. "I can't wait to eat this one's meat."

The man boils the crab and delivers it to us with butter, a nutcracker and a pair of flimsy plastic bibs. Boiled into submission, the crab seems less menacing now, more like a piece of art. I wrap the bib around my neck and fiddle with the nutcracker. Chizo handles the crab with her teeth, cracking open each piece, and retrieving the full portion of meat, with machine-like precision. She slides me big pieces and I devour them. What a wonderful crab, I think. We must do this more often. Love is sweeter around fresh, supersize Dungeness crabs.

I watch Chizo clean out a claw, her teeth cracking the shell evenly and efficiently. Then her fingers take over, dancing deep inside the crevices, retrieving the tender meat.

"I have mastered your crab," she says, happily feeding herself.

I ask how she mastered eating crab so quickly.

"We ate crabs in Owerri, when I lived with my grandmother," she says. "We caught crabs in the river with our own hands. We called them *inshikoh*."

She would chase *inshikoh* along riverbanks, barefoot, capturing a half dozen at a time and boiling them in a blackened pot. "Small, small meat on *inshikoh,* not like your giant crabs," she explains. "Everything small in Africa. Even our crabs."

I say nothing. She rarely criticizes her motherland. She invariably views everything African as sweeter, stronger, more soul-
satisfying. Now our encounter with Dungeness crabs has cracked
open another side of her psyche.

I hear the sea lions yelping again and the sour smell of the sea
suddenly overwhelms the sweetness of the crabmeat. Chizo squirts
lemon on a final piece of crab flesh and takes it into her mouth.

I gaze at her face, marveling at the delicacy of her features, even
while chewing. Then I watch a single tear roll down her cheek. Is
my Chizo crying for the lost crabs of her youth? Is her tear for the
merger of past and present, Africa and America, two distant places
coming together in a single meal?

I ask her why she is crying.

She says she isn't. The lemon juice got into her eye.

A few weeks later, back in Berkeley, I buy her a live Dungeness crab
as a present. I call her and tell her we have a guest for dinner: her
favorite crab. She arrives home with another unexpected food from
her childhood: chestnuts. "Let's roast them in the oven," I say. She
gets a tray and lays out the chestnuts, a few dozen of them. I take
a look, pleased at the large number, then go back to reading a book.
When I break away and return to Chizo, the chestnuts are baking.

We sit at the kitchen table, drinking red wine and watching the
crab move around in a big pot of water. We are waiting for the
chestnuts before cooking the crab. I sip wine and watch the crab
move and wonder about life. I look at Chizo wearing a colorful
African gown and a head scarf and wonder what brought us
together. I put on one of my African top-and-downs, the suit made
from the gorgeous thick material sold by the Woodin shop in
Accra. I put on my mahogany seed necklace. I don my Muslim wool
cap. I am decked out in my African garb, celebrating something.
Maybe the wine is thinking for me now. Maybe I become romantic whenever she wears African clothes. Or maybe she loves the crab
and I love making her happy. In this life, we can easily make the

ones we love so sad, so the simple act of providing her with a live crab, and making her happy, fills me with satisfaction.

I am lost in my thoughts, growing more satisfied, when the first explosion comes. Then two or three more bombs go off. The sounds come from inside the oven. As I stand in shock, Chizo flings open the oven door. Chestnuts come flying out, whizzing past my face, smacking into the ceiling, bursting against walls. One flying chestnut scores a direct hit on my chest. I fall to the floor, more shocked than hurt. Chizo comes over to me and helps me up. Her laughter ignites my own. We hold one another, laughing and laughing, relieved that the chestnuts are no longer exploding, glad to be safe.

I unravel the mystery of why we were attacked by flying chestnuts. I pick a dark roasted chestnut from the floor, hold it between my thumb and forefinger and deduce what went wrong. Chizo never sliced open the chestnuts before baking them. They were sealed. Without a small cut in each, too much pressure builds in the chestnuts—and they blow.

"We boil chestnuts in Africa," she says when I advance my theory.

"If only you hadn't opened the oven door," I say. Then I add, "No one is to blame."

She shakes her head and waves her finger. "I do blame someone for this mess," she says. Then she turns around, grabs the crab from the pot and holds it close to her face as if she is daring the crab to grab her nose with a claw.

"I blame you!" she yells at the crab. She stretches out her arm so the crab's claws, flapping in the air, come inches from grabbing her dreadlocks.

I am trying to open one of the exploding chestnuts, thinking I might eat one anyway, when I hear her issuing urgent instructions.

"Boil some water, Daddy," she says. "A rush order."

And then, holding the crab close to her face for a last time, she says sweetly, "Time for you to give us enjoyment."

* * *

We enjoy ourselves. Hours later, after the arrival of darkness, I lie in bed, reading, while Chizo sits on the redwood deck in the back of the house. The wide French doors are open, allowing a cool breeze to come my way. From the bed, I can see right through to the other side of the cottage. Chizo, wearing only a head scarf, is kneeling. I slide out of bed, creep behind her, hoping to surprise her. I think I am succeeding when, a few feet from her, I realize that Chizo is not alone. A large raccoon stands across from her, fumbling with the carcass of the Dungeness crab. The eyes of the raccoon shine in my direction and I hold my position, saying nothing. I have caught Chizo playing with raccoons before, though usually through the safety of the glass panes in the French doors. I've never seen her so close to a raccoon, so exposed. I have explained to her the risks of approaching raccoons; many prowl around Berkeley at night. I have told her of the consequences of receiving a raccoon bite: the inevitable worries over rabies and the need to receive painful shots. She's ignored my warnings. I am not surprised. Animals inspire no fear in Chizo.

Now she is presenting the carcass of the Dungeness crab to a neighborhood raccoon. Why? She wants the raccoon to enter our house. The crab shell is an invitation.

I quietly resist opening the French doors, pressing my body against the door handles. I don't want to spoil our lovely evening by rebuking her, so I try a little tenderness. I ask her about Jimmy, the orphaned chimpanzee she took care of in the Accra Zoo.

"Do you miss Jimmy?" I ask.

"I do. I miss Jimmy."

"Me too," I say.

I met Chizo and Jimmy at the same time, on a visit to the zoo, and I often remember them together. In our bathroom, we have a photo of Chizo holding Jimmy in her arms, so every morning I see them together and am reminded of their connection. Jimmy is friendly, funny, smart and, despite weighing about fifty pounds and standing only a few feet tall, as strong as a pro football player. He once bit Chizo so hard that she bit him back. When I asked her how she had the strength to retaliate after receiving a deep wound, she said, "African women are warrior, very big warrior."

Chizo adored Jimmy. She lavished fruit and peanuts on him, and served as a tireless playmate, even when his strength brought her to the point of exhaustion. Once, she fed Jimmy ice cream and then erred in telling the zoo's technical adviser, a chimp expert from Germany. "Is there ice cream in the jungle?" the adviser asked. Without waiting for an answer, she snapped, "No more serving ice cream to your baby chimpanzee." A disappointed Chizo complied, though she often recalled how much Jimmy enjoyed ice cream.

I used to wonder who would leave Accra first, Chizo or Jimmy. The German tried hard to find a better home for this lovely baby chimp. She wanted him to live in a chimpanzee sanctuary, where he would spend his days in the bush with other orphaned chimps, retreating to a cold concrete cage only at night. The government would not let Jimmy go and he remains in the Accra Zoo. Perhaps out of loyalty to Jimmy, Chizo is supernaturally friendly to animals. She stops dogs on the street and talks to them, which I find especially funny because, while talking to the dogs, she ignores the people walking with them.

"Look, the raccoon is eating the crab," Chizo says.

Turning her head, her eyes meet mine and our lips come together. For a moment, I forget the raccoon. The cool breeze and Chizo's touch take me far away. Then the sound of the raccoon scraping the crab shell brings me back to the perilous moment.

Chizo pushes me away from the French doors and opens them. The movement startles the raccoon and he retreats into the darkness, leaving the two of us, pressed against one another, peering through the glass panes of the door, searching for a final glimpse of the animal. We stand there for a long time, our bodies growing warmer, the moonlight reflecting on the panes. I fall asleep, my body propped up by Chizo. Then I hear her voice and I think I am awakening from a dream about the chimpanzee. "Did Jimmy bite you?" I ask.

"Come to bed," Chizo whispers, taking my hand. "Jimmy is gone."

Chapter Three

Cracking the Code

I don't like getting phone calls from my ex-wife that begin with her saying, "The police are surrounding your cottage, I've seen them draw their guns and, as best as I can tell, Chizo is inside."

I stop pedaling on the exercise bike at the YMCA and run out of the workout room, into a hallway, where cell phone use is permitted.

I ask my ex-wife to repeat herself.

"The police think there's a robber in your house."

"A robber? They caught a robber?"

"The cops think Chizo is the robber."

Oh, lord. I know my ex-wife is serious because she lives next door to me and is watching the whole situation unfold from a rear window. Worse, the cops came to Nora's house first and she's not happy about the unexpected visit.

"When they opened the door, they had guns out," Nora says. "Scared the crap out of me. Cops kept asking, Am I okay? Like why would I not be? They kept asking, Where's the guy? The guy? I say. What guy? They say, The robber, where's the robber?

"Get off the phone and get home," Nora says. I run to my car, which is parked a few blocks from the Y. My heart is racing, my emotions unraveling. I imagine Chizo in handcuffs, her face against the hood of a squad car, her legs spread, a cop patting her down, then pushing her into the backseat of his car. Then she disappears into a jail, while I raise her bail.

I get behind the wheel of my car, my mind racing. Home is less than a mile away, and even in this short distance anxiety overwhelms me. In the few minutes it takes to drive from the Y to my home, I panic. My fears are amplified because of Chizo's skin color. She never imagines her blackness as a handicap, but neither does she look beyond color. Rather she views her dark skin as the benchmark for humanity. She treats whiteness, instinctively, as an abnormality, a handicap that must be overcome. Her sense of blackness as normative endears her to me—and suits the politically correct atmosphere of Berkeley, where "people of color" are celebrated. Whites in Berkeley embrace Chizo, cheering her natural dreadlocks, fawning over the exotic "tribal marks" on her cheeks, perceiving her as authentic—a veritable "face of Africa," as a fellow African called her. With her winning smile and fetching style, Chizo presents a compelling image of African femininity: powerful and dignified, brave and improvisational, daring and sensual.

As I pull my car onto my street, I wonder whether Chizo can charm police officers. Six of them. There are three cop cars parked sideways in front of Nora's house. I park my car and cautiously walk up the driveway, passing Nora's house on my left. Then I push through the gate into the backyard. I live in the backyard with Chizo. That's right. We live behind my ex-wife's house, where my two children also live. My front door is about forty feet from Nora's back door. I even share the same legal address with my ex-wife, which is why the cops went to her house first. My cottage is wired to a burglar alarm system, and Chizo forgot to punch in the code. When the siren went off, she panicked. Then she screwed up a second time when the security company called the house phone.

Later, Chizo tells me what happened when the security company telephoned her. "I kept saying 'Africa.' The code word is 'Africa.' And the woman on the phone said, That's not the code. The code is a number. So the woman says, I'm sending the cops."

This is all my fault, I think. Our security password isn't actually "Africa." It is indeed a number. Africa is an easy way to remember the number 237422, as the letters correspond to the numbers on the keypad. Unfortunately, the security company wants the owner to give the number, not the word that helps you remember the number. When I showed Chizo how to work the keypad on the alarm, I drilled her on the code. I said "Africa," over and over again. I never told her the number. I never realized the security company would not accept the equivalent word.

I don't know any of this when I approach my cottage and see two uniformed cops leaning against the front door. Two more cops are inside.

Four cops in all. The one I talk to is tall and black. He's sitting in the swivel chair at my desk, which is a few feet from the kitchen table. "You the husband she keeps talking about?" he says.

"We're newlyweds," I answer. "Just married a few weeks ago. On a rooftop in San Francisco."

I smile, inviting his congratulations. He doesn't smile back.

"We almost arrested her," he says. "She was holding a knife when she opened the door."

"A knife?"

I give Chizo a worried look and she replies, defensively, "I was cutting a yam and they showed up."

"So what?" I say, irritated. Our front door has two large glass windows through which she could see the men in blue. "You see the police, and you put your knife down," I say. "Isn't that what she should do, Officer?"

He sighs. "I explained to her that in America a woman doesn't greet a group of policemen holding a knife in her hands. Especially a long knife."

I want to add the words "especially a black woman," but I simply thank the officer for his explanation, trying to sound as grateful as a guy surrounded by cops can be.

I'm still hoping for an encouraging response from the black officer and I know why I am. Sometimes when Chizo and I meet a black American, I hope to receive "extra credit" for our marriage. Sounds crazy, but at this moment I want to scream: I'm married to a black woman! Can't you cut me a break?

I keep waiting for the black cop to give me a sign that he considers me to be an honorary soul brother. Or at least a friend of the tribe. All the cop says is "How come she doesn't know the code?"

I can't help thinking that the cop is asking whether she lives here, whether she's really my wife?

I invite Chizo to explain and she says she gave the word "Africa"—the password—to the woman on the phone and the woman rejected the word. "She wants a number instead," she says. "I beg her. I beg and beg and beg. Please, lady, 'Africa' is the code. She says, No, no, no. The code is a number. She says, I'm calling the cops. I keep saying, 'Africa,' the code is 'Africa,' my husband says so. She says, Too late, the cops are coming, tell your story to them."

The cop looks at me. "My bad," I say. "I thought the password and the number were interchangeable. I never told her the number. Just the word 'Africa.' I'm to blame."

The cop shakes his head. "Your code spells 'Africa,'" he says. "That's cute."

He seems sincere, yet still no soul-brother sign. He drily explains that the city gives us one false alarm. The next time the police arrive and don't find a robber, I get fined a hundred dollars.

I tell him I understand and I'm sorry. I'm very sorry.

The cop gets up from the chair and hands me his card. He is out the door already when he turns and asks, "Is that really your ex-wife in the front house?"

The cop isn't the only person mystified by our living arrangement. My ex-wife lives in the front house with her boyfriend. She and I still own the entire property together, the front house and my cottage and the grounds in between. I'm supposed to sell her my half share and move somewhere else, but we haven't yet agreed on a price. Meanwhile, our two kids enjoy the ability to move back and forth between us in their pajamas.

Chizo understands we are living next to my ex-wife for the benefit of the children, and temporarily. She accepts the situation.

Her big complaint is that the cottage is too small—essentially a single big room, with one wall devoted to a thousand books and a balky wall heater that, combined with all the skylights and the super-tall ceiling, ensures the place stays cool, too cool for her liking. We are trying to make the best of a difficult situation and we are succeeding, though Chizo's mother would disagree.

Chizo told her family in Nigeria that my ex-wife lives on the same property, so that, in African terms, we all share a single "compound." The folks back home now expect Chizo to be poisoned. The clock in Nigeria is ticking. The death of their daughter, it seems to them, is inevitable.

Her mother, Edith, is terrified, praying constantly, fasting and turning to her minister in order to concoct some defenses. I become aware of both the inevitability of Chizo's demise and her mother's dramatic actions when Edith asks to speak with me on the telephone. I have spoken only once before on the phone with Edith— the first telephone conversation in her life. Now I listen closely to her, straining to make out her words. She speaks with a heavy Nigerian accent and uses many unfamiliar phrases and grammatical constructions. At times she slips back and forth between Igbo and English, so that the two languages sound indistinguishable to me.

I'm not sure I understand what Edith is saying, so I ask her to hold on and then summarize for Chizo what I think I've heard her mother say.

"Your mother is telling me I should not allow my first wife to murder you," I say.

I pause for suspense before the words "murder you" and allow a smile to form on my face. "Am I understanding her correctly?" I ask.

Chizo grabs the phone from me. She lets fly strings of Igbo, punctuated by English words, such as "ex-wife" and "divorce" and "California."

The conversation goes on for a while like that, Igbo mixed with bits of English. Then Chizo says, "Wait, Mother," and whispers in my ear, "Tell my mother no one is trying to kill me and you are keeping me safe. Tell her you're protecting me."

"From what?"

"Just tell her. I'll explain later."

Chizo gives me the phone. I have a statement prepared in my mind. "I love your daughter and I am keeping her safe," I say to Edith, slowly and clearly.

Chizo smiles, her eyes widening and skin glowing. Squeezing my hand, she says, "Tell her how well you're feeding me. From the pictures we've sent, my mother thinks I'm too skinny. I must have AIDS, she says. Or maybe your ex-wife is poisoning me and you are too stupid to notice."

I speak more forcefully into the phone now. "Edith, your daughter Chizo is healthy. I'm feeding her very well. She's eating all the time. She's strong and beautiful. She's gaining weight, fattening herself like an Igbo bride."

I'm lying now, but for a good cause. Actually, Chizo isn't gaining weight. She's thin like a fashion model, not even a pound heavier than when we were in Ghana, where heat and the intense humidity conspired to keep her weight down (and mine as well).

"Chizo is too thin. She is like a goat during a drought," Edith says. "Don't joke with me. You must make my daughter fat."

I ponder for a moment whether I should explain the epidemic of obesity in America and how her daughter is an object of envy of most of the women who see her. I decide I will only waste time trying to persuade Edith that in America thinness is a sign of health and high status, and fatness is viewed as a pathology of the poor and ignorant. Her tribe, the Igbo, are famous for fattening up women before marriage and consider heaviness a sign of prosperity and prominence. Heavy women are envied for their beauty and their sexual prowess. The Igbo man who marries a thin woman risks ridicule and unhappiness.

Edith herself is fat, so she knows the terrain. In the days of her youth, her parents sent her to a premarital fat farm, where she and other Igbo women ate prodigiously in order to add more "flesh." She is bewildered by the pride Chizo displays in her lithe body and personal fitness. To her mother, Chizo's petite stature—she can easily wear size one jeans and can fit into junior sizes, despite standing five feet five inches and weighing 110 pounds—is disturbing. In her mind, thinness is a cause for suspicion. Chizo must be ill.

And I am to blame for Chizo's condition, Edith insists. "You keep telling her how good she looks," she says. "Don't you know the devil preys on thin people?"

The devil? I have heard enough superstition from Chizo's mother. "What's the devil have to do with Chizo's body size?" I shout.

Before she can reply, Chizo grabs the phone and pulls my left earlobe so hard my teeth clench. The word "devil" has provoked Chizo's intervention. She lets fly another blast of Igbo into the phone and then tells me, "Don't argue with my mother about the devil. Okay?"

I nod my head. She isn't finished. "See what you've done. Her minister is on the phone now. He's concerned."

I am too. Nigerian ministers are tough debaters, very opinionated and rarely rational.

"He wants to talk to you," Chizo says.

"What do I tell him? That he's a trickish man. That he's trying to profit from the fears of a poor woman who has a daughter in America. That he thinks America is a place where people are gullible and money falls from trees? I bet the minister is charging your mother for protecting you from the devil. You think so too, don't you?"

Chizo waves a fist at me. "I think he can hear you."

I take the phone and greet the minister. I am greeted in return by a booming male voice singing "God Bless America."

I laugh. The minister laughs. "What state are you in?" he asks.

"California."

"Is that near Boston? I have a brother in Boston."

Close enough, I say, then break into song myself. To the tune of "God Bless America," I sing, "I love Nigeria and I love one of Nigeria's beautiful daughters, my darling Chizo."

The song and lyrics are a masterstroke. Many Nigerians are

romantic and with them my displays of affection for Chizo buy me quick acceptance.

"My dear minister," I say when I stop singing, "do you realize I don't have a first wife in America? Chizo is my one and only wife. She is not my second wife. She is my one and only wife. You know we don't get to keep two wives in America. Only one. That's law."

There is silence and then the minister says, "I am glad to hear of your words. Chizo's mother is worried. She says you have a first wife in America and that you keep her in the same compound as Chizo. We are all wondering whether you sex her too, because you whites have no morality. If you are not sexing them both, and you speak the truth about Chizo, then the devil must be at work. Only the devil could arrange to bring your old wife and your new wife so close together. The situation is dangerous. So we have been praying and fasting the entire week to save Chizo's life."

Wow. I'm speechless.

"Are you still there?" the minister asks.

"Yes. I'm thinking. Are only a few of you fasting and praying for Chizo's life or is your whole congregation doing it?"

"About fifty of us," he says. "We are stronger when we fast in large numbers. Fasting strengthens our prayers and stronger prayers protect Chizo from the devil."

Oh.

I thank the minister for his prayers and the prayers of his church members.

"There is only one way to do battle with the devil," he says, "and that is to win. We must defeat the devil. We must not let him take your new wife."

"Amen, Minister," I say with gusto. "Amen."

"Praise the Lord," he says.

"Praise the Lord," I repeat.

I raise my voice now because I must tell the minister something important and he must hear me loud and clear. "In the name of Jesus," I say, "please tell your people to stop fasting and praying for Chizo. Your fasting and prayers have worked. Chizo is safe in

America. No one is plotting to kill Chizo. Certainly not my former wife. Chizo is safe. She is thriving."

"Amen," the minister says. "Praise Jesus."

I am divorced, I explain, but in America many people divorce and divorces are governed by rules. Divorced wives do not try to kill the new wives of their former husbands, at least not usually.

"Good news," the minister says. "Praise the Lord." The minister sounds calmer now and his voice is friendlier. Maybe I have broken through his fog of anxiety. "Life is different in Nigeria," he says, "which is why we cannot stop praying for Chizo. In our culture, when you abandon a wife, you make sure she stays far away from your new wife. Otherwise, the old wife may murder the new wife."

"I'll make sure—absolutely sure—no one harms Chizo," I say.

I am expecting the minister to thank me, and he says nothing. I think the telephone connection is gone and then I hear his concerned voice and I realize I haven't persuaded him of anything. He still thinks that Chizo's life is in danger and that I am a fool not to share his fears.

"You are also in our prayers," he tells me. I thank him quickly and I hang up.

After the cops leave, satisfied that Chizo lives in the house and is not a thief, I am reminded that it's not just the minister who is worried. My daughter, Oona, arrives at the cottage with some chocolate-chip cookies that my ex-wife, Nora, baked.

I consider the cookies a friendly gesture, but Chizo won't eat them. Even after I eat one, Chizo won't touch them. So I eat another one.

My daughter eats a cookie too.

Chizo and Oona, who is ten years old, get along great. Oona first met Chizo in Ghana. They spent six weeks together in our house in Accra. From the start, Chizo and Oona were friends. At first they became close out of necessity. Our house in Accra had no hot water. Chizo boiled water for Oona and bathed her out of a bucket. The electricity went out, usually every day, and Chizo lit candles for Oona. The streets of Accra were thick with people, there were no sidewalks and dust and dirt were everywhere. Oona was afraid of the streets, and Chizo went everywhere with her, a constant guardian. Their partnership turned affectionate by the end of Oona's visit. When Chizo arrived in America later in the same year, on Halloween night, Oona greeted her like an old friend and they went trick-or-treating together.

Chizo is still upset by the police visit, and Oona tries to cheer her up. "Good cookie," she says, smiling. "Try one."

Chizo won't. I ask why, and she says, "I'll tell you later."

When Oona leaves, she tells me, "What better way for your ex-wife to poison me than with a cookie?"

"A chocolate-chip cookie?"

"She's always sending food back. Haven't you noticed I don't eat any of it?"

I hadn't noticed, actually.

"Nora is trying to be friendly," I say. "She likes to cook."

"I'm not eating anything she cooks."

"I've eaten it. I haven't gotten sick."

"You think poison is one-size-fits-all like a cheap hat," Chizo says. "Poison works on enemies, not on friends."

I ponder her reasoning and let the conversation die. Death by poison is one of Chizo's most persistent fears. The specter of juju, which I thought we left behind in Africa, persists in California. In Nigerian movies, someone always gets poisoned and Chizo views poison as part of the ordinary arsenal of weapons deployed by resentful people, home or away. Juju respects no borders; few escape its power.

Chizo's family is no exception. Her mother fears she will be poisoned if she ever visits her husband's home city of Calabar, an old colonial center in eastern Nigeria. Her husband will be powerless to protect her because somehow his ex-wife, who lives in Calabar, has mysterious powers to do harm. Chizo's sisters believe the woman represents a lethal threat of such force she can enlist their father in the nefarious plot against their mother. So Chizo's mother won't visit Calabar, not even to stay in the spacious, two-story home owned by her father in the city. The home sits empty.

I react with disbelief every time I hear Chizo speak of the empty house and the specter of evil in Calabar. Surely, she is joking. Can't her father simply promise to everyone in the family that he will never harm her mother? When I actually suggest that he declare publicly that he will never, wittingly or unwittingly, assist in the poisoning of his wife, Chizo starts laughing. She laughs for a long time and when she stops she says, "Is the devil talkative like whites? Does he speak with ten tongues? Is he a big parrot?"

She explains that promises are meaningless. Her mother's security depends on her staying far away from Calabar and her father's ex-wife. "Otherwise my mother will die," she says.

I can't persuade her to think differently. I decide that the subject is too much for us. We never discuss it ever again. This is one intercultural trip wire we avoid crossing.

Living next door to my ex-wife, Chizo cannot avoid meeting her. At first they keep their cool. They coexist without interacting. They watch each other, warily, from a safe distance. Then one day something terrible happens that upsets this tidy balance.

The story has nothing to do with poison. The story starts with a machete, and, as so often happens, I inadvertently lay the groundwork for what goes wrong.

I bought the machete for my son, Liam, in Africa. When he and my daughter visited us, we were out in the bush, far from the capital city, in a place where small monkeys roam like squirrels and bananas grow like weeds. Our driver, Stephen, took us to the bush in his ancient Honda. On a dirt road, he stopped to inspect some locally made charcoal, stacked up in piles alongside the road. As he negotiated a purchase, I spotted the machetes for sale. Both the blades and the handles were made in Ghana. Africans used to make a lot of their own tools, but now so much comes from China.

The rarity of these homemade machetes made me want one. I paid less than two dollars for it. The blade was heavy and dark, and the handle was not smooth, as if a man had carved it out of a piece of a tree he'd felled himself. Don't misunderstand me. The machete was no work of art. It was a tool and I gave it to my son. He was twelve years old then and in Africa he was old enough to have his own machete.

Later in the afternoon, Chizo taught him how to use it. They wandered into the bush and found some brush to chop. The heavy machete was hard for Liam to swing. The Chinese machetes are light and surer. He complained of the difficulty, but Chizo pushed him. "You're in Africa," she said. "You swing the African machete and you grow powerful like the African boys."

When the time came for Liam to return to America, we wrapped the machete in some old copies of the *Daily Graphic* newspaper, tied a cord around the bundle and put it in his suitcase. The machete made the long trip to Berkeley undamaged. When we showed up a few months later, we found the machete in our cottage. Liam stood the machete, blade down, in the corner behind the front door. He kept it there because his mother didn't want it in his bedroom.

"Have you used it?" Chizo asked him.

He said no.

"I will," she told him and kept the machete under our bed along with some old stereo equipment and boxes of books.

She laid the machete on its side so that she could grab it without lifting her head from her pillow. "I feel safer with the machete nearby," she said.

One afternoon I come home and see the machete, and Chizo, in action. I'm riding a bicycle and from the end of the block I see her lithe and powerful form slashing at the plants that surround the standing stones in the yard in front of my ex-wife's house. A week before I had told Chizo that the plants in the front yard had gotten too tall and that Nora ought to trim them. For an instant, I think that Chizo is helping my ex-wife. As I get nearer, though, I realize I am confused. Approaching the front yard, or what's left of it, I am suddenly stricken with horror. What have Chizo and her African machete done to Nora's cherished garden?

Piles of branches and plants lie everywhere. The carnage is immense. In the heat, Chizo perspires heavily. Her shirt is drenched. Her bandanna is soaked. The sweat glistens on her bare legs. She holds her machete high in her right hand as if waving to me in triumph. Could she be celebrating?

Oh my. Nora will surely poison us now. Her beautiful lavender flowers are gone, slashed to the stems. The fecund lemon tree, which I planted with her years ago, now looks like a bizarre dwarf; a long branch remains, the rest of the fruit-bearing limbs hacked away and stacked like firewood to one side of the front steps. The grasses are chopped to the ground line. All over, the cuts are so ugly, so random and irregular, that they look as if they have been made by a vandal.

They haven't. They have been made by an African who clears brush like a whirlwind.

"What have you done?" I cry. "What have you done?"

Chizo ignores me, possessed by her own overwhelming self-confidence. She keeps swinging the machete against a once-thriving bush. Once, twice, three times, the blade whacks against the bush. The bush looks sickly now. One more stroke of the machete, I imagine, and surely the bush will fall over, dead.

I am reeling, disoriented now. For a moment, I think we are in Africa and Chizo is slashing the small cornfield we maintained at one end of our compound. I close my eyes and remember the spacious cottage we had in Accra, set on Kuku Hill, a short walk from the State House and the beach. I linger on the delicious image, smelling the air blowing in from the Atlantic. Then I open my eyes and return to the horror. A knot forms in my stomach. I once more see Chizo standing tall in front of Nora's ruined garden, the machete hanging from her right hand.

Chizo, incredibly, isn't finished. She sets in motion again, the machete rising high in the air. I am afraid to grab her arm and stop her from taking another whack. I come closer, hear the thud of the blade against a bush. She has struck the machete so hard that the wooden handle has cracked down the middle.

"Darling, please stop," I say. "You're finished. You're done." My calm tone surprises me. I'm often poised in moments of danger and, make no mistake, we are in danger. Chizo has massacred my ex-wife's front yard and, worse, she doesn't even realize she's done wrong. Improbably, she insists she's done Nora a big favor.

"She'll be so happy. I have saved her work. She will thank me."

"Are you sure?"

Her answer is to swing the machete again, slicing another bush in half. I shudder at the size of the cut, yet I am helpless now. I watch her slash away at the few remaining healthy bushes. She slaughters them with the same random intensity she applied to the others. I look at her face and see no anger but I wonder whether anger fuels her outburst.

Back in our cottage I explain to Chizo the difference between pruning and slashing. I tell her that Americans expect their plants and trees to be pruned in straight lines, carefully and according to well-accepted practices. "There are special tools for this," I say. The machete is too blunt, too indiscriminate a tool for as delicate a task as trimming a front garden.

"Nora will be very upset," I predict.

Ever confident, Chizo disagrees. She expects praise for her toil. I fear the whirlwind instead.

It is not long in coming. The first intimations are loud knocks on the door. I imagine the police officers hammered away with the same intensity. I look through the window in the door and see Nora. Since I've moved in with Chizo, she's never knocked on the door, never crossed the imaginary boundary line between our two houses.

We are in big trouble.

I look at Chizo. She still doesn't get it.

She rises from her chair coolly and strides to the door. I can see the smile on her face. For an instant I think she'll have the sense to draw down the curtain on the front-door window and pretend we aren't home. I do a quick calculation and conclude we have enough food in the cottage to hide out for a few days. We can turn off the lights, stay quiet and convince Nora we've gone on a long trip.

Chizo swings open the door.

"Who destroyed my front yard?" Nora asks.

Chizo acts like she hasn't heard the question.

"I said, Who destroyed my front yard?"

Chizo raises her hand like a child in school.

"Why did you do it?"

"To help you."

"Help? You used a machete."

"Yes, the one we bought in Africa."

Nora looks past Chizo and our eyes meet. "I didn't know anything," I say. "She didn't tell me. I come home and find a big mess."

"A very big mess," Nora says.

"The garden will grow back," Chizo says.

"You don't use a machete on a garden."

"I thought you'd be happy," Chizo says. "We use machete in Africa."

Nora shakes her head, glares at me and says, "Tell her she's not in Africa anymore."

Sometimes the worst brings out the best in people. Nora leaves the cottage, satisfied with issuing a verbal rebuke. Chizo is silent the rest of the day. Nor does she speak the next morning. Lonely, I think that our experiment in communal living—done for the sake of the children—is imploding. Must Chizo and I move? On the move all day, I ponder this question. I return home for dinner and pass Nora under her kitchen window on the way to the cottage. I hear her inside, preparing dinner, but she doesn't notice me.

Pushing open the cottage door, I am assaulted by a strange

odor. I find Chizo at the range, stirring African spices into a broth. From separate bags, she takes dashes of *oziza, ehiri* and *uda*. They are spices from home that she buys from a Nigerian grocery store in downtown Oakland. She gets hunks of goat meat from the same store. And the *egusu* seeds she so adores. And the inimitable *dawa dawa* seasoning that looks like wet dirt and stinks so bad that I must leave the house when she includes it among her ingredients. With a paring knife she chops the goat into small pieces and tosses them in the soup. She sprinkles in salt, stirs the soup and waits for the goat to cook.

She is making pepper soup, the national dish of her Igbo tribe. She dips a spoon into the pot and gives me a taste. The spices are strong, and the soup is salty. I'm grateful she refrained from using *dawa dawa.* Flashing her a smile of relief, I ask for a small piece of goat meat and she tells me to wait. "I want to give Nora first."

The sound of her name makes me shudder. I call my daughter, who sometimes acts as a courier between the two houses. When she arrives, Chizo fills a big bowl with broth and then carefully selects a large, fleshy piece of goat that's had all the fat and skin stripped away. "Your mother will like this soup, oh," she tells Oona. "It gives the eater extra-extra large power. Bring it to your mother fast-fast."

Oona leaves with the bowl. A few minutes later, she returns with an empty bowl. "My mom wants more," she tells Chizo.

Chizo fills another bowl, once again carefully selecting a piece of goat meat. Off goes Oona with the bowl. A short time passes and she returns, again with an empty bowl. Oona also carries a small steaming loaf of bread.

"My mother says you'll like this," Oona says. "It's an American specialty. Banana bread. I helped my mother make it."

Oona sets the bread down on our small kitchen table. I get a knife and cut pieces for Oona and myself.

We start to eat the bread. Chizo sits down. "Nothing for me," she says. Then she cuts herself a thick piece, and Oona looks astonished. After Chizo takes her first bite, she looks around and laughs. "I'm funning you," she tells Oona.

Something is different now. "I am relaxing my skin," Chizo says, laughing again. Oona and I join her in laughter, and she takes another bite of bread and another and then another. Soon, Chizo eats the whole piece and declares, "Cut me one more."

Oona rushes to do the cutting. She hands Chizo the piece and says, as if making an announcement, "I'm glad you and my father are married."

Her declaration startles me. I look at Chizo and she puts her index finger against her lips. She wants me to stay quiet. There are times when she enjoys freedom from questions, when life rolls on without analysis, when she simply experiences the joy of the moment. She wants me to experience the joy with her. I do—for a few seconds. Then my anxieties take over, and my joy vanishes. Nervously, I reach for a piece of banana bread, and Oona starts to speak. I think she's going to say I've had too many pieces already or I should save the remainder for Chizo.

Instead she asks me a familiar question. "Since you married Chizo, does that mean I've become half-black?"

"Do you want to become half-black?" I ask my daughter.

She nods her head eagerly. "My skin isn't really white anyway," she says, stretching out her arm. "I'm brown already." She tugs at her skin, which is the olive color of my father's Italian parents.

"So now that you're married, am I half-black?" Oona asks.

What a question. I pull Oona close to me. I am reluctant to supply an answer, and I signal to Chizo to stay quiet. I know she thinks Oona cannot alter her skin color out of solidarity for our marriage. Chizo thinks white is white and black is black; skin color isn't a new set of clothes. I am not so sure. This is America, after all. Here freedom trumps inheritance.

I want Oona to feel free to discard traditional views of race. I hold her tightly and I give her the answer I believe she wants to hear. "Yes, you're half-black now," I say brightly. "And for as long as you want to be."

Chapter Four

Chukwu

I have this persistent sense that I knew Chizo when we were both children. We were somewhere together long ago and that explains why we are together now. I can't quite place where we grew up together, and I feel we are now like those old friends who no longer recall how they met. In the rambling house of my memory, Chizo is everywhere she shouldn't be. She is in my kindergarten class, in the stands at my Little League games, at my Bar Mitzvah, across the dance floor at my high school prom, in the philosophy stacks at my university library. I see her on the Green Tortoise bus that carried me from New York to California thirty years ago. She is the person ahead of me in line when I interview for a vacant room in a San Francisco Victorian. The list goes on. Chizo is woven into my memories of places and experiences we never shared together.

About six months after Chizo and I arrive in America, I visit one of the places of my own past—the majestic Multnomah Falls, just east of Portland, Oregon. The falls sit above the mighty Columbia River, which is swollen from winter rains. I've been at Multnomah Falls before, more than a few times, though I've never been here with Chizo. She is with me now. In Portland, I worked my first solid newspaper job twenty years ago, on *Willamette Week*. Our offices were less than an hour from the falls. I came here often and yet I never climbed to the top. Not once.

Chizo and I plan to reach the top today. Looking at the falls, hearing the roar of crashing water, I grudgingly accept that we have never been here together. I ponder the possibility that love tricks the mind by creating pleasing illusions. They invariably give way to the rock of reality. Love blinds, but not forever.

I look at the real rocks studding the hillside above the Columbia River and I imagine the collision of water against stone and the sharpness of the stone slowly giving way to the smoothness of age and experience. I think of how lovers who succeed lose their sharp edges over time—and ease their way to a common future.

We are some distance from the entrance to Multnomah Falls, our rental car parked on some rough ground alongside the winding tarred road. There is a low wide wall, made of rocks, that runs along the edge of a cliff above the river. Chizo stands on the wall, while I snap her picture. "Stop moving," I say and she does, though only long enough for me to take a few shots. Then she hops on one foot, then on the other, trying to frighten me. She leans to one side, half her body seemingly aloft in the airspace over the mighty river. I scream and she ignores me, once more daring me to interfere, to plead with her to come down, to persuade her to halt her horseplay. I am afraid that she will fall off the low wall and tumble down the steep incline. I think about shouting out a warning, advising her that, if not careful, she can slip off the wall and hurt herself. But such warnings she doesn't like to receive from me. I swallow my shout and dismiss my dark thoughts.

Chizo thinks positive, visualizing success, not failure, even when facing imminent danger. I should do the same, she always says. I content myself by thinking she is giving me another lesson on self-control.

I stay quiet, admiring her confidence, marveling at her abandon. I envy her courage and her strength too. As I watch her display of balance, she jumps into the air, landing solidly on both feet, her body steady, as if racing along the tops of walls was her occupation, an activity as familiar to her as climbing a flight of stairs.

It is late May. Portland is blessedly dry today, the sun is shining brightly and the weather is unusually warm. Chizo is dressed in white. She wears white JLo denim pants, a white silk blouse from Jones New York and a Liz Claiborne denim jacket. The jacket is white too. Only her skin is dark, the color of chocolate. Her skin shimmers in the sunlight, and with her white attire, she appears like an angel descending from heaven, trying to decide whether she belongs on the ground or in the air.

I take more pictures and admire her openmouthed. She jumps again and once more lands securely on the top of the wall. Her jewelry jingles, drawing my gaze. On her wrist, she wears a silver bracelet. Large silver hoops hang from her ears. A silver heart hangs from her neck. She's in silver and white today, except for her black cap. The brimless cap gives her a touch of danger, a sense that her sartorial purity is a phantom. That she is not an angel after all. Her Bebe shoes are black too, though the laces are white and a white stripe runs down the middle of each shoe.

Did she match the laces with the rest of her outfit by design, or is it serendipity?

I pose my question when she gets down from the wall. She makes a face that says my question is silly. Of course she matched the laces on purpose.

We walk along the road to the base of the waterfall, where visitors gather. We stand and wait, admiring the falls high above, close enough now to feel the chill of the water in the air.

Chizo strikes an aggressive pose, the mouth of the waterfall squarely behind her. "They are watching me," she says, "admiring my dressings, right from time." I ask whether she feels cold and wants to put on the long Larry Levine coat we left in the car. "Don't bother me about my wearings," she says. A small café, selling hot drinks and sweets, catches her attention. She buys a chocolate ice-cream cone. As she eats, she brushes the cone against her jacket, leaving a trace of ice cream. She pouts. The dark spot on her white jacket bothers her. I get a cup of water and a paper towel from the café and rush to her rescue. She wipes away the spot. She hopes there won't be a stain.

of worshipers to a vast, unfinished building on the outskirts of the city. I managed to contain myself until the minister asked all the unmarried women to stand up, hold out their arms and pray.

"Pray to ward off evil spirits," the minister shouted. "Pray for Western Union to bring you money. Pray for God to deliver you a husband."

After each exhortation, the congregation bellowed, "Amen." The loudest "amen" came last, for the single women to be delivered husbands.

The minister's exploitation of the unmarried drove me out of the church. I read a book in the hot sun, while Chizo stayed inside. At the end of the service, she found me in the dusty parking lot. I made the mistake of telling her to stop attending this church. She exploded and we argued until dinner. In those days, we argued often about religion and religious ideas until I realized that while specific churches and ministers might offend me, Chizo's direct relation to God should not. Chizo needs God, and I do too, if I'm going to share her world, a world where good and evil do permanent battle, and the forces of evil, or bad "juju," constantly attack the forces of good. God is on the side of good, naturally. And without God, Chizo says, humans are destined to serve the devil, which is why she unashamedly declares that "Christianity is my juju."

Hiking in the Oregon forest, we need to marshal some positive juju to ward off the negative juju that Chizo says is on the loose. In short, we need God.

I want to ask a question. She won't let me.

"Be quiet," she says. "I'm talking to God."

I have a bad habit of interrupting people, but when Chizo talks to God, I stay quiet.

She turns away from me and looks at the clear blue sky. I sigh and let my mind wander. I am thinking about nothing when Chizo grabs my hand. "Get moving," she says. "God wants us at the top of the falls. We aren't safe until we get there."

Chizo breaks into a fast walk and I struggle to stay close to her. When I finally draw even, I ask, "Are you sure?"

She looks at me like I'm nuts, shifts her eyes away and walks faster. I strain to stay with her. My legs are sore now. My neck is stiff. My left foot is cramping. I am tired, frustrated, angry at God, or rather angry at Chizo for turning a walk in the Oregon woods into a divine encounter. I want to shake my fist at God, rail against his selfish domination of my wife, when I remember something that happened to me years before, in Africa, when Chizo and I went on a nocturnal search for wild chimpanzees in a coastal jungle near Ghana's border with Ivory Coast.

We searched all night for the chimpanzees, hoping to get near enough to observe their interesting habits, handicapped of course by our own need for lights and the great difficulties of moving in the dark. Just before dawn, as we cuddled together in the dense forest, unable to sleep, our hopes of hearing or seeing chimpanzees at night fast vanishing, Chizo made an extraordinary confession to me.

"I talk to God," she said. "A lot. I ask Him how to settle difference we have and also to help me understand you when I don't."

"What does He tell?"

"To be patient."

"Really?"

"Yes. He also tells me that you are His gift to me."

Chizo took my hand and her words sank into me.

"What else does He tell you?"

"Whenever I feel unable to appreciating your culture, whenever I lose hope that I will understand you and you will understand me, He tells me that our love is enough to make our differences tolerable."

Chizo's stunning confession of course eased the disappointment of our fruitless nocturnal search for chimpanzees. That night in an African forest, I learned that God, in Chizo's mind, is the first cheerleader for our relationship. He is the glue that holds together our love affair. He is the balm Chizo applies to every cut, wound and scar that I inflict on her. In short, since I am flawed, imperfect and undeniably mistake-prone, God is my best friend. He is my redeemer.

I decided that the more Chizo talks to Him, the better.

* * *

As we draw nearer to the top of Multnomah Falls, I think of this conversation with Chizo about God and Africa and us. Ascending a steep path, I am tired but I do not wish to display weakness to Chizo and so I persist. My method is persistence, I decide. I won't rest until Chizo rests.

Fortunately, Chizo rests. I rest too. As she relaxes, stretching her arms toward the sky, I bend over, huffing and puffing, taking in big gulps of air. I am still thinking about her conversations with God.

"You ready?" she says, interrupting my thoughts.

I'm not. I want to rest longer. Chizo says we'll rest at the top. She heads off around a bend. The falls are roaring. The air is moist. We are close. We round another bend, our pace quickening. We reach a platform rimmed by a low railing. The mouth of the falls seems near enough to touch.

The setting is gorgeous, the power of the falls majestic. I draw Chizo near me. I am overcome, once more, with the sense that she and I have been here before. A smile comes over my face and I suddenly feel light, like I can fly. Maybe I am simply glad to have reached the peak. Or maybe my elation is more profound. Looking at Chizo, set against this giant waterfall, I think how beautiful she is and how lucky I am that we found each other—and keep finding each other. I'm falling in love with her all over again.

Something else doesn't make sense to me. I feel a breeze blow past. I feel the cool air on my face. I feel a third force, a presence, standing with Chizo and me.

I pull her close to me and gaze into her eyes. "Is He nearby?" I ask.

Her answer comes in Igbo. "*Chukwu du anyi,*" she says. "God will lead us."

I try to repeat the phrase and stumble.

"*Chukwu du anyi,*" she repeats, more slowly this time.

I say the Igbo words and I smile. A sense of peace comes over me. I feel light. My worries have vanished suddenly. I say to myself, without knowing why, that I can die now. I can die right here and now, with Chizo next to me. I don't mind going.

I am startled by the words coming from inside me. So long I've chased life, trying to squeeze all I can from my days, and at the same time I've feared death. Chasing life and fearing death have been my twin beacons, illuminating my path. I suddenly realize I've lived my entire life out of fear. Fear everywhere, always expecting the worst. I start to cry.

I feel the presence again. The breeze is caressing my skin. Or is that Chizo? Is she caressing my cheek, wiping away my tears? I can't tell.

I feel like I'm in a gospel song and Aretha is singing, Can you feel it?

Can I?

I ask Chizo, "Can you feel it?"

The roar of the waterfall swallows her answer.

She repeats herself, this time louder. "*Chukwu* is with us," she says. "We're safe."

The way back down is easy. Our legs are flying. I say I know why. Gravity is pulling us down the steep path. We are rolling like rocks down the side of a hill.

Chizo disagrees. She knows why the way back is so easy. The evil spirits are gone. God has visited us. We're safe. We're happy. And aren't safety and happiness all that we want?

She holds out her arms and spins around. She takes my hand and spins me around.

We dance. All the way down, we dance.

PART TWO

Accra

July 2001

I went to Accra in July 2001 to write a mystery novel set in an exotic West African city that was fitfully reviving after decades of romantic and rueful decline. My life was like the city. I wanted a new sense of purpose, new challenge. Soon I would abandon The Wall Street Journal, for which I had worked for many years, most recently as a foreign correspondent. Feeling that journalism was an inadequate response to what I saw in my travels around the world, I wanted to strike out in a different direction, as a writer and a person.

That summer I wrote every morning in a busy hotel near the center of Accra, I had a small room on the second floor near the front desk. The window overlooked the courtyard, where a band played a few nights a week and the restaurant served a mix of Ghanaian, Italian and Lebanese food. A friendly family, of Lebanese descent but born and raised in Accra, owned the hotel. I took my breakfast in my room, and invariably stayed inside, writing on my laptop at a small desk, well past noon. Taxis gathered outside the hotel gates, and there were newspaper kiosks and young girls selling cards with units for my mobile phone. I went to the ocean in the afternoon, taking my lunch at the beach. I ate spicy goat kebabs and drank tall bottles of Star beer, while peering out at the Atlantic, trying to imagine Africa's impenetrable and vanished past. In the evenings, the sounds of highlife music filled my ears, and Africans swept up in the moment crowded my view.

It was much later that I realized the folly of my literary ambitions. My *novel proved to be a failure. My story was too vast, sprawling, undisciplined, out of control and confusing—a lot like Accra, my inspiration. I wanted a Hemingway moment, and I would be denied. I would not finish the novel, not that summer, not ever. Instead I was drawn into the heart of a city by the sea, and in a zoo, of all places, I met an African woman.*

She wore the face of her continent. She moved according to the rhythms of her place. She felt comfortable in her skin. She was beautiful, daring, powerful and upsetting. She robbed me of my routine.

I sensed I could learn important lessons from this African woman, at least about living in the present. Until I met her, I had lived only in the past and in the future. The present was a faraway land, where I could not comprehend the language spoken by the inhabitants. This woman immersed herself in the fullness of the moment with a curious ease that I took for wisdom. She seemed to possess neither a past nor a future. To her, the present loomed so large, in all its splendor, that the past and future appeared pale, brittle, even illusory. I wanted a present and, I would later come to realize, she wanted a past and a future.

We each had something the other one needed. And, like needy men and women everywhere, we borrowed from one another. We tried on each other's traits and habits. We swapped disguises. We fell in love.

Chapter Five

Zoo Stories

The parking lot of the Accra Zoo is flattened earth, pocked with moon-size crater holes. The ground is yellowish brown, baked from months without rain. My driver, Stephen, at the wheel of his ancient Honda, finds a smooth spot, kicking up dust in his wake. It is late afternoon, the air is cooling, and I step out of the car and into the haze. A few small children run up to me and ask me for money. I ignore them and Stephen shouts something in Twi, the local language.

The breeze from the Atlantic is blowing, and the heat of the day is giving way to the relief of the evening. I adjust the white wool cap on my head and straighten out my clothes. I am wearing my third outfit of the day. It is so hot in Accra, even at this time of year, that I usually make my first wardrobe change by noon. I am wearing a pure white, cotton top-and-down, the drawstring pants held tight to my waist and covered by a long-sleeved smock. There is gold-colored embroidery across the smock and a matching pattern at the bottom of my pants.

"You are looking like one slick *obruni*," Stephen tells me, using the Twi term for "white."

I smile. Stephen has been my driver since I first visited Accra nearly a year before, and I enjoy his teasing. He is from the genial Fante tribe and his father was a fisherman. If Stephen weren't so funny and patient, I might have left Accra in disgust long ago.

I ask him to wait. I don't know how long I will be but he is used to waiting and doesn't say anything. Up ahead is the entrance to the Accra Zoo. There is no one at the small gate because the zoo is closed. I push past the turnstile and jog to the right. I take four or five steps and I can see the lion getting fed and the two crazy old chimps eating bananas. The zoo is small, and the animals stay in small cages with steel bars. The place has the feel of a pet hospital: the animals crowded together, their smells hitting you in the face, a sense of desperation in the air. There are no zoos like this in America any longer. This one seems out of the 1950s, when the British designed it.

A tall thin man watches me from the shadows. He is one of the zookeepers, in charge of the chimps and monkeys. He is also Chizo's boss. He calls out to her. She is in a cage with an orphaned chimpanzee, an eighteen-month-old baby named Jimmy.

I peer into the cage and see Chizo wrestling with the chimp. The cage is eight feet high and ten feet wide. The floor is concrete. This is where Jimmy lives. He shares the place with some rats.

Chizo is in a squat, a position from which she can lift Jimmy in the air and turn him upside down, all the while keeping her balance. She is laughing and imitating the strange noises that Jimmy makes.

"When will you be done?" I ask her.

I speak softly, trying not to upset Jimmy.

She doesn't answer. The chimp jumps into her arms.

I ask again.

"Don't rush me," she says. "You can see I'm busy."

I go sit down on a bench and wait. Africa is teaching me about patience. I keep my eyes on Chizo. When she stands, her carriage makes her seem like royalty. Jimmy is on her shoulders now and once again I am awed by her physical strength. Even through her stained green overalls, I can see the outlines of her thighs. They are thick and sculpted, like the thighs of an Olympic sprinter.

Chizo eases through a small door in the cage, the chimp in her arms. She lets him slide down her leg and run off to climb a tree.

He sits at the top for a long time and I look at Chizo. I see past the long jagged scars on her face—her tribal marks—and to the beauty of her features.

Chizo beckons and I come closer. "I want to take him for a walk," she says. "Come with us."

I think of asking her if she is allowed to take the chimp for a walk but I've been in Accra long enough to know not to inquire about rules. There usually are none, or none that matter.

The three of us walk along an asphalt path that snakes through the zoo, Jimmy holding Chizo's left hand and I holding her right hand. We stop at a cage full of ordinary mona monkeys. Jimmy stares at the monkeys. I stare at Jimmy. There is something very funny about Jimmy watching these monkeys, knowing he is free, unfettered by a cage. Perhaps I am dreaming but he seems to be taunting the monkeys with his hands, saying to them, Hey, I am free and you are not, isn't that cool?

This chimp captivated me from the moment I saw him four days ago. Or perhaps I am captivated by Chizo, whom I first saw at the same time as the chimp. They are a striking pair. Jimmy is the first orphaned chimp ever to be nursed in the Accra Zoo. Chizo is the first African, in the zoo's entire history of nearly fifty years, to come in intimate contact with a Great Ape. Many Africans eat chimps; only a rare African plays with them. Chizo is that rare African.

When I think Jimmy is absorbed fully by the monkeys, I ease Chizo toward me and kiss her on the lips. Our first kiss. Jimmy notices, makes irritated noises and tries to bite my hand. I pull away and Chizo chastises Jimmy. I pretend to be upset but mainly I am afraid that I botched my first kiss with Chizo.

Jimmy has big teeth. He likes Chizo's full attention and is upset to share her with me. Chizo says he's jealous. He seems to grasp that I have designs on Chizo and that I am not an ordinary visitor to the zoo. I came out of sheer curiosity; zoos are unusual in African cities. I wandered over, hoping to kill some time on a slow afternoon. I've ended up visiting four out of the last six days, timing my arrivals around Chizo's schedule and each time raising my level of interest in her. Until I started coming around, it seems to Jimmy, he was the only man in Chizo's life. Now I'm visiting Chizo every day, hanging around so long that he has to share her with me. No wonder he's upset.

I kiss Chizo again, Jimmy tries to bite my hand once more. I am frightened now, and not of botching kisses either. Chizo laughs and laughs. "Jimmy is funning us," she says. She tells me to go away while she finishes walking Jimmy around the zoo. She holds Jimmy close and I see his penis grow erect. I turn and go.

I wait in the car with Stephen. He doesn't believe me when I tell him the chimp is jealous of me—and that he has an erection. "Serious?" he asks. I repeat myself and he gets me and smiles. We've both been thinking that Chizo has an African boyfriend stashed somewhere; we never imagined that my most aggressive rival would be a chimp.

Before leaving the zoo, Chizo must get rid of the chimp, who usually doesn't want to get back into his cage. It is dark now, and I'm tired of sitting in the car with Stephen. I go back inside the zoo, through the still-open entrance. Except for the night watchmen, Chizo and I are now the only people around. I watch her routine, which is to get into the cage herself and then lure Jimmy in with some zany antics or peanuts and fruit. Once Jimmy is inside the cage with her, she escapes, while holding him off until she locks the cage door. The sad part comes when Jimmy realizes he's locked in and Chizo is out free.

Tonight Chizo fumbles her escape. Repeatedly, Jimmy refuses to let her out. On her fourth try, she escapes, slamming the lock shut before Jimmy can push open the door. I watch him peering at Chizo through the bars of the cage. He wails, he pounds the floor, he pouts. Chizo sits just outside of his reach. Frustrated by Jimmy, I decide to make him upset by kissing Chizo again. As I do, he presses his face against the cage, one arm stretched out toward me.

He can't reach me. He snarls. I'm not worried about him biting me now, and I kiss Chizo again. She kisses back, grabbing my lower lip with her lips and squeezing hard. I feel a mix of pleasure and pain. Chizo again squeezes my lower lip, releases it, then presses it again before letting go entirely.

I am smitten.

Stepping away from Jimmy's cage, Chizo flashes a glorious smile that lights up her face and makes me feel lucky.

"I like your dressing," she says.

She means the top-and-down. I smile and take her hand. Our plan is to have dinner and go dancing. Because we are on our first date, I've asked Stephen to spend the evening with us. I usually do without him in the evenings, picking up taxis on the street. Tonight I don't want to deal with any strange drivers.

Stephen asks Chizo for directions to her house. She tells him. The streets are all blacktopped until the last turn. We go onto a road with no name. It is little more than an alley that is interrupted by a huge hole. The car disappears into the hole and then emerges. Chizo and I, sitting in the backseat, fall forward and then backward. We are like riders on a boat, hitting a big wave and bracing ourselves.

Chizo's house is behind a tall gate. She gets out of the car, opens the gate and waves Stephen in. She closes the gate behind her.

We are here only for her to change into clothes for the evening.

The first thing I notice is a woman bathing in a stall. I can see her pretty face, but the rest of her is covered by the stall.

"*Kedu,*" Chizo shouts, greeting the woman. She says something to Chizo in their Igbo language, which I happen to know a bit of because my favorite Nigerian musician is an Igbo, Stephen Osita Osadebe. The Igbo are one of the great tribes of Africa. They tried and failed to secede from Nigeria in the late 1960s, creating a short-lived state called Biafra. George Harrison of the Beatles made Biafra famous by holding the first rock concert to raise money for starving Africans there. Chizo was born to an Igbo mother after Biafra collapsed in 1970. Her mother's firstborn, a boy, had died during the war, probably of malnutrition, as many other babies did.

I am not surprised Chizo has an Igbo neighbor. The Igbo are often called the Jews of West Africa. Their native area of Nigeria is packed with people, and many move up and down the west coast of Africa. There are many Igbo in America, refugees from the Biafran war who stayed. And the Igbo are prominent in the Catholic Church. Only a year before, I wrote a front-page article for *The Wall Street Journal* on Igbo priests who travel the world, filling vacancies in churches, even in Ireland, of all places. Irish missionaries converted large masses of Igbo one hundred years ago, and the Igbo remain enthusiastic Catholics.

We move past Chizo's friend to the apartment building. We pass four doors. The fifth is hers. The door is unlocked and Chizo pushes it open. I follow her into a small room. There is a single lightbulb hanging from the ceiling. There is a thin foam mattress on the floor. A large black suitcase sits in one corner and two more suitcases are stacked on a shelf extending out from the wall opposite the window. Below the window, covered by a screen and no glass, is a small table. A gas cooker sits on top of the table. A rubber tube runs behind the table to a canister of gas below.

This is where Chizo lives. There is no kitchen. No bathroom. No running water.

I watch Chizo open the black suitcase in the corner. She pulls out clothes. I watch her study various combinations of them. She views herself in a cracked mirror hanging sideways on a wall. I am surprised at how many clothes she can fit in a single suitcase, but then most of her clothes aren't large. This is the tropics after all. People don't wear much.

She continues to experiment with different combinations. I squirm. I say she looks great. She keeps trying outfits. I keep saying she looks great. Finally, she says, "Rushing man. Wait outside."

I step outside—and nearly crash into the woman from the shower. Her name is Chichi and she is Chizo's roommate.

"You are the American," she says.

She wears a single cloth around her body and a matching scarf on her head. She is cooking fish on a grill. Her skin is the lightest possible shade of brown, the color of the sand on Accra's Labadi Beach.

I do not know what to say to her.

I wonder how these women share such a small room.

Chizo joins us outside carrying a plastic bag with her clothes for the evening. She will take a shower and get dressed at my hotel room while I wait in the hotel restaurant.

Back in the car, I ask her how they manage to live together in the tiny room with one bed.

"We sleep in the same bed," she says, pausing, inviting a reaction from me.

I start to speak and she cuts me off, laughing.

"We are African women. We are used to it. We don't know lesbian. That's for you whites."

I'm sipping a large Star beer when I see her come down the steps from my room inside the hotel. She wears a backless skintight top, cut low on her chest, and a short black skirt, revealing her thighs, which now seem sexy rather than simply powerful. She wears black vinyl boots with spiky heels, making her seem much taller. I put the beer down and stare at her as she comes toward me. I've never seen her before in anything but her zoo clothes. Now I see what's hidden underneath those clothes.

I like what I see.

"Wow," I say when she sits down at my table.

"These are my club clothes," she says.

She drinks a Coke and we talk about dinner. I let her choose the restaurant. She picks a fish place called Blue Gate that I don't know. But Stephen does and gets us there in ten minutes. The restaurant, which is an Accra favorite, specializes in a fleshy, bony fish that the locals call tilapia (though it is quite different from the better-known variety of the same name from South America).

When we arrive at Blue Gate, we find two women are cooking dozens of tilapia on a long grill on the side of a crooked street. Storm drains rim most paved roads in Accra, including this one, and juices from the grill spill into the drain below. Customers walk to the grill and pick the fish they want, then return to their seats, either inside the small dining room or across the street, where they eat on plastic tables in a vacant lot. Chizo spends a long time choosing our fish, as if she relishes the chance to do so. Or maybe she is picky. She selects two large fish and the chef slow-cooks them while applying plenty of spicy sauce from a tin can that looks a hundred years old.

From time to time, Chizo visits the fish to see how they are doing.

When the fish arrive, Chizo dabs on more hot sauce. "I like hot," she says.

I do the same. I like hot too.

She takes fried plantains and white rice with her fish. I take boiled plantains, white rice and a diced tomato salad. A well-prepared plantain is a delicacy in these parts, and I don't let a day pass without eating one or more.

"I'm happy you like plantains," Chizo says. "I cook them well."

I hope she gets the chance to cook some for me, I think.

I am drinking another Star beer, washing the fish down, looking up at the stars starting to assemble above in the wide African sky. The cool air kisses us, a relief from the heat of the day. I decide not to ask Chizo many questions tonight. I decide to turn off my reporter's brain. I force myself to stay silent.

When we finish eating, we linger. She drinks two shots of whiskey, quickly, which we obtained from the outdoor bar across the street from Blue Gate. I have a shot myself while marveling at how so much of African life can take place in the wide open, out-doors. I drink another shot and look at Chizo. Her eyes dance. The night is cool and her calm makes me calm.

"Relax your skin," she says and looks away.

She doesn't want to talk but there is something I need to tell her. "I'm only in Accra for three more weeks," I say.

I haven't told her this before and expect her to say something, but she sits quietly, relaxing her skin, I suppose.

I feel I must speak. "I go back to California in three weeks."

Her eyes focus on me, reluctantly. "Is that America?"

I nod, pull out the pad I always carry around and draw a quick map. "California is here," I say, pointing at a spot on my map.

"When I first came to Accra, I stayed in a place in Adabraka called Hotel California," she says. "I know California is in America. I only don't know where."

"I'm from California. My adopted home. I'm originally from New York."

She doesn't understand.

"You don't know where New York is?"

She doesn't. I make a note to find her a map of the United States.

I want to say more about my travels, about how I just moved out of London, where I worked for the *Journal,* and how I am returning to California to be near my children, who live with their mother since my divorce, and how I will be teaching journalism at a large university while I figure out what to do next. I want to tell her all these things, and more, but I see she is absorbed in studying my mouth. I ask her why.

"I like the gap between your teeth," she says. "Very beautiful."

Many people in Ghana have similar gaps. They go to specialists who widen the space between the two front teeth. They consider these gaps to be a special kind of loveliness.

My gap comes from a botched orthodontics job done in my youth. I tell Chizo that I don't consider the space between my teeth to be beautiful and that no one in America does either.

She disagrees.

I explain to her how the gap came about by mistake. An expensive mistake.

Maybe because I suddenly feel vulnerable, with all this body talk, I impulsively ask Chizo to tell me about the scars on her face. These scars are what I first see when I look at her. They are the size of quarters: unusual, prominent and arresting. They immediately wrap Chizo in mystery. They demand an explanation.

Chizo says her marks were a mistake too. As a baby, she took sick, and her grandmother carved them into the fleshy part of each cheek—when her parents were away. Her grandmother meant the marks to protect her against evil spirits and to ensure her good health. Her father and mother were horrified by them, furious with the grandmother for doing this without their permission. The cuts were made with rough razors, and when they healed the marks were large and enduring. On her right cheek is a scar that resembles a teardrop. On her left cheek is a jagged scar that looks like the letter *w* written twice.

"The marks spoil my face," Chizo says.

I shake my head and tell her the marks enhance her beauty. They make her appear exotic, special, otherworldly, like a heavenly creature. I don't know whether I have said the right thing but I have said the only thing I can say. I am moved by her facial scars, which I think give Chizo a terrible beauty, not unlike the beauty of Africa, where the wonderful and the awful—the divine and the devilish—coexist, and often happily. What surprises me is that I believe what I say. The scars on Chizo's cheeks, easily dismissed by locals as "tribal marks," stemming from her ethnicity, are to me an integral part of her face. They are as much a part of her as her captivating eyes, which already exert an unaccountable power over me. Honestly, I cannot imagine Chizo without her facial scars. They inspire in me a sense of the profound, endowing Chizo with a wisdom that I imagine she acquired through suffering, through experiencing the straight turn crooked, through her own unacknowledged loss of innocence.

Chizo grows quiet again. I look at the stars, sip my beer and wonder whether I am the first person to insist the scars on her face enhance her appearance. Perhaps I am because she is looking at me in disbelief, her eyes wide open. A long time passes and finally I can't stand the silence. Looking at her looking at me, I ask what she is looking at.

"The gap between your teeth," she says. "It makes you more handsome."

I choose the dance club. A place I've never been called Chester's that on Wednesday nights has live music in an open-air courtyard. Chester's is named after a lawyer in Accra who has his own TV talk show. He is a homosexual, probably the most important and interesting gay man in Ghana. But since homosexuality is illegal here, Chester is in the closet, though barely. He often comes to the club and dances better than Michael Jackson. He's short and wiry, likes wearing tight black clothing and is known for grabbing the mike and leading the excellent house band in some American pop songs.

We get to Chester's early, just after 10:00 P.M., and take seats under the sky along the whitewashed wall that forms one perimeter of the club. Chester himself is here tonight, and the energy is already high. At a large table bordering the dance floor is a tall, stout man with a furry beard and light skin. He is the most famous man in Ghana, instantly recognizable as the country's former dictator and later twice-elected president, Jerry Rawlings. Just a few months ago, J.J., which is usually what people call him, gave up power and allowed voters to choose his successor. Even though a political opponent was elected in his place, Rawlings stayed, making himself the only former dictator of an African nation to live in his country after surrendering power.

He is sitting less than twenty feet from Chizo and me.

She notices him. "That's J.J.," she whispers.

I am excited. I have been trying for months to get an interview with Rawlings, who talks only with the BBC. I tell Chizo that I must speak with him, though I won't bring up my interview request here. I rush over to Rawlings and congratulate him on giving up power. "A great act of statesmanship," I say. He smiles and shakes my hand. Rawlings is strikingly handsome. His father is Scottish, making him, in the local parlance, "half-caste," or half-white. I tell him I am an American journalist and want to interview him sometime. He tells me to see his press agent, the very man who has been refusing to arrange a meeting with him. I smile, touch his shoulder and then go back to my seat.

I listen to the music, a mix of reggae, West African highlife and a bit of American pop. Everything the band plays is happy music, soft and lilting, relaxed, easy to follow. The band is confident, hungry for attention and energized by the presence of the former dictator. The crowd is made up of about half Africans and half foreigners, mainly aid workers and assorted other do-gooders. The entrance fee is nearly three dollars, high enough to keep out the ordinary Africans—and a relative bargain for the city's elite.

I ask Chizo to dance. She says no, not yet. There are only a few people on the dance floor. "I don't disgrace myself by being the first," she says.

She drinks a locally brewed Guinness while I sip bottled water. A half hour later, I ask her to dance again, and again she says no.

As midnight approaches, the dance floor gets crowded. When the floor is packed with dancers, Chizo takes my hand and brings me onto the floor. She starts to shake, shimmy and roll—the embodiment of grace and power. She lowers her behind until it nearly touches the floor. She slowly rises to meet me. Her spins are crisp. She pretends to sing to me, mouthing the words of the song played by the band. Her eyes widen, as if to beckon me inside her. I am moving as little as I can, afraid to do something stupid, watching her and not my feet.

We keep dancing through a slow song and the singer moves away from his musicians and mingles with the dancers as he croons. My clothes are soaked with sweat. Though the air is cool and we dance in the open, fans are whirring above us because the heat from the crush of people is intense. I take hold of Chizo's hands for the first time and we sway gently to the sound of highlife. I'm intent on not stepping on her feet. I hear her voice singing in my ear. The singer comes near us with his microphone, dancing and singing, coolly serenading us.

The ex-dictator, Rawlings, is on the dance floor now, and he and his wife are near Chizo and me. I watch his feet, see his steps, look him in the eyes. Chizo tugs at my arm and moves close to me. "Don't stare at him," she says. "Look at me."

At that instant, she kisses me, throws back her neck, beckons me with her eyes and lets me kiss her, a glancing kiss that catches the side of her neck. To the beat of the music, she shimmies down the length of my body, bringing her butt to within a few inches of the dance floor. Her butt is still shaking. I am motionless, watching her flesh hover above the ground, wondering how she will rise up, until I watch her do so, my mouth open.

The next day Stephen and I pick up Chizo at the zoo near closing time. She is waiting for us at the front gate, already wearing her street clothes. She looks fetching in leopard-patterned overalls that expose her rounded shoulders and narrow frame. On her head she wears a wide hat in matching material. Though wearing spiky heels, she deftly moves across the dirt parking lot, never wavering as she walks over rocks and holes. I tease her about Jimmy and she suddenly stops. She asks me for a two-thousand-cedi note, which is about twenty-five cents, and goes over to the food stand in front of the zoo's entrance. She buys a bag of peanuts and takes my hand.

"I promised him a treat," she says. We are still a hundred feet from the front of his cage when Jimmy starts screaming. "Jimmy," Chizo shouts. "Groundnuts."

She hands him a handful of unshelled peanuts, then gives me the bag. "You try."

Before long Jimmy's reddish hand is reaching through the bars. I hand him a peanut, then another and another. He's happy. Emboldened, I hold his hand, alert to the chance of a mishap. Chizo laughs. "He won't bite," she says.

I stroke his hand and then pat the hair on his arm. He looks at me and I look at him, all while Chizo is singing to him. I finally hand him the bag and we take off.

Stephen is asleep in the car when we get there. I wake him and, seeing Chizo, he asks to hear the story about Rawlings. She tells him that we danced right next to the ex-president and his wife. Stephen is impressed. He drives us back to my hotel, passing the large metal gate at the entrance and parking near the restaurant. I have something to show Chizo and we go up to my room.

Inside, I hand her a small CD player, wait while she adjusts her hat to put on the headphones, and then press the start button. Instantly, she is transformed. She is whirling, swaying, sashaying to the music. I am playing my favorite Nigerian album, by Osadebe, the Igbo Frank Sinatra. The album is called *Kedu, Greetings from America,* recorded during a visit by Osadebe to Seattle. In a voice alternately gruff and sweet, light and intense, Osadebe sings of peace and community, love and yams, the sacred food of the Igbo. Lilting guitar lines mix with a jazz-inflected brass section. His swinging songs are sung in Igbo and in English and sometimes both. Chizo excitedly shoves one of the earplugs into my ear and now we are both listening to the music, dancing close to one another.

We fall on the bed, the music still captivating us. We kiss one another, holding tight, our hands intertwined. "Where did you find this music in America?" she asks. "Do Americans know our culture?"

Osadebe is singing in Chizo's native language. He is her favorite musician, which surprises me since his style of music comes out of the 1970s, when Chizo was only a child. Osadebe is groaning out another greeting from America now, this one in English, something about a secret and why his lover asked him about the secret in public. Chizo laughs and pulls me tighter. We are kissing now and I forget to tell her how I found the Osadebe album in the Africa section of a Berkeley music store some months before. As we touch each other for the first time, she tells me of her pride in being Nigerian. "We are the giants of Africa, the Super

Eagles," she says. But the Igbo are special. "They are my brothers and sisters," she says. "They are my people."

Her joy over my knowledge of her people—even my superficial knowledge of Osadebe, the Igbo troubadour—washes over me. I suddenly cannot form thoughts. I go speechless, robbed of the capacity to admit to her that she is the first person I've ever met who has even heard of Osadebe.

My silence gives her the chance to speak, and she explains the meaning of the Osadebe song. He sings about the impossibility of escaping from gossip. We are all doomed to be talked about, Chizo says and then translates the Igbo lyrics into English: "In this world people will be saying if you eat, they will talk about you. And if you don't eat, they will still talk about you."

Chizo smiles now, holding me tighter, letting herself go. "How strange," she says, "that an American brings me a CD of my favorite singer—songs in my own mother tongue."

"There's a great music store where I live," I say, beaming proudly. "A shop called Amoeba. They have a huge Africa section."

"What magic do your people possess to collect in a distance place the music of my people?" Chizo asks.

Her question silences me. Magic? I don't understand. I simply marvel at my good luck in finding a woman who can decode Osadebe for me. Whatever magic I may possess is nothing compared to Chizo's.

Or is something else happening here?

Chapter Six

Bushmeat

Love is an adventure, I think, as I walk on the side of the main road in the hip Osu neighborhood of Accra. I dodge young men—and some women too—who call out, *"Obruni, obruni."* One man stops and breathlessly tells me that one of my shoelaces is untied. I look down and find that he is indeed correct. When I bend over and tighten the knot, he cheers. He is still clapping when I walk off.

A guy selling necklaces and colorful shirts calls out to me, "Hey, *obruni,* be my customer." I look at him warily, weighing whether to approach his roadside stand and inspect his goods. I start toward him, thinking I may purchase a piece of local jewelry for Chizo, when I catch sight of her standing across the road in front of a taxi. She sees me and my step quickens. I cross over a sewage drain and then hopscotch my way past potholes the size of surfboards. When I finally cross the street, I hug her.

She doesn't hug back. Instead she pushes me into the backseat of a waiting taxi, blindfolds me and stuffs a gag into my mouth. I try to speak. I can't. I worry about breathing. Everything is dark. I can't see. And I'm held down by her powerful arms. I struggle, but I can't free myself. Chizo can carry an eighty-pound bucket of water—on her head. She wrestles with a chimpanzee without breathing hard. She hacks at thick bush with a heavy machete. Her grip on me is so tight that I feel I have no chance of escaping. I am thinking about faking a heart attack when she shoves my arms behind my back and ties my wrists together with what feels like a head scarf. I am her prisoner now. The taxi is rumbling over a pockmarked road and Chizo steadies my head, maybe so I don't smash it against a door. She is whispering something to me in Igbo. I catch her phrase the third time. *"Afran ganaya,"* she says. I love you.

I love her too. Tonight is my last night in Accra. My plane leaves Africa for America in seven hours. I have to be on that plane. I have got places to go, people to see. Besides, there is a big penalty imposed by British Airways if I miss the flight.

The taxi is on smooth road now. Where are we going? For an instant I fear Chizo is abducting me. My last night, her last chance to grab me. Chizo and I have spent twenty-five days together, seeing each other every day since we first met at the zoo. I suddenly wonder how well I know her. Maybe she plans to hold me for ransom? Maybe she has an accomplice? My fears are running amok. Chizo's swift seizure of power terrifies me.

My head is spinning, and the blindfold hurts too. Just as I near my breaking point, Chizo calmly says, "You whites don't joke with planes. I know that. You won't miss your plane."

Her words jolt me back into reality—and chase away my ridiculous anxieties. I try to tell her I'm grateful—I try to thank her for realizing the importance of airline schedules—but I can only hear myself grunting nonsensically. Then the taxi jerks and I fall against her body, gagging. She holds my face against her chest. I wonder what she is wearing. I smell her perfume. I feel her necklace against my skin. The taxi is speeding now and I concentrate on the sound of Chizo's heart. I can hear her heart beating. She holds the back of my head and I am still, hearing her heart, tasting her skin and growing calmer from breathing in her scent. Even bound and gagged, I like being near her.

I suddenly don't want to leave Africa.

The taxi slows, rumbles over a rough road and comes to a stop. The engine cuts. I hear a door opening, then Chizo is pushing me out of the backseat. My legs are unsteady and she helps me stay upright. I feel the ocean on my face. I smell the salty air. Chizo unties my wrists and holds one hand. She leads me onto sand. I am wearing sandals and I can feel the sand on my toes. I feel the spray of water on my face and hear the dull thud of the waves hitting the beach, the sound growing louder. I'm at Labadi Beach. Relieved, I want to shout. I am elated. Chizo is a stranger to me no more. My fear vanishes.

She sits me down in a plastic chair and removes my gag. I heave a sigh, then breathe deeply. The air is cooler than in the city. My eyes flutter when she removes the blindfold. Tears of joy run down my cheeks.

There's a table in front of me. A bottle of a local gin, a Coke and a tall Star beer. On a plate are goat kebabs and roasted plantain. Labadi Beach is where we often go to relax. I take a long drink of beer. I dip a kebab into a pile of loose pepper next to the kebabs. I like the taste of goat. I shove a stick in my mouth and chew the mix of pepper, tomato and meat.

Chizo kisses me on the cheek. She is smiling, the biggest smile in the world. I understand now why she didn't visit her chimp today. She's been busy, planning my farewell event, my last night in Accra.

The tide is rolling in. We are at one of a row of restaurants that sit on the beach. On weekends, they are jammed, but it is a Wednesday. The beach is almost empty except for the people working there.

We are at my favorite restaurant, nearest the entrance to the beach. Robert, the manager, is a friend. On one of my first trips to the beach, he pleaded with me to eat at his restaurant, promising me happiness. He delivered. I go back now, most times. Today he greets Chizo warmly, then disappears.

I sip my beer. The sun is setting. There's nothing off in the distance. Peering out, I imagine the slave ships working this Gold Coast hundreds of years ago. I imagine New York on the other side of the Atlantic. I think of Africa and America separated by a single body of water. I think of the suffering of the slaves carried over this ocean. Then, gulping my Star beer, I tell Chizo she's full of surprises.

"I'm not finished," she says.

I shudder. "Please don't blindfold me again," I say.

She puts her hand on my lips and I stop begging. We get up for a stroll. Some small boys follow, asking for money. We don't give them any and they leave.

The big hotels are to the north and we walk south, all the way to the lagoon, where men sell sticks of pot for pennies. Chizo goes off alone and buys a stick for us to smoke. I had not smoked pot for many years before coming to Accra. The pot is weak, but, at three dollars an ounce, it is ridiculously cheap. Weak is good too. I don't get, as Chizo says, "overstoned."

We sit down on the bare sand. The heat of the day is finally relenting. The air is invigorating and there is no breeze and I hold Chizo close to me. We smoke. The small fire from the match burns long like a candle. She draws deeply on the pot stick, then blows smoke in my mouth. I hold the smoke and swallow. She blows another mouthful into my mouth.

We've had enough. We rise to walk again. We let our feet touch the water. The sea laps against the bottom of my cotton drawstring pants. In my left hand I hold my sandals, and in my right hand I hold Chizo's hand. I can't remember when the three boys started to follow us. They do cartwheels and walk on their hands. Behind them are two older men. I now realize that one is the leader of the comedy troupe that works the beach on weekends, delighting crowds with gymnastics and curious tricks.

How did Chizo find them?

Back at our table, the comedians give us a private show. When the glass eater is done, after he's swallowed and regurgitated a six-pack of (broken) Coke bottles, he comes over to me and wishes me a safe trip. "Come back to Ghana," he says.

I dig into my pocket, looking for bills to give him and the troupe a dash, or tip. Chizo stops me. She's taken care of it.

"Where do these guys come from?" I ask her.

"They come from Ada," she says, a village about two hours away, on the coast.

I await further explanation. There is none. I tell the glass eater I admire his skills. He is happy. I thank the rest of his crew. They smile. Then the smallest of the boys, in a kind of finale, tucks his legs behind his back and under his arms. Then he rolls on the sand like a ball. He stops, and the glass eater lifts him in the air and then drops him onto our table.

Chizo breaks into laughter. The boy smiles. I wonder whether the boy really wants to be a contortionist or is pressured into participating in what might be a family business. Before I can ask the boy anything, he unfurls his body and bursts into the air as if shot from a cannon. He lands on Chizo's shoulders. Swaying in her chair, she laughs uproariously. My doubts about the boy vanish. He looks so intently at the ocean now that I turn and search the horizon for whatever he is looking at. I find nothing, and when I swing back around, the boy is gone. The glass eater and the other comedians are gone too.

Alone with Chizo, I am still hungry. We've had only goat kebabs and a couple of roasted plantains. "Dinner is coming," she says. She is cooking it. Robert has let her use his kitchen. Chizo has never cooked for me before. Actually, no African woman has ever cooked for me before. I do not know what to expect.

Chizo leaves me to prepare dinner, while I continue to walk on the beach. The waves are lapping against the sand, and the sun is dropping. The water is warm enough to swim in but I never do more than put my feet in. Locals use the sea as a toilet, and the ocean floor drops steeply after fifteen or twenty feet. The combination is unattractive.

I apply my bug repellent. The superstrong stuff I buy at REI in the United States. You can't find anything so lethal here. Malaria is a constant peril, and limiting the number of bug bites I receive is prudent, even when taking my daily malaria medicine, which I am.

I slip off my sandals and walk along the water. Soon I am joined by Felix, the batik artist. He has a limp and a beard. He makes large batiks, the size of bedsheets. I bought a few earlier this visit, and he asks me if I want more. He keeps a shop at the edge of the beach, where the sand meets the bush, and the beach gives way to a tropical forest.

The shop is made of discarded wood planks, the color bled out of them by the wind and the sun and the sand. He brings me there and offers me a stool. I sit down. On each wall of the shop there is a large batik. Earlier in my visit, Felix showed me photos of designs and I picked a couple and he made the batiks expressly for me, taking about a week to do so. I have no time for ordering now and I am looking at the wall coverings closely. One of them I like: four elephants, their trunks extended, marching west against the backdrop of a blue sky.

"Beautiful," I tell Felix. "The colors are wonderful. And the elephants are magical, like out of a movie."

He smiles broadly and agrees to accept the same "best" price as before. I give him the money, about twenty dollars. As he folds the batik, I make a mistake. I tell him I am leaving for America this very night.

His face falls. Perhaps he thinks he's losing a good customer.

I tell him I may return.

He still looks disheartened. He shakes his head and launches into a story. Felix likes telling stories about his difficulties as an artist, about having to leave Ivory Coast because of the civil war, about how he moved to Ghana and struggled here. Most nights he sleeps under a tree behind his shop. To make the batiks, he goes to a village a few hours from here, where a friend keeps the materials. He makes the batiks with his friend, then returns to the beach with them. He has no phone. The only way to find him is to troll the beach. "I wish I had a proper shop, with electricity and a phone," he says.

I say nothing. I look at my watch. I should get back to Chizo. Maybe her dinner is ready and she needs me.

I look at his sad round eyes, and then I look at the ground. I have only one rule in Africa whenever I meet very poor people. I have only one rule and I am about to follow it.

I hear a voice in my head reminding me of the rule: Only make promises you can keep, and make very few promises.

I hear Felix's voice overwhelming the sound of my own. He is practically shouting. "Take me to America," he says. "I will repay you when I become a famous artist there."

I clutch his lovely batik against my breast, stand up from the stool and look him in the eye. He stares right through me. I can feel hope on his breath. "I'm hungry," I say. "Tonight is my last dinner here, and my friend is cooking for me. I wonder what she's making."

"Something special," he says.

I nod and say, "I can't take you to America. But the next time I visit, I'll buy more of your art."

Felix is unhappy. "Are you bringing your girlfriend to America?" he asks.

I tell him no, she's not coming. "I'm not bringing any Africans to America," I say. "I don't have room in my luggage."

He laughs. I can see the space where his front teeth should be. The idea of my leaving without any Africans stashed in my luggage seems to please him. He shakes my hand the West African way, with the finger snap at the end.

I botch the snap and walk away.

I feel the sea at my face again. The breeze brings relief from the smells of Accra, where the intense heat and the crush of people, cars and waste can make for a bracing brew.

When I reach the table, I find Chizo drinking a Guinness. The plates are covered with paper napkins, so the sand doesn't get on them.

Chizo removes the napkins. She piles white rice on my plate and a large portion of stew. We sit close to one another. I start eating, first the rice, then I mix in some forkfuls of the stew. I notice that Chizo isn't eating yet. When I pick up a piece of meat from the stew, she edges closer to me. I think I've got a leg, though I can't tell for sure because of the sauce. I eat the bone clean. The meat tastes salty, smoky and unfamiliar. Definitely not chicken, not even one of those scrawny, bony African chickens. No, this is another meat.

"What is this?" I ask. "Goat?"

Chizo doesn't say. Her eyes are smiling. "Do you like it?"

I'm not sure, but I say yes anyway.

She kisses me lightly. "I was afraid you might not," she says.

"Why?"

"Whites don't usually eat this."

"No?"

My voice betrays my fear. I remember how enthusiastically she blindfolded me. Once again, I feel out of control, a stranger in a strange land, the familiar ground giving way.

I'm about to learn anew that Africa is not what it seems. The meat in my mouth is unexpectedly tough. I chew on it seemingly forever. I can't get it down. I suddenly accept that something else is going on here and I don't know what it is.

"You're eating bushmeat," Chizo announces. "The best bush-meat in Accra."

Her eyes are shining brightly and I think her declaration is meant to help me. I try again to chew the meat in my mouth. I do not succeed. I stop chewing and ask, "Am I eating jungle rat?"

"You deserve it," she says.

In mock horror, I bury my face in my hands and slump in my chair. "You should have warned me," I say.

She looks into my eyes and I am filled with regret over my complaint. "You deserve bushmeat," she says. "That's what rich African men eat. The big men. The chiefs. Tonight you are one of the big men of Africa. You are my chief!"

I like the sound of this and I sit up in my chair, ready to try again. I resume eating, thinking about my bigness and forgetting about what I am chewing on. I do feel bigger than usual. I do. Chizo is making me feel extra special one last time. She is giving me a great send-off. I stab another piece of bushmeat and put it in my mouth. The meat tastes saltier now, and my mind is filled with an image of a dead jungle rat, being roasted on the side of a road, having been caught in the bush, then killed, skinned and seasoned for smoking. I've seen these dead rats many times along the road. Once, with Chizo in the central Makola Market, I held a prime piece of bushmeat in my hands. The market woman edged near me as if afraid I might abscond with her pricey meat. I remember my surprise at how much she wanted for this one piece alone: almost ten dollars. For West Africans, bushmeat is a delicacy and Chizo's jungle rat is only stage one in the meat riot that is the African palate. Big men yearn for antelope, African deer, zebra, baboon, even chimpanzee or gorilla.

The thought of eating a chimpanzee of course makes Chizo sick. She loves jungle rat, though, and tonight she's in bushmeat heaven. I watch her tackle her piece, stripping the bones clean and practically devouring them too. Her face glows while she chomps. I am silent now, letting the sea breeze and the spray of the ocean wash over me. I look over at Chizo and wonder what she is thinking. I wonder what I will tell her at the airport, when my driver, Stephen, drops me off, in those moments when we are fending off the porters looking for tips and possibly plotting the theft of my luggage. I wonder whether, in that last instant I see her, I will be strong or weak. I wonder what promises I will make in the final moment, having not made any to her. Will I even promise to return?

"Would you like some more?" Chizo says, interrupting my thoughts.

She wants me to eat more bushmeat, though she is too proud to insist. I cannot disappoint her. "Pile it on," I say. "The more I eat, the better it tastes."

*　　*　　*

At the airport, Stephen pulls alongside the curb. I promise Chizo I will return.

"Next time," she says, "I'll cook you bushmeat again."

I smile but cannot hide my sadness. There are no bushmeat leftovers for me to take to America. No Chizo either.

I look at her for a final time, then Stephen opens the trunk and the porters commence fighting over my luggage. I have two large suitcases, each weighing about fifty pounds. I want to ask Chizo to help me handle them but she's in the car. Since she's not an airline traveler, she's not allowed to accompany me into the airport.

I choose one of the porters. "I'm coming," he says, then walks off, leaving me with a half dozen others. When one porter tugs on my shirt, I raise my voice, issue a vague threat, and they all step back as if I am about to attack. By the time my chosen porter returns with a luggage cart and grabs my two suitcases, I am ready to leave.

I want to see Chizo again but my porter is moving now with my luggage and I must chase him. In Africa, I never let my luggage out of my sight. When I catch up with my bags, I turn around and I don't see Stephen's car. He's gone. Chizo is not. She is standing alone, watching me from a distance. I push forward through the crowd around the entrance, keeping one hand on my porter. When I look back again, I'm startled to find her right behind me. She kisses me on the lips.

I hold her close and I don't want to let her go. My arms are around her waist, my hands on her behind. My face is buried in her hair. "Rushing man," she whispers. "How can you behave this way in public of people?" Her question makes me stand back and I see the Africans around us. There are many and they have formed a tight circle, giving Chizo and me space enough to move. They are staring at us. When they see me watching them, a chant erupts.

"Harry! Harry! Harry!"

Not again. Chizo and I laugh. The crowd thinks I am Harry Zakkou, the general manager of the most successful soccer team in Ghana, Hearts of Oak. Harry is the African equivalent of George

Steinbrenner of the New York Yankees. He is flamboyant, wealthy (from a local business) and married to an African woman. Of Lebanese descent, Harry is a local hero, rare among the Lebanese for having mixed-race children and embracing African society. Even better, the Hearts usually win the league championship and this year they are competing in a special tournament to crown the best club team in Africa.

The funny thing is I actually look like Harry and I am flattered that I've been mistaken, once again, for this local celebrity. Harry is fair-skinned, tall, thin and keeps his hair short. Me too. We don't actually look very much alike in the face, though. I know. I've met Harry. We've lunched together, and he's taken me to a couple of soccer games. But to the Africans here, Harry and I are near twins.

"We whites all look alike, don't we?" I say to Chizo, teasing.

The crowd is growing larger now, and the chanting louder. "Harry!" I hear. "Harry!"

I wave my hand and pretend to be Harry. There is no point in explaining who I really am. People would only feel sad to hear the truth.

Chizo wants to move on. "Don't joke with your plane," she says. She pushes the porter, urging him to get me inside the terminal. I hold on to his waist and inch forward, keeping my eyes on my bags.

I feel Chizo against me and then I don't. I suddenly fear I will never see her again. I fear that while I am away something will happen to her. She will be caught in a car crash and she won't get the medical attention she needs. She will be treated like an anonymous African and not my special African.

A man in a uniform asks for my passport. We are at the point where only passengers can proceed.

I don't feel Chizo's hand anymore. I am afraid to turn around and see that she is gone. I don't turn around. Instead I concentrate on getting my passport back. I need my passport. The man returns it, and I push forward, following my luggage.

PART THREE

Grand Bassam and Cape Coast

December 2001

*I*n the fall of 2001, I began teaching at the University of California's School of Journalism in Berkeley. I wondered when I'd next see Chizo Okon, or even whether I'd ever see her again. She might forget me. I might forget her. We lived eight thousand miles apart, roughly one-third of the Earth's circumference. The flying time from California to Ghana totaled seventeen hours—with the wind! We were at least eight time zones apart. When Chizo sat down for dinner, I was just waking up.

E-mail made forgetting each other harder, and exchanging greetings easy. Before I left Ghana, Chizo created her first e-mail account. E-mail helped because she had no phone. To speak with her I had to call one of her friends with a cell phone. But her friend then had to find Chizo, which did not always happen and often chewed up costly minutes on the phone. E-mail became our lifeline, but even it was a challenge, at least for Chizo. To get online, she traveled by bus or taxi to an Internet café in the center of Accra, where for about a dollar an hour she sent e-mails and surfed the Web—on those days when the whole system worked at all.

In late August 2001, I sent Chizo my first e-mail from California, I did not know what to expect. Two days later, I received an e-mail from her while I sat in my office at the university. A quick glance at the screen made my heart leap. I closed the door and opened her first e-mail to me. Her mail went straight to my heart:

HONEY, I'm so happy to receive your words. I hope your
journey didn't cause you too much stress. I'm fine and ok, only
I'm missing your presence. I'm always thinking about the way
you love whole of me. Whole of me wants whole of you.

Two weeks later, the planes hit the World Trade Center and the world changed. I faced a choice. I could chase the biggest story of my time. Or I could choose a different path. I could marry Africa.

I couldn't decide. Then one day a famous journalist told me he planned to travel to Afghanistan in December, after the semester ended. He invited me to join him. We would report on the U.S. invasion of Afghanistan, on the hunt for Osama bin Laden, on the future of the war on terrorism. I thanked the journalist for his invitation and thought over his offer.

I was tempted to go with him. For days, I weighed my options and finally decided to buy a ticket to Kabul. I decided that Chizo could wait. I decided that Africa would be there when the war on terrorism ended, or at least until bin Laden was captured. Romance was exciting, but I had a career to sustain. I had articles to write and a reputation to enhance.

I made plans for an Afghan trip and anxiously counted the days until I would have to confess to Chizo that I would spend Christmas in Kabul. I imagined her asking me where Kabul is on the map and then struggling to describe the location to her.

Before I informed Chizo of my decision, I received an e-mail from her with only these words: "Whole of me wants whole of you."

The e-mail kept arriving in my mailbox. "Whole of me wants whole of you." After reading these words many times, I closed my eyes, heard Chizo's voice, visualized her face, saw her smile and felt her touch. Then I opened my eyes and listened to my heart.

I didn't go to Kabul. I bought a ticket to Accra, intending to spend New Year's in Africa.

Chapter Seven

The Little Red *Blolo*

When it is winter in America, it is summer in Ghana. I walk unsteadily in the midday heat, protected from the sun by my canvas Tilley hat. I wear a zippered cotton vest, laden with pockets, over a thin white T-shirt; both are soaked through with my perspiration. The heat is relentless. I've already changed my clothes once today and I am soggy again anyway. My hat, which I never remove, is soaked. The hat fails to dry fully during the night and sports spots of green mold. Moldy or not, my hat and I are inseparable.

Though I am a short walk from the ocean, the heat remains intense and the Harmattan wind provides no relief, beating on my body like a broom. Near the end of each year, the Harmattan blows hot from the Sahara desert into West Africa, sweeping through the day, carrying tiny particles of sand from faraway places. At this time of year, the sand and the heat are twinned and inescapable. My Tilley hat provides the smallest of defenses. Long pants, despite the heat, are essential. To wear my open-toe leather sandals, I must don socks in order to protect my skin. Against the Harmattan, my pale skin is indeed useless. I envy the dark-skinned people around me, though even for the Africans the only true defense against the heat and dust is resignation.

It is December 2001. I am back in Africa, reunited with Chizo for the first time after a separation of nearly four months. I knew I must return to her when I began sleeping with her picture under my pillow, and a piece of her clothing alongside me, in my cottage in California. Before I could tell her that I shared my bed with these articles, she told me in a phone call that she slept with a photo of me, and fell asleep holding one of my shirts in her arms.

Because my visit comes a couple of weeks before Christmas, Chizo and I celebrate by leaving Ghana in a hired car for the neighboring country of Ivory Coast. We drive north along the Atlantic, veering off the main road to reach the old French colonial capital of Grand Bassam, which lies on a thin peninsula jutting into the Atlantic. The town—long ago abandoned by the French colonialists, who came to favor Abidjan as a commercial hub—is today merely a pleasant curiosity. On the ocean side of Grand Bassam, many clean and comfortable hotels run by French expats line the sandy beach, set behind low stucco walls. The water is arresting, green and blue and clear, rolling toward the land in gentle undulations.

That night we stay at one of the modest beachfront hotels, owned by a retired French butcher and his wife. We take a small room close to the water. Chizo goes inside ahead of me, surveys the room, nods approvingly and then, with a single swoop of her right hand, she grabs a green-gray gecko running along the wall. She snaps the gecko's neck and, before I say a word, tosses the dead reptile outside.

Chizo has never been to French-speaking Africa before, and I have a selfish reason for visiting Ivory Coast. The former French colony is one of the best places to find traditional African art at reasonable prices. The country's ethnic groups, especially the Baule, are famous for the style and skill of their art, which has a great following in France. Close to the center of Grand Bassam, there are a few art dealers who specialize in the carved statues, figurines and masks that endlessly intrigue me.

In the heat of the day, I am walking the ruined streets of Grand Bassam, searching for an art dealer known for offering unusual and authentic works. Soon, I am surrounded by dozens of statues and masks, in all shapes and sizes. A tall Malian man, his skin the color of coal, gives me a tour of his unimposing gallery, which is actually housed in an old wooden garage with a concrete floor and exposed rafters.

His name is Toumani. Though he looks younger, I learn he is my own age, late forties. While his English is heavily accented, he speaks confidently in a low voice. I stand close to him, while Chizo keeps her distance. She thinks these statues contain evil spirits, and the priests of her Catholic upbringing told her to stay away from them. Indeed, the longer I remain among the statues and masks, the farther away from me she stands, until she is outside in the blazing sun.

Toumani sends a small boy out to her with a Coke, which Chizo accepts. She calls out, *"Merci beaucoup,"* which is probably the only French she knows. I thank Toumani in English and he flashes me a wide smile. He is happy to see me, he says, because life is hard in Ivory Coast, what with the military government, rising crime, strife among the country's distinct Muslim and Christian regions. All these factors have combined to reduce the number of French people living here, stifle tourism and depress the art trade.

I have about a hundred dollars with me, in West African francs, and from a quick look at the things around me, I know I could spend it all in one visit. I am dazzled by the possibilities but aware that I must carry back to Ghana (and ultimately to the United States) anything I buy. My eyes are drawn to smaller pieces, in particular a foot-long statute of a big-chested, long-necked woman. The carving is not fine. What's striking about the statue is the paint. The woman is painted red, except for her hair, eyebrows and the ends of her breasts, which are painted black.

"She is spirit lover. In the world beyond," Toumani explains. "She is *blolo* in the Baule language."

From my reading on African art, I already know the term *blolo*. This red woman, with a crack running through the left side of her face, represents the otherworldly lover that every Baule wife or husband secretly desires and ultimately must possess. The otherworldly lover offers a refuge from the disappointments of love in the real world. Now I have a *blolo* too. She might come in handy, I think, bringing me peace of mind because I know she awaits my arrival in the world of our ancestors. I decide I must buy her.

Toumani accepts the price I offer. Though he wants more, he also wants me to return and purchase more pieces, so the goodwill between us matters to him. And I have my own dignity to respect. I don't wish to be seen as the foolish *obruni,* the privileged white foreigner who can lavish money on trinkets. I have learned not to overpay for art in Africa for a practical reason as well: no matter how old a piece looks, it may be a fake. The red woman, my *blolo,* seems decades old, and the paint pigments surely are indigenous. The statue is heavy, carved from a hardwood, and the cracks, at the base and across the face, testify to its age. Yet things are never what they seem in Africa, and I must content myself with the existential pleasure provided by the red woman, and not fantasize that I've purchased a valuable artifact.

I step outside the shop and show Chizo the statue. She purses her lips and brightens only when I slip the statue into my vest pocket. "Out of sight now," I say to Toumani, who wishes my *madame* a good day.

Before leaving, I ask Toumani to visit me the next day at my hotel. It is a Sunday and he would not ordinarily open his shop. I tell him I will be at the beach behind my hotel the whole day and he can find me and bring me back to his shop. "I want to see more," I say, and without Chizo.

Chizo's ultrablack braids, extensions to her own hair, swing across the back of her neck, weighted down by polished brown-and-white cowrie shells attached to the ends. From across the main street of Grand Bassam, I wave to her. We have left the art shop to wander about the town, and I want her close to me now. In a strange place, I don't wish to appear to be alone. A lone *obruni* attracts an unwanted crowd.

She crosses the road, leaping over large potholes with ease. She joins me in front of a street vendor's stand. We are surrounded by crumbling colonial buildings, the heat of the day finally easing, late afternoon giving way to early evening. I breathe deeply, the sea air invigorating me.

No longer fearing the intense sun, I remove my hat, exposing my newly shaven head. At the sight of my naked scalp, Chizo shouts "Sunshine," teasing me. On this visit, she persuaded me to shave my head close to the skin, the way many African men do, and even though I obeyed her, she teases me about my close cut. I wonder whether Sunshine is an affectionate moniker or not. She insists she is genuinely proud of me for shaving my head. African men seem to share her view. On streets, I am stopped over and over by men who wish to congratulate me on my styling. "His head is beautiful shape," Chizo tells these men in an admission that excites me.

Chizo calling me Sunshine does too, though I am more excited at the moment by the small original paintings hanging on a portable board in front of me.

"Are you the artist?" I ask the man standing next to the paintings.

He shrugs, not understanding my English. I try again, this time pointing at him, cocking my right hand as if holding a brush, and then waving the brush in the air in the manner of Picasso. He smiles. "No, no, no," he says. "I am brother."

"*Magnifique,*" I say, trying at least to sound French if not make sense. I point to a group of four small portraits, all of women in different settings. They are painted in oil on small canvases and all in the same style: bright colors, cartoon images, slightly dangerous action. My favorite shows three women, with very large behinds, dancing in a popular manner known in Ivory Coast as *mapouka.* The dance depends on a woman's ability to shake her bootie in such a way as to simulate the act of copulation, done in time with a polyrhythmic beat. To underscore the illustrated dance, the artist painted the words "Mini show/Mapouka" on a white banner in the upper-right corner of the canvas.

I take the painting from the nail on which it hangs and let

Chizo have a close look. She points at the large behinds of the women and pats her own, smaller behind. "You want bigger?" she asks, forcing me to smile and shake my head.

I decide to buy the painting and ponder the rest. There are three other paintings by the same artist, all the same size, six-inch-by-six-inch squares. They are less attractive to me, but they possess the same cartoon style and convey some of the same energy. Each painting is eight thousand francs, or about fifteen dollars, and the price is fixed. The man won't accept any lower, even if I buy all four.

I decide to take only the *mapouka* ladies. I hand the man ten thousand francs and he looks upset. He has no change and must search for some. He asks a small boy to scour the street, looking for a hawker who can break my two five-thousand-franc notes. Forced to wait, I look away at Grand Bassam's crumbling colonial buildings, which reassure me that I am indeed in an alien place. When the boy arrives with my change, I deposit the money into my pocket—and then I hear an American voice.

"These paintings are cool," a man says. "You bought one. How much?"

I turn in the direction of the American voice. The man wears a beard and his hair is shoulder length. I introduce myself and he does the same. He's a doctor, and the woman with him is from Sweden. She's also a doctor, and his wife. They greet Chizo warmly, as if they meet Africans all the time. They are not tourists but rather work as doctors at the same hospital in Nairobi, doing some kind of charitable work. I spot a big diamond on the Swede's left hand. She and the Yank are newlyweds, she says, and on holiday. Just like Chizo and me.

"Your honeymoon?" I ask.

"Yes. That too," the woman says.

Their arrival is a relief. I immediately like them. For days I've been surrounded by Africans and French speakers, and these two people are neither. They speak English fluently and we instantly share an understanding of which we are only partly proud. We

The next morning, I awake well before Chizo and sit outside our room, watching the ocean. I order breakfast, and when it is ready I place a café au lait and a croissant on the night table next to the bed where Chizo is still sleeping. I watch her breathing from across the room. I am still afraid to touch her. After we were robbed, we came back to our hotel, escorted by the French couple. In the safety of our room, we could not fall asleep for a long time and Chizo would not speak with me. After a while I forgot about wanting to hold Chizo and I slept fitfully. I left the bed this morning without even kissing her and had café au lait and croissants. Returning to the room, I sit across from her, still smelling the coffee while she sleeps. Streaks of light, streaming through gaps in the drawn curtains, fall on her face.

I don't want trouble now and leave the room, closing the door quietly. The ocean is my only friend this morning. I head toward the low rear wall of the hotel, push through a gate and go down a few steps to the beach. The air is cool and inviting, the sun is strong enough, and the sand is cool on my feet. I roll up the bottoms of my drawstring pants and let the water run over me. Then a man selling tie-dyed women's clothing greets me in French. I reply in English and he says, "Designed and made in Côte d'Ivoire." I look at his stuff and he says, "I give good price to you, English man."

I tell him I am not English. "You are German," he says and smiles. "Your English is good for a German."

I don't bother to correct him, happy that I'm not instantly recognizable as a Yank. I hold in my hands an orange-and-white skirt that ties around the waist of a woman in the manner of a traditional wrapper. The skirt is light cotton, good for the beach. I ask him for the top. He doesn't understand me, so I rummage through his stuff and find the match, a sleeveless blouse, narrowly cut.

I offer him half of what he asks for and he refuses. I hand him the clothes and walk away. I have taken ten steps, maybe more, when I hear him running after me. "German," he says. "German, get good price."

I turn and he's standing behind me, so close that our noses

almost touch. He asks for a thousand francs more, and I give him a single note, worth about ten dollars, and take the outfit.

Chizo will be pleased, I think. I want to return to the room and give her the clothes, but I still fear her mood. I stay on the beach, walking back and forth, never straying too far from my hotel, watching the sea roll toward me, sucking in the air, feeling the water on my legs. The beach is clean. The sand is pristine. There is no trash. No one is washing clothes on rocks.

A man selling CDs interrupts me. For a moment I think it is the same man who sold me the clothes but this man does not call me German. He carries a pile of CDs in a plastic bag. I motion for him to come closer and say, "Franco, Franco," giving him the name of the late Congolese *soukous* star.

"Mamou," he says. I nod in approval and he digs into his bag and pulls out a Franco CD by that name. I check the case. There are six songs from the mid-1980s, made at the peak of Franco's popularity. I take a thousand-franc note from the pocket in my shirt and give it to the peddler without asking the price.

He accepts and I turn my back on him and search the beach for the entrance to my hotel. In a few minutes I am climbing the stairs again. I find the staff are preparing lunch. They are putting white tablecloths on wooden tables, arranging them for the maximum views of the ocean. The glasses are stuffed with napkins to prevent too much sand from collecting inside. A short, dark man introduces himself as Jean-Paul and asks, in English, "Will you have lunch?" I tell him yes and he points to a table in the middle of the row nearest the ocean. "I keep," he says, smiling. I wonder if he knows I was robbed last night, or perhaps he is always friendly.

In the room, I find Chizo awake. She wishes me good morning from the bed and then leaps toward me, kissing my lips. Her body brushes against mine and I suddenly feel wanted again. I hand her the clothes and she smiles. She is naked and puts on the skirt first, tying it tightly against her small waist. The way she stands tells me I have made a good choice. When she slips her arms into the blouse, she runs to the small mirror and proclaims the outfit a success.

* * *

Toumani finds us at the table facing the ocean. It is nearly noon when he arrives, and the red *blolo* stands tall in Chizo's lap. Toumani brightens at the sight of the statue in the embrace of another African. He wears a long dark gown with silver embroidery across his chest and a white woven cap that fits his skull. He looks like a holy man today; his dress reminds me that he is Muslim.

He sits down in the chair across from me and looks out at the ocean, saying nothing. The sky is clear, there is a small breeze, and the air smells of lavender from the hotel's gardens. Two orders of crepes arrive and a plate of grilled fish and mushrooms. I order a bottle of Flag, the country's most popular beer. Toumani asks for fish and rice and a bottle of water.

I look away for a moment. When I look back I see a small, dark statue of a comely woman, squatting slightly, near my beer bottle. The statue is carved in the Dan style, instantly recognizable from the large lips on the woman's face, the narrow eyes, the long jaw and the meticulous arrangement of the hair. Dan artists, who are well-known for masks, are also admired for their statues.

This statue is wonderful. The patina is smooth and dark and even, and the condition is excellent. The only flaw is a long crack down the back of the woman's left foot. Part of the foot is missing; the toes are gone. Still, the statue can balance and stay upright. Whatever caused the removal of the toes happened long ago, judging by the aging of the wood along the crack.

I reach across the table, lift up the statue, which weighs less than a pound, and turn it around. I am surprised by the beauty of the woman's back, the intricate scarification along the spine and the masterful curves of her pronounced buttocks. Each cheek shows signs of special wear: rub marks that suggest the previous owner often touched the cheeks of the statue, perhaps for good luck or as part of an unknowable ritual.

I clasp the Dan statue to my breast and peer out at the ocean. I feel a mixture of sadness and anger over the robbery, but also gratitude that Chizo and I are safe and there is beauty in the world and a man like Toumani wants to share it with me. I am happy Toumani brought the statue and sad that I have little money to pay for it. I start calculating in my head what I have left and I conclude that I can afford to spend only a pittance on the beautiful lady that I hold against my chest.

"The statue comes from far," Toumani says. "The man who give me, his father has . . ." He pauses as if to give himself a moment to rummage through his limited English, then he shrugs. *"Ancien,"* he says.

I agree. Running my fingers over the statue, I inspect the cracks and discolorations and the dirt and dust gathered at the joints and I agree that the statue is old. My problem is not the condition of the statue, I tell him. The statue is lovely and I thank him for bringing it. My problem is my lack of money.

"We were robbed last night," I say.

He is unsure of what I am saying and Chizo intervenes, rising from her seat, setting down the red woman on the table, then acting out the story. She shows him how the three men took us down, waving their guns, forcing us to hand over money. She acts out how she pleaded for the return of the *blolo,* how she took it back, how our white friends surrendered much, even their wedding rings, and how she lost nothing because the men only had eyes for the whites.

Toumani is sad for us. He is also sad for himself. He realizes the robbers stole from him too, by robbing me, his customer. My loss is his loss. His face turns cloudy. He pushes his plate aside and takes a long drink of water. He seems far away and for a long time is quiet. Then suddenly he returns. He throws his hands in the air, shakes a fist, mutters in French. I don't understand him. I call over the waiter who spoke English to me earlier and ask him to translate. Toumani launches into a dissertation and, when he stops, the waiter explains how Toumani's country—Côte d'Ivoire—was once great and prosperous and the people enjoyed life and prospered. The whites were plenty, and there was money and jobs and happiness and peace. Now the young have nothing and must steal, and the whites are fewer and fewer and even many blacks are leaving. The waiter goes on, talking about military coups and bad politics and growing tensions between Muslims in the north and Christians in the south. Everyone fears that a civil war will break out and that the country will be split between north and south, Muslims and Christians, and that life will grow even worse, all the foreigners will go away, and the people will remember simple robberies, when no one was physically harmed, as part of the good times, so badly will things fall apart.

The waiter is out of breath and now I know that he is not merely translating but talking from his own heart, sharing his forebodings, providing details and distinctions and amplifications that elude Toumani, who is after all only a trader of art and not a sophisticated waiter like this man who speaks with Europeans every day and finished secondary school. I thank the waiter and expect him to resume his duties. He puts a hand on Toumani's shoulder and points to the statue and Toumani speaks to the waiter in rapid French and the waiter speaks back. Then Toumani nods and the waiter smiles and delivers to me an unexpected boon: Toumani has decided to sell me the statue for whatever money I can spare.

I reach across the table and clasp Toumani's hand. *"Merci,"* I say. *"Merci beaucoup."* He returns the thanks, keeping my hand in his. We hold hands for a long time and finally I tell Toumani we must leave the hotel. We have no money to remain in Ivory Coast, and it is the last day of the year, the thirty-first of December. We want to spend New Year's Eve in a calmer place, where we feel safer. I tell Toumani that Chizo and I must go by taxi to the border and return to Ghana, where she lives. I stand up and place a single ten-thousand-franc note in his hand.

He slips the bill into his pocket without looking at it and offers to walk with us to the taxi place. I am happy for his company because I fear that a driver will conspire with others to rob us and I wish to leave this country without being robbed again.

Toumani guesses my thoughts and, at the taxi place, talks with a few drivers before we choose one. Toumani settles the price for our transport to the border and waits while we seat ourselves comfortably in the car. There is another passenger in the front seat and Chizo and I have the backseat to ourselves (having paid extra for the "middle" seat). We stow our small backpacks on the floor.

The driver asks if he can drive away. I lower my window and shake Toumani's hand. He asks me when I will return and I say I do not know.

"Care for African queen," he says.

I hold the Dan statue in the air, my eyes meeting his eyes. He salutes the statue as if he is saying good-bye, then shakes his head and points to Chizo. "Care for African queen," he repeats.

I understand him now, and gently pull Chizo toward me and kiss her cheek. She waves at him and shouts, *"Inshallah."* He salutes us, barks at the driver in French and steps back from the car. *"Bon voyage,"* he says.

The sound of the tires grinding against the dirt road swallows his words. The car speeds away. I turn my head and watch his tall, majestic figure grow small in the distance until finally he is gone.

My eyes turn to the front and the journey ahead, but Toumani stays in my mind, and for a long time I see him when I look at the statue.

Chapter Eight

Midnight Mass

When riding in an automobile in West Africa I can't decide what worries me more: the bad roads, the bad cars or the bad drivers. Usually, I worry about all three. On the road, I find myself visualizing death and destruction, sometimes my own. Because I never drive a car for even a minute in Africa, I clearly am not ready to take responsibility for my own safety. But my worries as a passenger are immense, and at times overwhelming. I even worry about other passengers, especially Chizo. In the months of separation from her, my biggest fear is always that she'll be killed in a car crash. My worry isn't simply about the harm from an accident but rather about the medical attention provided afterward. Emergency medicine is poor to nonexistent in West Africa and road accidents are the biggest single killer of otherwise healthy people.

I have rules about drivers in Africa, since I use so many of them. My most important rule is rather drastic: If a driver does anything I consider hazardous—and I have a low bar for hazards—I ask him to stop the car and I get out. I am especially cautious in the first few minutes because a bad driver, at least in Africa, often will betray himself quickly. Especially in the matter of locating my destination. I don't mind getting lost. Too often, however, drivers, who invariably are men, will abandon the hunt prematurely. I want a driver like Stephen, who knows how to get to everywhere from anywhere and has an indomitable spirit. Tasked with finding a destination, Stephen will never quit until he does.

I can't always be choosy about drivers. Even in Accra, Stephen isn't always available, and I must find a stand-in. Sometimes Stephen has a customer who pays more. Or sometimes the relative who leases him his car needs him or the car, leaving me to hunt for a replacement. Looking for drivers, as it turns out, is my most essential activity, and my biggest headache, because in addition to safety and reliability, there is the matter of money. Dickering over money indeed often overwhelms all other considerations, since African drivers presume that an *obruni,* a white, must have lots of cash. Let a driver overcharge, and what's lost is more than money. The overcharging driver is also the one who will abandon a search readily and, harboring an inflated sense of his value, will not realize he is lost when he actually is.

There is one final issue over which even the best driver has no control: the darkness. I try to avoid driving in Africa at night. Some nocturnal trips are of course inevitable, but I almost never drive outside of the city at night. The bad roads, treacherous by day, can be lethal in the dark. I've seen potholes big enough to swallow entire cars. And the police or army checkpoints are invariably scarier in the dark.

All these thoughts run through my head as we drive south along the coast, back to Ghana. The route is flat and the road is smooth. In the backseat, Chizo leans against my left side. I feel her dreadlocks against my cheek and smile. In my right arm, I cradle my red *blolo.* The passenger in the front seat turns up the *mapouka* music. Chizo dozes, her body limp against me. I raise the *blolo,* holding it in front of my face, and start a conversation. The music is so loud no one can hear me speaking to the statue—or the statue speaking back to me.

The *blolo* tells me we've begun our journey too late in the day. It is New Year's Eve, after all, and while the ritual of one year passing into the next is celebrated more quietly in West Africa than in the United States, the passing is not routine. There are three or four hours of light remaining, enough time to reach Cape Coast, the old colonial capital of Ghana, before nightfall.

The driver keeps going, not stopping for food, or even to allow us to relieve ourselves. We are all eager to get out of this country before dark.

At the first checkpoint, the soldiers wave us through, and I give thanks to the *blolo,* my otherworldly guardian, rubbing her large pointed bosoms with exaggerated enthusiasm. I keep one eye on Chizo, making sure she is sleeping, because if she catches me touching the statue in a sexual way, she surely will grow angry. Luckily, when she does awake, the statue is tucked neatly between us on the seat.

Our driver stops at the next checkpoint, and Chizo closes her eyes, slumping against me. A man with an automatic weapon greets our driver. The gunman wears sunglasses. He nods, waves and we are moving again. At a third checkpoint the driver slows only briefly before rolling by men with guns. Then we go a long time without stopping. We pass the last large town before the border. Now we have only thirty miles until Ghana, where things are much calmer. Inside Ghana, the road police are only checking for smugglers, and they never bother passengers. The petty bribery is mild and, with an *obruni* in the car, the chances of harassment by police are small indeed. Ghana is fine.

Not so in Côte d'Ivoire. Even though we are close to the border, my anxiety is rising. I retrieve the *blolo,* stroke her repeatedly and then clutch her against my chest. I am singing softly to the statue when Chizo opens her eyes and grabs the *blolo,* stuffing it into my backpack. I wince, try to kiss her, and she turns away.

We are near the border when the driver stops at another checkpoint: five soldiers with weapons. A half dozen empty oil drums strewn across the road. A narrow space for cars to stop. A low, wide shack on the roadside, maybe where the soldiers sleep.

The driver rolls down his window. A soldier barks out words in French. The driver cuts the engine.

Not good.

The driver turns his head, looks at me in the backseat and waves his hand.

I don't move.

He says something in French.

I think he's telling me to leave the car but I ignore him. I don't move.

Then a soldier leans his head into the driver's open window. "Out, white man," he shouts. "Out. Out."

The soldier is older than most, hatless, and his camouflage shirt is untucked. I get out and show him my passport, opening the cover so he can see my picture. I am careful not to let him touch a page, much less hold my entire passport.

He looks away from me at the other soldiers, and I think I am finished. I start back toward the car and he shouts, "Woman! Papers!"

As it happens, Chizo has no passport, only a phony identity card. She gets out of the car and gives him the card.

The soldier doesn't like it. Shaking his head, his gun swinging loosely in his right hand, he asks me for money.

I refuse.

"No pay," the soldier says. "You no pay."

Before I can speak, he shoves me against the car with his free hand. Another soldier rushes me, sticks his hands in my pockets and pulls out some West African francs. He holds them high and laughs. The other soldiers laugh too.

I tell the driver to start the engine. He doesn't.

The soldier waves his gun at Chizo and points at the shack.

She doesn't move.

"Go, go," he shouts.

Chizo stands still. Two soldiers, without guns, approach her. I get in front of her before they reach her.

One of the soldiers bumps my chest with his chest. Excuse me, he says in French and steps away from me.

I turn to the soldier speaking a bit of English and tell him I won't allow Chizo to be taken into the police shack. I tell him—pointing my finger hard at the ground where I stand—anything that he wants to do will have to happen here, on the side of the road, in plain view. I grab Chizo's waist and draw her close to me.

I want the soldiers to realize I am her hero.

My eyes search for the soldier's eyes, hidden behind his sunglasses. I am not afraid, absorbed in the task of maintaining eye contact. Make him see me, I decide, even if in doing so I provoke him more. He presumes I am too afraid to call him to task. I am not. I am beyond fear. I learned long ago in Africa, as anywhere else, that I am safest in a dangerous situation when I act as if I have nothing to lose. In this moment, I cannot see past these soldiers and Chizo and my own vulnerability. I cannot ask myself why, on an impulse, I crossed into Côte d'Ivoire so soon after a military coup and with Chizo lacking proper papers. Her lack of papers becomes an invitation for mischief and undermines my one undeniable asset: the color of my skin. No serious European would travel without proper papers, so in this soldier's eyes I am either stupid or disrespectful. I am, in short, the rightful object of his derision.

I stagger forward when his butt smashes my stomach, struggling to stay on my feet, and take solace in the belief that the soldier could not have hit me with all his strength because I feel no bones are broken. Instinctively, my hands move to shield my face. Chizo does not help me. She knows that I am alone now and that we are both better off if the soldiers believe she cares nothing for me. Better for her to wink at the soldiers and encourage them to believe that she is merely another African trying to take advantage of me.

This thought crosses my mind when the bottom of Chizo's foot blasts into my backside and I sprawl forward, my face suddenly in the dirt, eating dust.

The soldier with a little English laughs. He tells Chizo to help me up. She raises me to my feet and I steady myself. The soldier comes close to me and removes his sunglasses with his right hand. His gun swings easily in his left, and he says to me, "Hit her."

I slap Chizo across the face, and before she can stagger backward, I pull her toward me. "Hands off," I shout. "She's mine!"

I turn my back to the soldiers and pull Chizo along. I open the rear door of the car, waiting for something. I push Chizo onto the backseat and I follow. I keep expecting to feel the soldier's gun against my back but I never do.

I slam the door shut and tell the driver to move. For once, he obeys me. I kiss Chizo on the spot on the part of her cheek that is red from my blow. The driver travels rapidly now, passing the checkpoint and kicking up dust that blows in the faces of the soldiers.

I stroke Chizo's hair and she leans against me, calm and quiet.

For a long time, she says nothing and then whispers something I did not know about her past. "My first boyfriend raped me," she says.

I let out a loud sigh, feeling the stress from her confession and the encounter with the soldiers. "Why are you telling me this now?" I ask.

She doesn't answer.

The delay at the checkpoint means we cross into Ghana as the sun sets. We move on foot. Cars from Côte d'Ivoire aren't allowed through without a special pass, and our driver lacks one. Anyway, travelers generally walk across the border and find new drivers on the other side. The Ghana side is crowded with shoppers. Stuff is cheaper here, and English is widely spoken. I am on firmer ground.

I think about how safe I feel in Ghana, how I've never been robbed here, how Chizo always tells me that I scare the locals with my aggressiveness and haste. I feel a wad of Ghanaian money in my right pocket, when a couple of dozen teenagers rush toward Chizo and me. The kids are selling kebabs, roasted plantains, bottles of water, laundry soap, coconut milk, nail clippers, batteries, even toilet paper. I point to Chizo, trying to divert the attention of the peddlers from me to her. She begins bargaining for the provisions we need for the next leg of our journey. We must drive several hours along the ocean to Cape Coast, the first British capital of what was then a colony called Gold Coast.

Abandoning Chizo to the peddlers, I find a collection of drivers standing by their funky cars on the side of the road. I'm eager to move, anxious to get a new driver. The road on the Ghana side is awful, as bad as any in the country, and while there is no chance now we will avoid darkness before arriving in Cape Coast, the later we are on the road, the more hazards we face. In Ghana, the threat is an accident, not a robbery; I fear other drivers and the bad roads much more than I do criminals.

My jacket gone, I wear a money belt across my hips. In the pocket of my loose-fitting drawstring pants is a wad of Ghanaian money, the only cash I have left. I calculate its value at about seventy-five dollars. I will need every cedi to get us back to Accra; besides the carfare, we will need money for a hotel and food, since the drive cannot be completed this night. I may even have to pay the last driver with money stashed in Accra.

I start talking to the drivers, alert to the quality of their English. A young baby-faced man named John speaks so well, I ask him whether he attends university. Not yet, he says. He wants to attend the university in Cape Coast, where he lives, but he is short of funds.

At the mention of his aspirations, I hire John to drive us. His car smells musty and is so decrepit I can't even tell the make or model. The front seat belts have been ripped out, the windshield is cracked in a hundred places, and whatever used to serve as roof padding is gone. The raw metal is exposed. A prudent person would wear a helmet in this car.

I tell myself to ignore the condition of the car because I know that on New Year's Eve, at this busy border crossing, there are no better cars available. What matters, actually, is that John is clean and well-spoken and offers to drive us all the way to Accra—with an overnight stop in Cape Coast—for fifty dollars. That's a fair price, especially since I can pay him out of money I keep at home, freeing up the money I have on hand. Just then Chizo shows up with food. She hands me a few sticks of goat kebab and a bottle of water. I introduce her to John and she gives him a kebab and a small banana. He is happy.

We are John's only passengers and we take off, hugging the coastline. As the sun sets, Chizo and I hold each other tightly in the backseat, and I speak loudly to John to make sure he stays awake and does not drive too fast. The real trick is to avoid the holes in the road. There are so many, and the road is only two lanes, one in each direction. Even good drivers cross over to the wrong side in order to avoid holes. The chance of a head-on collision, what with many drivers passing to gain speed and with parked trucks often protruding onto the tarmac, is too great for comfort. Perhaps because of my fretting, John drives slowly and I surrender any hope of reaching Cape Coast early enough to do something exciting on my first New Year's Eve in Africa. I will merely be happy to live through this road trip.

My confidence in a positive outcome is not raised when John begins praying, aloud, asking Jesus to protect his car and his passengers. Every time he invokes the name of Jesus, Chizo shouts, "Amen." Listening to the two of them, I am not sure whether to grow more relaxed, because we have God on our side, or more fearful, because our driver believes he benefits from divine intervention.

My own earthly vigilance also helps. Twilight has given way to darkness and John still drives without headlights. I ask him to switch on his lights and he refuses. "I don't want to drain the battery," he insists.

I ask him again and he repeats his answer. I've heard his reply before from African drivers. Incredibly, they usually want to be paid extra for turning on their lights. Or they actually believe it is best to use the lights sparingly. The first big fight I ever had with Stephen was over his refusal to drive at night with the headlights on. Stephen also believes that headlights drain the battery, even when the car is running. At first I tried to persuade him that his reasoning was flawed, insisting a moving car generates sufficient

We step outside and are met by the sea air. There is a breeze blowing in from the Atlantic, and the waves crash loudly against the beach. I tell John to drive to the castle. There is a restaurant next door, set back from the beach, where I've been told the food is reliable and fresh.

He knows the place and we arrive in minutes. We pass a high stucco wall and enter the restaurant. There are no walls; the restaurant is like a large covered deck. Only a few tables are full and we take one nearest the ocean, on an uncovered veranda on pillars above the beach. To our left is the castle, whose outer walls are illuminated at night. The castle is perched on a massive rock, waves crashing against it. The castle was first established by the Swedes in 1653, then seized by the British twelve years later. The structure was used as a prison for captured slaves, who awaited loading onto ships bound for the New World.

Chizo has never visited a slave fort, even though many of them dot Ghana's coastline, in various degrees of ruin. I want her to see the inside of one.

The waitress brings me a bottle of Star beer and Chizo gets a Guinness. When I ask for fish, I learn the kitchen still has some. I am so relieved I don't bother to ask what kind, just say fish is fine, bring it fast and grill, don't fry. I am drinking a second bottle of beer when the plates of grilled fish, rice and plantains arrive. The smells of fish and the ocean mingle together, and my first bites are intoxicating.

After dinner, I find John asleep in the car. I rap on his window and he snaps to attention. We slide into the backseat. It is thirty minutes until midnight. John looks at me in the rearview mirror and I tell him I want to go somewhere, anywhere, that permits Chizo and me to experience the ending of the old year as people in Cape Coast do themselves. "We must hurry," I insist.

John seems unconcerned with time. Apparently, the pace of things in Cape Coast is much slower than in Accra. After the British moved their capital to Accra, Cape Coast reverted to its roots as a sleepy fishing village dominated by the Fante tribe, of which John is a member. Many Fante still fish in the waters along the beach, paddling out into the Atlantic early each morning in small home-made boats and returning by early afternoon, loaded with fish (on a good day). For these fishermen time seems to stand still. Most don't speak English, the one television network broadcasts only about five hours a day, and even radio programs are scarce. When I ask John whether any live music is being performed in town, he looks bewildered.

"Then what can we do?" I say, flashing my impatience.

John is silent for a long time and then he turns toward me, a wide smile covering his face. "You go to midnight mass," he says. "With me."

Before I can answer, Chizo agrees and excitedly tells me that on many holidays, in West Africa, midnight masses are held and the attendance is often large. "You can't miss midnight mass," she says. "And we dressed for the occasion," she adds, tugging at her clothes.

John starts the engine before I even agree to go to church. He soon veers onto an uneven dirt road. We sway back and forth, up and down, as if on an amusement ride. John knows now to keep his headlights on, so he can see ahead, though not very far because the surroundings are dark. John is small and well-spoken or else I might grow fearful, moving into the dark recesses of Cape Coast, easy prey for any of his confederates to rob us of our cell phones, my passport and ATM card that's useful at a few banks in Accra and the little cash we have left. The Fante are peaceful, and robberies of this sort are rare here, so I am calm, expectant, wondering what New Year's surprise he has for us.

I do not wonder very long. We pull up to a concrete church and hear inside the shouts and murmurs of a congregation gathered in prayer. There is no place for John to park, so we get out and he promises to collect us later. I watch him reverse and then follow Chizo toward the church entrance. As the mass is under way, I expect us to slip unnoticed into seats in the rear, from where I will quietly observe the coming to an end of the year 2001.

How wrong I am! We move through a doorless opening and see the congregation seated before us in plastic chairs, on a concrete floor, under the open sky. The walls are bare and there are gaps where windows may one day be. The only religious symbols are a large wooden cross and a picture of Jesus at the front of the room. Presiding over the gathering is a short, slim minister, dressed in dark pants and a white short-sleeved shirt. His hair is cut close to his scalp. Despite waving his left arm, he spots my entrance so quickly that I almost wonder if John has called ahead and alerted him to my impending arrival.

Before I can even sit down next to Chizo, he booms out, "Praise the Lord! The whites have come to bless us!"

Every head in the half-built church turns and searches for me. I am the only foreigner present, the only white, and my plan to sit in the back, and go unnoticed, is ridiculous. I am easy to spot.

"The whites have come to bless us," the minister booms again. "Praise the Lord."

I sink deeper into my chair and Chizo nudges me with her elbow. "Get up," she says. "Get up."

Once more, the minister repeats himself and now he is beckoning me to rise to my feet. I pretend not to notice and then hear Chizo importune me again. I rise unsteadily and wave to the crowd, their bodies twisted and necks turned trying to take me in. I wave once more, longer this time, though I fear that any show of friendliness on my part might be misinterpreted.

I need not worry. The minister has his own design, spinning a riff on my appearance that suggests his zeal for exploiting even the least propitious opportunities for fund-raising. "I'm so proud the whites have chosen to join us tonight," he says as I collapse into my seat and clasp hands with Chizo. "Yes, Lord, the whites have chosen to bless us and we cannot let them down," he continues. "We cannot let them down."

His listeners respond with encouraging words, and the minister walks down the main aisle. "Let's make ourselves proud in front of the whites," he shouts. "Let's show the whites we are generous. Let's show them we are rich in spirit. Let's show the whites we can dig into our pockets and give. Praise the Lord!"

The woven baskets come out and move from the first row toward the back, and the back row toward the front, and again the minister praises Jesus for sending a white man to witness the generosity of his congregation. "Praise Jesus," he shouts. "Let this white man tell the world about our faith!"

Shouts of "Amen" erupt again and the dirty bills come out of the pockets of these poor people and the minister shouts for more money. "Shame on us if the white tells the world we are not generous with our Lord," he shouts. "Shame, shame, shame!"

The minister falls quiet and his flock is quiet too. I tug on Chizo's hand and hiss, "Can we leave?"

"Are you stupid?" she replies.

I stand up and Chizo stays seated and in an instant I decide she has made the right decision.

"White man!" the minister shouts, catching me on my feet. "Are you proud of us? Are you proud of our faith in the Lord?"

I say nothing but the people around me shout with joy at my presence, cheering the very beneficent Lord who has delivered me to them on this special occasion. I am frozen in place, embarrassed to have been singled out by the minister and afraid to do something stupid again. How I wish to say something smart and sincere, yet I am speechless. I fear the minister has mistaken me for one of those freelance Bible thumpers who march around Ghana presuming to save souls. Or, worse, maybe the minister honestly believes I can teach him and his worshipers some lessons about life.

"White man! White man!" the minister booms. "Tell us you are proud."

My body sags. I can't move. I hope he does not ask me to join him in front of the congregation, where he might beseech me to lead a prayer or a song or share a few thoughts on the festive occasion.

Now everyone in the room is looking at me, and my eyes are

moving, from one to another, my brain tuning out their chanting: "Tell us, white man. Tell us!"

Even Chizo is standing now. Even she wants to hear from me.

I open my mouth and, without thinking, I deliver an old Hebrew benediction, in English. "May the Lord bless and keep you. May the Lord bring His countenance upon you and give you peace!"

The worshipers cheer. I let out a breath and begin to breathe normally. I think I have escaped the worst when a crowd of men rush me and lift me off my feet. A dozen of them have hold of my extremities and are pushing me higher and higher until I tower over the group.

There is something strange about them holding me so high. I feel embarrassed, scared and also powerful. I relax and imagine myself as a village chief presiding over my people. Everyone is chanting in the Fante language. I am swept up in the moment and begin babbling myself in fake Fante, pretending to have found my own "lost" tribe.

Chizo persuades the men to return me to earth. I am drenched in sweat, breathing hard and feeling dizzy and swaying from side to side. Chizo helps me to my chair. I sit down, at last steadying myself. She sits down next to me. Are these the same chairs we had? I can't remember. The minister, framed underneath the cross, beams and launches into a song.

I look at my watch. In the commotion, I've missed the clock striking midnight. It is now ten minutes into the new year, and I want to kiss Chizo. I lean toward her, expecting my lips to meet hers in romantic union.

She recoils from me in shock. "In church?" she whispers. "You want to kiss me in church. In front of all of them. You will shame and offend them. And me."

Even a small kiss is impossible, I think.

I plant my lips on her cheek, thinking she will now submit and her lips will meet mine.

No way. She flashes me an angry glare, then says, "Here my lips are only for God."

Chizo spits out her words as if she means them. I pull away from her and suddenly feel someone behind me. Weird. I am afraid to turn around and see who is there. I am afraid that God or some other jealous suitor of Chizo's (a chimp?) is behind me. Is this the beer talking? Or am I cracking under the stress of the past few days?

Slowly I turn to face the presence behind me.

It is John, the driver.

"Praise the Lord," he says.

I blink and take his hand. "Let's get out of here."

I pull him along with me, out the door and into his car. I sit in silence until Chizo arrives. "Now you can kiss me," she says, brushing her lips against mine. We kiss for a long time, the car starts and I feel a new year—and perhaps a new life—has begun.

Chapter Nine

Use It for Laughter

The singing drives me from bed to the window. I push my neck out into the bright sunshine and strain to see where the singing is coming from. I can hear voices of men and boys, chanting, repeating the same Fante words, in time with a simple beat. They must be praying, I think.

I rush out of my bungalow—too fast, actually, because I smack my head on the low archway. I stagger outside, dizzy and in pain. Chizo is in town to do her braids. New Year's morning and I am alone. I lean against the low wall that marks the start of the beach, panting. Men in Ghana are generally short, and these bungalows were either made for these men or wrongly made. I feel the blow to my head and rub my skull gently. Slowly my eyes focus on the sea and sand before me. Cape Coast Castle, perched on a massive rock, gleaming in the morning sunshine, lies to my left. I am seeing the castle for the first time in the daylight and I feel I am in a dream, perhaps because of the blow to my head or the jarring majesty of the castle. The whitewashed buildings are long and low, and the structures seem perfectly positioned on the rocks. I can't take my eyes off the castle, even though I once more hear singing. I turn in the direction of the singers and see a crowd of men and boys, too many of them to count, in front of a long line of tall coconut trees.

They sing and beat the side of a wooden boat. The boat is filled with fish, and they are dragging it away from the sea, pulling it high and hard onto the dry sand and then abandoning it to its three-man crew. They empty their fish and a small boy quickly runs his hands over the net, looking for new tears. He sets out to repair them while the crew begins sorting the fish.

I move down the beach, closer to the surf, and watch a crowd of men race to another boat. There are three small men in the boat and the man in front, who I suppose is the skipper, is holding the boat in low water, his paddle stuck into the sea floor. His boat is long and narrow and seems made from a single tree. There is no motor or sail and all three men have paddles. The man in front shouts in Fante and the crowd of men on the beach wade into the water and grab hold of the sides of the boat and pull it onto the shore. The boat goes airborne for a moment, then smacks the sand with a thud. The men inside jump out and the singing begins again. All the men sing and drag the boat and the boat groans along the sand, leaving a track behind it.

I am closer now, yet not so close that anyone will ask me to help drag the boat. The midday sun is hot, and the air heavy, so that even the breeze from the Atlantic provides small relief from the heat. My Tilley hat, faded from long use, protects my head, and I wear a long-sleeved white smock, with gold embroidery across the chest, and a matching pair of drawstring pants, with the same embroidered pattern at the bottoms of the legs. Most of the local men wear only shorts and are hatless. I look back at the sea and another boat making its return, the pattern repeating itself, the men wading into the water, grabbing the boat and hurling it onto the beach. I smile, though I don't know why, and I greet the crowd of men, acknowledging their labors.

One of the men waves at me and, moving closer, says, "White man, can I have your hat?"

I turn away from him without answering and am startled to see, coming out of the cluster of coconut trees, a group of women and girls. They carry woven baskets, propped against their hips. They wear wrappers and matching shirts and laugh with one another.

I see they have come for the fish. They are fishmongers of various degrees of significance. Some must have customers in town. I approach one of them; she carries a basket with a pile of live fish. A little girl holds on to the woman's wrapper. I pull a five-thousand-cedi note from my pocket and offer the bill in exchange for the fish in her basket. She accepts. I point in the direction of the restaurant where we dined last night and begin to walk, holding the cedi note in my hand. She follows, and her daughter follows her. We walk toward the low wall that separates the restaurant from the beach. I get the attention of a waitress, who sends out the cook, a man who speaks English.

I ask him to cook me these fish, along with some roasted plantains and white rice.

He agrees, and vanishes with the basket. The woman looks stricken, until he returns and gives her the empty basket. I give her the bill. She smiles, and I smile back. Her daughter tugs at my pants. I bend down and she touches my face, then runs her fingers along the top of my head. I wonder whether this child has ever seen a white person before.

I sit down on a wooden chair at a wooden table that faces the sea. When I look up, the woman and child are gone, and the men are dragging another boat in from the sea. Their singing is fainter than before.

After lunch, I walk into the center of town, lingering in front of the heavy doors of the castle, which is closed today. I think I will visit the next day. Now I want to spy on Chizo while she's getting her hair braided. But where is she? She left in the morning, early, without telling me her destination, saying only that she would return in the evening. Braiding can consume an entire day, even two days, depending on its complexity—and yet the cost might be only the equivalent of three dollars. I don't know what style Chizo wants and accept that she could return after dark. I miss her and want to find her. How many braiding shops could there be in Cape Coast?

I set off toward the central market. Approaching it, I see a group of women braiding hair in the open air, their customer obscured from view. There are six braiders surrounding the customer, working in tandem. I come very close to the braiders, wondering if I will find Chizo. Then I get a glimpse of the customer, and she isn't Chizo.

"Who else braids hair?" I ask.

No one replies to me. Rather the braiders laugh nervously and speak in Fante, looking away. Then a man standing nearby says, "*Obruni,* you want your hair braided?"

He is a small young man with eyes that twinkle.

"My hair is too short for braiding," I say, smiling. I am pleased to have someone to speak English with. In Accra, most people speak English, of one sort or another. Not here, where the Fante dialect rules and I struggle to make myself understood.

I ask the man where is a proper shop, inside a building. He looks at me blankly and smiles. I fear I have exhausted his pool of English words.

I take out my cell phone and call John, the driver who took us to church. This is one of those times when I wish Chizo had her own cell phone. John answers and I wish him happy new year, then ask him to come and find me.

He tells me he's busy. "Get over here now," I shout. "I need you."

Cape Coast is small. Ten minutes later John pulls alongside me and I get into the front seat. I tell him my problem: Chizo is in a braiding shop, somewhere, and I want to find her. "How hard can it be, she came on foot," I tell him. "She must be near."

John shakes his head. "Problem," he says. "How much will you pay me if I find her?"

I shrug. I decide that John is hustling me. Coming to someone in Ghana with a problem can be an invitation for abuse. Usually, when I ask for help here, I pretend I couldn't care less what happens. Today, perhaps because I am on holiday, I make a gross error, conveying to John an urgent personal need. I now confront a man seeking to strike it rich at my expense.

"I find her, I get ten dollars," he says.

I tell John I'll pay him the normal hourly rate of three dollars, and I'll include the time he spent driving to fetch me. As a bonus, when we find Chizo, he'll get a bottle of Star beer (worth thirty cents in American currency).

John tries to speak and I stop him. "Start the engine," I say.

He does. The car coughs, then jumps forward. We head up a hill and snake our way through the center of town, ending up on a cliff overlooking the castle and the Atlantic. Ahead are a row of shacks, built out of plywood and lacking roofs. We have arrived at a small braiding ghetto.

"She must be in one of these," John says.

I ask him to wait in the car, get out and enjoy the ocean view. The day is clear and I can see for miles. I stare absently at the sea, then turn my gaze north. In the distance, jutting out on a small peninsula, is the town of Elmina, home to its own gorgeous slave fort, founded by the Portuguese in 1482 and, like the fort in Cape Coast, restored to something resembling its original awful grandeur. I linger, scanning the horizon, spotting a few fishing boats and wondering whether Chizo will welcome my interruption or feel I have broken some secret African code of gender relations. The appearance of a man, even her *obruni* boyfriend, in a braiding shop might unsettle the braiders and cause her embarrassment. I turn back toward John and reconsider my plan of action. Then, as usual, I forge ahead.

A dirty, sun-bleached curtain covers the entrance to the first braiding shack. I duck inside and bump into a braider. The customer isn't Chizo. I apologize, retreat and enter the next shack more carefully, lifting the curtain this time and leading with my feet, not my face. This shack is also jammed with women, but not one I know. At the third shack, I simply call Chizo's name from outside on the road. No answer. I wait. I call again, and her voice calls to me from the next shack.

I venture inside, ducking my head through the doorway and creeping slowly forward. Chizo sits at the center of seven young women, each clasping a piece of her hair. They twist a small tuft into a braid, then attach a long hair extension to the base. On some braids they attach colorful beads. About two-thirds of the extensions are attached. Hours of work remain.

The women laugh among themselves, chattering in Fante. Chizo does not speak the language, and neither do I. I watch the women silently and they look at me with what seems like a mixture of awe, admiration and fear. The Fante have an old saying, "Use it for laughter." The first man I ever met in Ghana, a Fante doctor with the Ministry of Health in Accra, taught me this adage. He explained that it means people should see the brighter side of life, even of inevitable setbacks and frustrations. I think of this piece of Fante wisdom as I stand, inches away from the braiders, trying to keep eye contact with Chizo while wondering what to say.

Chizo rescues me. "Go away," she says. "You're making the women nervous. I will meet you on the beach when I'm finished."

The women stare at Chizo, amazed that she has the power to speak to me. I can see from their faces that they've instantly revised their opinion of her. "See what you've done," Chizo sneers. "Now they will charge me more for braiding."

I should know better than to visit Chizo here. She often complains about the penalties she incurs from "moving" with me—and how she can't qualify for the "Africa price" once locals realize we are together.

I leave quickly, without saying good-bye.

John drops me near my bungalow, and I pay him (enough for him to get his bonus Star beer too). I walk down to the beach and then turn toward the castle. I am barefoot now, my drawstring pants rolled up to the knees, my Tilley hat on tight, a pair of Teva sandals in my left hand. The sun still beats hard and I dab sunscreen on the tip of my nose. I want a cool place to sit. I wade in the warm water, drifting along in the direction of the large rock that juts out from the castle. At the base of the rock I put on my sandals and climb, taking short steps to avoid toppling over. I reach the peak and sit, feeling the breeze, facing the Atlantic, looking out, trying to divine the vast expanse of the ocean, imagining the eastern seaboard of the United States at the other end, imagining the rigors of traveling the watery highway in front of me that connects Africa with New York, my place of birth.

Two young boys interrupt my reverie. The taller of the two gains my attention with the crispness of his English. "Would you like a stick of ganja?" he asks.

The boy looks to be nine years old. Did he say what I think he said?

The boy smiles and repeats himself. He wears a torn Nike T-shirt—a fake probably—and a pair of shorts with rips in them.

I ask how much.

The price is three thousand cedis, or less than fifty cents, for two sticks.

I tell the boy to bring me four sticks.

He holds out his hand. I wave him off and he goes, the smaller boy trailing him down the rock.

Marijuana is illegal in Ghana, but farmers grow the herb in the hills and forests. Local demand is small and most of the crop goes to Europe, where pot restrictions are relaxed. Local consumers are chiefly foreigners and members of the small community of wannabe Jamaican Rastafarians, fans of Bob Marley, who make a show of wearing dreadlocks and peddling ganja. The police usually look the other way, and I have never heard of any foreigner arrested for buying small quantities of weed. Alone on the rock, I of course wonder about the chance of police enlisting children in a sting operation.

Undercover kids? I laugh. The gambit depends on a degree of cleverness, and zeal for strict legality, that I have yet to encounter in West Africa. More likely, I think, the boys may be in league with adult entrepreneurs.

Perched on the rock, I enjoy the breeze and the sea air—until I realize how easily I can be trapped out here, forced to jump from the rock into the sea. I try to banish these ill thoughts and lose myself in the wind and waves, but I can't. I impatiently wait for the boys to return.

They come with the four sticks of pot, and before paying, I want to test it. I realize I have no matches. I throw up my hands, and the taller boy instantly knows my problem. He pulls matches out of his pocket. I put a joint into my mouth and motion for him to give me a light. He strikes the match, cupping his hand around the flame. I take a draw. He lights another match and ignites the stick again. I draw deeper this time. The herb is mild, and the smell is good.

I pass the taller boy his payment, dashing him an extra two-thousand-cedi note. He is pleased. "You are my favorite customer," he says.

I marvel at his English and contemplate starting a conversation. First, I address the remainder of my smoke. The stick is thin and fast burning. I face the ocean, close my eyes and take another toke. The pot is hitting me now, supplying a gentle buzz. My mind wanders. I think of Chizo's head full of extensions. I imagine her hair swaying from side to side, the multicolored beads clicking together. The afternoon is giving way to twilight now, and the heat is relenting. The sun sets early in Ghana, and I want to stay on the rock to watch it go down.

I turn around, expecting to talk with the boys. They are gone. Only the matches remain.

When Chizo returns, the sun has set and I'm outside, on the low wall separating our bungalow from the beach. The darkness prevents me from seeing her braids. She rests her head against my chest and I let my fingers run over the beads and listen to her complain about the pain in her head. The tightening of the hair, and the process of attaching the extensions, she says, pains her scalp. What an ordeal. Ten hours in a chair, circled by female hands, poked and pulled. "No sleep tonight," she says.

"I have pain relief," I say and put a stick of weed in between her lips. I strike one of the remaining matches and she takes a toke. While she smokes, I walk down to the restaurant and order her dinner. Stars fill the sky; I can't recall ever seeing so many, so

Chizo's race consciousness cuts both ways. She's also attracted to me partly because I am white. She wants to be near whatever whiteness means to her, and undoubtedly those meanings include privilege, opportunity and a freedom from stigma. I also know that I am drawn to her African heritage, which I associate with grace and beauty. When I was growing up in America in the 1960s, communion with blackness seemed difficult, and black women seemed especially out of bounds. As a teenager, I fantasized about having a black lover, and in college, I once did, a girl from Jamaica whom I dated for a few months.

The explanation of my attraction to Chizo's blackness eludes me; there is something unseemly even in my acknowledging that black femininity excites me. I am reminded of this hard truth when Chizo and I reach a small inner courtyard, where we stand beneath a wide balcony that leads into what once were the private rooms of the commander of the castle. The tour guide explains that newly enslaved women gathered in this courtyard in the evening and the commander would observe them from his balcony. In this way, he chose his concubines.

I shudder. Chizo and I are the only interracial couple on the tour, and I fear that the guide disapproves of me. I walk near the guide and, in a pause in his presentation, I reveal to him that Chizo is neither Fante nor Ghanaian. She is, I say rather loudly, from Nigeria. "Wonderful," the guide says. He smiles and shakes my hand, as if relieved that, while I may have stolen an African, at least I have not stolen one of his sisters!

After the tour we enjoy the bright sunshine by standing at the castle's ocean edge, near a row of ten cannons that threaten to greet attacking ships. The vistas from the castle are spectacular and the rehabilitation of the whitewashed walls and stone floors is almost too stylish. The castle has a terrible beauty, and in response I force myself to hear the screams of pain and anguish that filled these spaces for so long. Tens of thousands of slaves were exported from this fort before the British abolished their legal trade. In an instant, I wish to hear the sad cries of all.

I do not ask Chizo for her own thoughts now. She points to the large rock outside the castle, where I bought the sticks of pot yesterday. We stand far apart, alone with our private impressions, until I creep up behind her, linking my arm around her waist as she bends over to touch a pile of cannonballs neatly laid out on the ground. I have an idea, and when I tell her my idea she says, no, she has a better one.

I march back to the courtyard where the female slaves would gather for inspection by the castle commander. On entering, I get down on my knees and run my hands along the stone floor. Then I touch the whitewashed walls, pushing my whole body against the cold surface, somehow hoping to unlock whatever secrets are contained in these walls.

Then I hear someone laughing on the balcony and look up and see Chizo smiling. It is time for our plan to unfold. Per her instructions, I am to pretend to be a male slave, milling about with other male slaves, all of us white! I do my best to look frightened, lonely and confused.

The role play does not have its intended effect on me, however. I simply cannot channel my "inner white slave." Rather I identify with the real slaves of the past, the women who suffered here. I begin to divine their helplessness, the violence done to them, their own shocking incomprehension of the bad turn in their lives.

I am crying and the sound of my cries echoes around the courtyard. I look up and there is Chizo on the balcony, beckoning to me. "Why are you crying?" she asks. "I'm picking you!"

I double over, the tears streaming again. I am still crying when I feel a tap on my shoulder. I turn and collapse into Chizo's arms. She brushes the tears from below my eyes, calms me, and our lips meet. We kiss, long and gentle.

I decide later that our kiss is a solitary attempt at performing an exorcism. We have disguised a moment of private passion as a symbolic repudiation of history.

PART FOUR

Port Harcourt and Accra

September 2002 and September 2003

*I*n the summer of 2002, Chizo and I rented a bungalow together on Kuku Hill in Accra. The house was less than a mile from the Atlantic, overlooking Independence Square and the State House. The nearness to the ocean kept the air fresh and took the worst edge off the relentless West African heat. A short walk down the hill, toward the ocean, there was a vista point from which to view a renovated slave castle that once served as the British head office in Ghana and now houses the offices of the country's president and staff.

Our bungalow was in the rear of a large walled compound, behind a larger main house and set back from a winding quiet street. Chizo extravagantly called the bungalow "our love palace." We had two bedrooms, a living room and a kitchen. I had a desk in the living room, where I wrote. Every day a young woman came to cook and clean a bit. Once a week, a boy selling coconuts turned up. My favorite tailor, whose shop was a short walk from the house, also visited frequently. A carpenter, who took a fancy to Chizo, made much of our furniture by hand and charged shockingly little for it. The oddest visitor was an electrician who, for a small fee, would adjust the antennae on top of our television so we could receive passable reception on the two over-the-air channels available in Accra.

Living together was a necessary experiment, but finding the house proved unexpectedly difficult. For some weeks we wooed a Muslim man named Ali who was building a bungalow on one of the side streets in Accra's trendy Osu neighborhood. I visited Accra in March, escorting a class of journalism graduate students on a reporting tour of the country, and after meeting Ali, I thought I could craft a lease agreement with him in days. We agreed on a price, I showed him a pile of American dollars, and waited for him to finish the bungalow. Our deal called for him to be paid—a full two years' rent in advance—on the day we together deemed the bungalow ready for occupancy. By my crude reckoning, four or five capable workers ought to have finished the bungalow, including the inside fittings, in five or six days of steady labor.

Day after day, Chizo visited the bungalow, and each of her reports grew more dour. After a week, the electricity remained unfinished, and the windows remained uninstalled and there was no sign of plumbing. I complained to Ali and he shrugged off my complaints. Chizo kept visiting the site, and we endured a second week of Ali's paralysis. The day before I expected to leave Accra to return to California, we met Ali's sister, who sold raw peanuts and bottles of Coke on the side of the road in front of the entrance to this bungalow. She confessed that her brother would never finish the bungalow because he felt remorse over the deal we'd struck and believed he could fetch a much higher price from some other foreigner. I said I could reopen negotiations but she said we should give up because Ali's pride would not allow him to do that.

The next day, my last in Accra for a few months, Chizo and I found another bungalow for rent, the one on Kuku Hill. The house, which was owned by Ghana's ambassador to Canada, was literally empty. There were no floor coverings, no kitchen appliances, no curtains or drapes over the windows, nothing.

A relative of the owner, a widow in her fifties, lived in the main house and was responsible for finding a tenant. She met with Chizo and me. We quickly agreed on a price for two years. Then she promised to paint the outside of the bungalow and its inside walls. She also promised to install a tile floor on the bare concrete. Any other improvements we would have to pay for. I knew by then that the woman's proposition was standard. Renters of local homes in Accra—homes without air-conditioning, a backup generator, a dedicated water supply and all the other accoutrements of expat lifestyles—were invariably offered as empty shells.

The woman, named Constance, was unprepared or unwilling to sign a deal on the spot. She wanted to get approval from the owner and complete the minimal improvements. Besides, we were not the first to show serious interest in the bungalow. A Lebanese man had seen the house and was deciding whether to rent it, she said.

Our hopes sank on hearing this. The specter of competing with the Lebanese inspired dread. In the minds of West Africans, Lebanese were loaded with money. Even though I was white, and presumably comparatively wealthy, I was no match for a Lebanese.

I left for California with the house hunt unresolved. Week after week, Chizo kept visiting Constance and Kuku Hill. She began to call Constance "Auntie," a term of respect and affection in Ghana. On visits, Chizo brought her pepper soup and sweets. She also began to counsel Constance on strategies to defeat her feelings of loneliness.

"You must look for a man," Chizo told her.

When Constance explained she could not properly pursue male companions, Chizo dismissed her sense of propriety as a hollow pretense. "Are you a piece of wood?" Chizo asked. "Are you a stick?"

Constance explained to Chizo, over and over, that she was too old to attract an African man. "There are so many young ones to choose from," she said. To which Chizo replied, "You can still have a good time with men, married or not, and the young ones might be fun too."

Before long, Chizo and Constance became friends, and their visits no longer turned on the fate of the bungalow. Constance waited patiently for a sign from the Lebanese man, whom she actually had not heard from for many weeks. She didn't know the name of the man, she had no cell phone number for him, she had no idea whether he even remained in the country.

I wondered whether the man existed and asked Chizo to inquire whether our offer was too low and more money was required. "Be patient," Chizo told me, and refused to sweeten our offer.

More time passed. One day, I called Chizo, who now had a cell phone, and learned the glorious news: Constance had accepted our money and given Chizo keys to the bungalow. When I arrived in June, I saw a house transformed through the force of Chizo's will (and the labors of local men). The next month we held a housewarming gathering that doubled *as birthday party for Chizo, who had never celebrated one. In her honor, I slaughtered a goat, which was then served to our guests.*

The visit to Chizo's hometown was opportunistic. I got an assignment to help a researcher at Amnesty International with an examination of Nigeria's oil industry. The industry's heart sits in Port Harcourt, where Chizo's parents live and she'd spent her childhood. Amnesty flew me from California to the Nigerian capital of Lagos, two hops on British Airways planes. Then I switched to a Nigerian airline and flew—along with two chickens in the seat next to me—to Port Harcourt. On my arrival, in the middle of the morning, a Nigerian who'd lived for years in Los Angeles took me on a tour of the city. I told him I was in love with a woman from Port Harcourt and he told me he'd been married to an African-American for many years.

We bonded. The man, John, had worked at a defense contractor, and lost his job in a downsizing. In his early forties and divorced from his American wife, he decided that, rather than start over in California, he'd collect his assets and return to Port Harcourt, the city of his birth.

I told him I planned to meet my girlfriend, coming in from Accra, and her family, who lived somewhere near the city center. He said nothing about my prospective rendezvous but, as he drove me about Port Harcourt, he shared his misgivings with me about Nigeria in general and this city in particular. He complained that the roads were awful; there were electricity and water shortages; sewage spilled onto the streets; and the police, while ubiquitous, were frightening, casually carrying automatic weapons. Corruption was rampant, and the government's ample revenues (from royalty payments on crude oil) seemingly existed solely to be looted by a favored few. "The governor won't take advice from anyone—until someone tells him another way to steal money," John said. "Then he starts listening."

His pessimism depressed me, yet his observations seemed unerring and I remained rapt in his presence. "One of these days Nigerians will get it right," he said. "But at the rate they are going, there won't be change for another forty years. I hope I live to see it."

Why isn't there more anger and despair? I asked him. "You can't be hostile in this situation," he said. "Who are you going to be hostile toward? You go four steps and you see someone who has worse problems than you."

After the tour, the Amnesty researcher—a pleasant Spaniard with a terrific command of English—took me to a series of meetings with prominent politicians and lawyers in the city. I tried to concentrate on the matters under discussion, but I kept thinking about Chizo. From the house on Kuku Hill, I knew she would take a series of cars to Lagos, and then a bus to Port Harcourt. I worried about accidents and breakdowns that might leave her stranded for hours, even days. If all went well, her journey should have required no more than twenty-four hours, so long as she drove through the night, when roads were clearest, however dangerous.

As I listened to a lawyer discuss the merits of burning to death captured thieves in a public market—the preferred method locally was to strap the accused to a discarded tire and then set him on fire—my mind took refuge in sunnier thoughts of Chizo and our latest reunion. Just how we would find each other was no small concern since we had no way to telephone each other. Her parents, at the time, had no phone and neither did I.

From California I'd arranged to meet Chizo in my hotel, only that plan was shot since the hotel was full. The Amnesty guy and I went to another hotel, so I expected Chizo to visit the wrong one.

Our meetings ended at about five in the evening and we went to our new hotel. I walked into the lobby and she was sitting there. She'd smartly called a journalist in Lagos, a friend of mine, who told her where to find me. We hadn't seen each other for a month, and after we hugged, I asked how her journey went. She said fine, and I told her about John, the refugee from L.A. I wanted Chizo to meet him, so she could hear about his experiences in America.

But first we had others to meet.

Chapter Ten

Guess Who? (1)

At long last, I meet Chizo's parents.

We are in Port Harcourt, the oil capital of Nigeria and the country's second-largest city. It is a warm September evening, and Chizo and I sit shoulder to shoulder on a wooden bench, inside a dark, windowless room large enough to fit two beds and a great number of plastic bags.

Edith and Samuel, Chizo's parents, have rented this single room for the past twenty-five years. It has no running water, no bathroom, no kitchen. Her parents cook and bathe outside, in a courtyard they share with about a dozen other families, who also live in windowless rooms.

Two kerosene lamps illuminate the room in which Chizo's parents live. Two bare lightbulbs hang from the ceiling, but the power is out or maybe the bulbs are dead. I am afraid to ask.

I don't want to ask questions, period. I don't want to draw attention to the poverty of Chizo's parents. I don't want to reveal my shock over finding them in these conditions. Chizo had told me her parents were poor, but I am still shaken by seeing them in these rough quarters.

I realize I am staring at her parents with my mouth wide open. Embarrassed, I look down, at the dirty concrete floor. Chizo nudges me. "Feel your eyes," she says. "Go ahead."

I lift my head and study Samuel. He is a wiry man with deep-set eyes, high cheekbones and very dark skin. "I am photocopy of my father," Chizo once told me. I now see she looks like a female version of her father, only younger.

He and Edith live in this room with three of their six children: two sons and a daughter. Chizo, their oldest child, and two married sisters live elsewhere. I know from Chizo that once all six children lived with their mother and father here. Only Chizo escaped when her grandmother invited her—at the age of ten—to live in a spacious, clean and well-ventilated house in a university town called Owerri. Chizo came of age in Owerri, doted on by a loving grandmother.

Lucky her.

Her brothers and sisters remained in this room, sharing the two mattresses at night with their mother and father and somehow coexisting during waking hours, seven of them jammed together.

All of her siblings now crowd into this room, looking me over. Our arrival is a big event, and Chizo's two married sisters have traveled by bus to be here.

Everyone is quiet. Everyone looks at me. I feel their eyes.

I am the first European or American—the first white, to put it bluntly—ever to sit in this room.

Everyone seems to be waiting for me to speak. I say nothing and my silence makes the room seem smaller.

I hunch over and grip the wooden bench with my hands. I hold the bench tightly out of fear that otherwise I will either bolt from the room or collapse onto the dirty linoleum that covers the concrete floor.

Chizo breaks the silence. She explains to her family that business brings me, her American boyfriend, to Nigeria. She talks in a mixture of Igbo, her local language, and English. I am working on an assignment for Amnesty International, she explains, accompanying a staff researcher from the group's London office on a tour of Nigeria's oil-producing Delta region. The goal is to produce a report on human rights, oil companies and the government. Chizo goes on to describe the work I do, where I do it, who I am, where I came from, how we met, where we live in Accra and something of the life we share. She goes on for a long time, actually, and is still going strong when Samuel interrupts her.

"When did my daughter become a big parrot?" he says.

Chizo says nothing.

Her sisters laugh.

"You talk like the whites now," Samuel says. "Have you forgotten that the quietest women are the most desired?"

Chizo still says nothing.

"And your skin is so dark," Samuel continues. "Can't you use a cream to lighten it?"

Chizo doesn't answer.

He points to her Rasta-style braids, her dreadlocks. "What have you done to your hair? Can't you straighten it the way you used to?"

Her sisters shift nervously.

He pauses, looking at her, demanding an answer.

"I'm living a natural life now," she says. "Hair, skin, everything."

"Why?" Samuel asks.

"I love my blackness," she says. "My skin, my hair, everything black. I love it all."

"Why?" Samuel repeats.

"He makes me live a natural life," Chizo says and points at me. "He is why I love my blackness."

I am stunned by her confession, but fear that Samuel will blame me for the changes in his daughter's appearance.

Chizo doesn't give him the chance. "You will shut up your mouth a little, Father, and stop acting like an uncivilized man from the village."

"Don't disrespect me," he says.

"I will do more than that. I want you to be crying."

I am proud of Chizo for defending herself, but I want to avoid a family battle. At least not until I've done what I've come to do.

"Kedu," I say to Samuel, offering the all-purpose Igbo greeting while squeezing Chizo's hand.

"Kedu," Samuel replies.

"Kedu," I repeat, my eyes now scanning the room, connecting with everyone, feeling them with my eyes, taking in their smiles.

I've taken the focus off Chizo and brought myself back to center stage. I feel a surge of confidence and tell myself I've got the situation under control.

"Afran ganaya," I say, continuing in Igbo.

My words mean "I love you" in English.

The sisters laugh, and I kiss Chizo on the cheek, smacking my lips theatrically, so that they know for sure I mean to say that I love her, not all of them. On seeing me kiss Chizo so passionately, Edith and Samuel rock back and forth, their mouths wide open.

"I am here to tell you an important story," I say, speaking English now, having exhausted my Igbo vocabulary.

I lean toward Samuel because he is, after all, my principal audience. "I love your daughter and I plan to marry her," I say. "She will come with me to America, and we will marry in America, according to the rules of the U.S. government."

I go on to say that Chizo and I will keep our house in Accra, Ghana, until her "fiancée visa," which permits her to enter the United States, is issued. Since I have yet to apply for Chizo's visa— I expect to do so soon—I explain that she won't leave for America for at least a year.

"She will likely visit Port Harcourt again before she travels to the States," I say.

I wonder whether anyone understands me. Am I speaking too quickly?

Chizo sighs and, looking at her parents, says, "This is what I want."

Her parents remain silent. Chizo then utters a phrase in Igbo. Her father takes a long breath, clears his throat and rises from his seat.

"You may marry her," he says.

I thank him and say I am pleased to receive his approval. From a plastic bag, I remove the bottle of Nigerian-made whiskey that Chizo told me to bring along. The Nigerians call this local whiskey "schnapps," because Europeans planted a taste in these parts for a scented brew. I give Samuel the bottle. Edith rises to her feet and grabs two small glasses and hands them to Samuel. He pours me a full glass and then pours himself one too. We touch glasses and down the whiskey.

The whiskey is harsh and I cough loudly. He smiles and our eyes meet.

"I am happy you are marrying my daughter," he says. "But tell me, what does your first wife think of my daughter? Will she welcome Chizo into your family in America? Will Chizo have her own house to live in or will she share the same house with your other wife?"

My other wife?

My jaw tightens and I suppress a nervous smile. I motion for Samuel to pour me another glass of whiskey. Chizo shifts uneasily on the bench and I squeeze her hand. Samuel hands me a full glass and I sip from it and then kiss Chizo on the lips, quieting her and making a loud smacking noise when my lips retreat from her lips. Her mother squirms and I wonder whether the whiskey is starting to talk.

Samuel stares straight at me and I calculate how much about American romance I should explain to him. From his question, I know I must tell him firmly and clearly that I have no other wife.

"I have Chizo only," I say. "I have no other wife. Only her. In America, she alone will be my wife."

I sip my whiskey again and hold Chizo's hand, waiting for the room to erupt in cheers. Perhaps I have failed to make my position clear.

"White man, tell no lies in my house," Samuel says. "There is no shame in admitting to having another wife. I only have one wife because I cannot afford to have more. You, white man, with your wealth, you can have many wives, you can even have other African wives."

I look at Edith, who has been staring at me, her mouth open, and when our eyes meet, she looks away. I wonder if her husband embarrasses her. I must remember to ask Chizo later. I wonder whether Chizo should explain the real situation to her father, but I decide I must.

I am afraid now, realizing that all along I've been out of my depth. I down another glass of whiskey, rise to my feet and take two short steps toward Samuel. I grab his right hand and pull him toward me. He lets his body fall into mine and the two of us are standing eye to eye, nose to nose, holding one another. I edge back, creating some space between us, and then take his hand. In West Africa, male friends often hold hands in public. I am making a conciliatory gesture, I think, not an intimate one.

Chizo helps by pulling out a disposable camera and snapping the two of us, now standing arm in arm, shoulder to shoulder. "Samuel, your daughter is my only wife," I say. "My one and only wife."

"In America we have one wife, one wife only, one wife at a time, only one."

"Only one," he says.

"Yes, only one."

"I accept," Samuel says.

I want to shout out, hooray, but instead I pour whiskey for Chizo's two brothers, who use the same glasses that Samuel and I used. I have drunk enough and start to worry about how Chizo and I will get back to our hotel. Perhaps my new Nigerian friend, John, will collect us. Otherwise, we will have to find a taxi on the dark streets and, inevitably, the driver will be a stranger and we will be vulnerable.

"Are you divorced?" Samuel asks.

"I am."

"I am also divorced," he says. "My first wife lives in Calabar."

Calabar is a day's travel away. Samuel was raised there. He explains that neither he nor Edith ever visit Calabar. They want to stay far away from his first wife, whom they fear will harm them if given the chance.

"Sounds like a good idea," I say.

Samuel nods in agreement and asks, "What will you do to protect my daughter from being killed by your first wife?"

"Killed? By who?"

That's all I can say before going mute. I suddenly feel dizzy. I fall away from Samuel and sit down next to Chizo. The room seems to be spinning. Is it the whiskey? Samuel remains on his feet and his voice is rising.

"We know you Americans enjoy killing people," he says. "How can I be sure you are not bringing her to America for your old wife to kill her?"

He sticks the index finger of his right hand into my belly and says, "Bang bang!"

Samuel fears his ex-wife and Edith does too. She tells Chizo this in Igbo and then Chizo tells me in English. Edith has soft brown eyes. Her face is fleshy and round. Her English is poor; she has nothing close to the facility possessed by her husband, who once worked for a British oil company—he was a pipeline security guard—and still carries the nickname "Little British."

"Edith won't go to Calabar," Samuel says. "Never. I have a house there, a large house."

He shakes his head, takes my hands and draws me close to him. "The sad part is that I cannot protect her in Calabar," he says.

I assure Samuel that I will protect Chizo in America. He nods. Then Edith asks, "Are you Christian?"

"No, I am not," I say.

Edith is disappointed. She edges away from me.

"I told you he is not Christian," Chizo says. "He is Jewish."

"Jewish?" she asks. "What is Jewish?"

Chizo tells her mother in Igbo that being Jewish is like being Christian only without the worship of Jesus.

Edith looks alarmed. Tears form in her eyes. She says something hurried in Igbo.

"What did she say?"

Chizo explains that her mother fears that, without the help of Jesus, I may become a tool of the devil, even if I don't want to, "because the devil is trickish."

I tell Edith that the devil won't get me. Never.

"All she knows is Islam and Christianity," Chizo says of her mother. "She thinks that if you aren't a Christian or a Muslim, you must follow juju."

I look Edith straight in the eyes. "No juju," I say. "No juju."

Chizo lets forth with another round of Igbo, supporting her words with a complex series of hand motions and facial expressions that, taken together, reassure Edith. She smiles. She pulls Chizo against her expansive body and begins to sing, first softly and then louder until Chizo's three sisters join in the song. Chizo is singing too, softly into my ear, our bodies pressed against her mother's ample body, the Igbo words unexpectedly soothing me. In the darkness, in the smallest home imaginable, I am being serenaded by a family of strangers in a language I can't comprehend.

I feel confused, disoriented. "Praise the Lord!" I cry out.

Everyone sings louder.

Only Samuel is silent, watching me intently, his lips pursed.

Chapter Eleven

Guess Who? (2)

The men in funny hats are looking for a minyan and I decide to help them. "I am Jewish," I say to the Hasidim.

"You're Jewish!" the taller one exclaims.

"A miracle!" the shorter one declares.

The conversation takes place in a popular restaurant in Accra called the Country Kitchen. The restaurant is close to the ocean, and the tables are set on a large covered patio. The ocean breeze is refreshing. During the daytime, politicians eat here in crowds, but at night there are rarely more than a half dozen tables filled and the service is slow. The waiters and cooks operate on what locals distressingly refer to as "Africa time."

It is past six in the evening, and darkness envelops the restaurant. The smell of burning citronella—an oil that repels insects—fills the air.

I walked here. My house is nearby, and I have no fear of walking to and fro, even in the dark. At least no fear of being robbed. My constant concern, while on foot in the dark, is stepping into the deep drainage ditches that line the road.

Because the mosquitoes feed at this hour, I wear a long-sleeved shirt and jeans. The only parts of my body uncovered are my hands and neck, and I have smeared bug repellent—the good stuff I bring with me from America—on my exposed flesh. I am overdressed, and perspiring as a result, but my aim is to avoid bites, even at the cost of feeling hot.

The headwaiter at the Country Kitchen seats me in a corner, where I can view everyone else in the joint. I watch the Hasidim enter the restaurant, get comfortable in their chairs and begin to puzzle over the curious menu, which consists entirely of Ghanaian fare. Fufu is a specialty. Various forms of cassava, a starchy root akin to a potato, are served. I long ago concluded I would eat neither.

Tonight I have ordered my usual chicken and rice, with fried plantains on the side. While I wait for my food, I drink a large Star beer and ponder the presence of the Hasidim.

In my years in Accra I've grown accustomed to the presence of a small number of Israelis. Most are in security, ex-Mossad, guarding mining operations or managing road construction or other building projects. These Hasidim stand out because of their long curls and black hats. The Israelis in Accra are secular and strong, with a large capacity to endure heat and dust. Not these pale-skinned Hasidim, who I imagine will wilt in the intense midday heat.

I walk over to their table and greet them. In the United States I make no special effort to commune with Jews, but in Africa I always identify myself as Jewish (for the benefit of the evangelical Christians who are prone to anti-Jewish comments, and perhaps to test my Muslim friends in Ghana, who invariably turn out to be tolerant of non-Christian faiths and relaxed about their own).

The Hasidim rise to greet me, and I tell them that I am curious, what they are doing in Accra. The High Holidays are upon us, and it turns out they are from Brooklyn and have flown to Accra to preside over religious services—first Rosh Hashanah and, ten days later, Yom Kippur.

"I was born in Brooklyn," I say, then add that I received Bar Mitzvah too, although so long ago that I confess I can no longer remember the correct way of reciting prayers.

The men smile. They must meet plenty of Jews of my sort in New York. I ask if they are rabbis, and they say no, they are ordinary members of a Hasidic congregation who have volunteered, actually, to help the very small number of Jews in Accra celebrate the holidays properly. And help is needed. There is no rabbi in Accra, no synagogue, no cantor, no Hebrew school, no Jewish venues of any sort.

"Accra is a hardship case," the taller Hasid says. "No rabbi will come for the holidays. Not worth it. There are too few Jews. So we come instead."

I flash a smile of understanding and the shorter one admits that Accra is not what he expected. "We were promised more Jews," he says. "Even with the two of us, we have only nine men. For a minyan, we need ten."

"You would be the tenth man," the tall one says.

Wow. In all my years as a Jew, I have never felt so important.

"You've done well to assemble even nine Jews," I say, smiling. Except for the few Israelis and a motley collection of foreigners posted here for professional reasons, Ghana is essentially Jew-free. Most Ghanaians, like Chizo's mother, don't even know Jews exist.

"We need you," the tall man says.

"You must help us," the short man says.

I know what they want, and I say yes without them having to plead further. I haven't done any favors for religious Jews for a long time. I am due.

I ask how many services I will be required to attend.

"Two," the men say together. "Only two."

One for the new year and one for the Day of Atonement. I am fortunate. I am getting off easy. I haven't attended a Jewish service for at least a decade. Maybe longer. I can't even remember when I last sat in a synagogue.

"I will attend both of the services," I say.

I give them my phone number and tell them I live nearby. "Call me," I say. "Please."

Both men smile, and before I return to my table, I order them bottles of Star beer, the big ones. Back in my seat, I suddenly feel lonely, and I wonder whether I am lonely for Jews, for my own tribe.

* * *

My chance meeting with the Hasidim explains why, a few days later, I find myself preparing to visit the home of the International Monetary Fund's director for Ghana. The IMF, which loans money to the government, is one of the most important international agencies in the world. The Jewish country director hails from Latin America. When he telephoned and invited me to his home for dinner—my reward, I suppose, for agreeing to round out the minyan—I asked whether I could bring a friend. He said fine.

I want Chizo to join me, if only because she has never attended any Jewish gatherings. I attend few myself. In advance of the dinner, I am anxious, worrying about the tedium of listening to so many Hebrew prayers and whether my long alienation from the faith will leave me open to ridicule. Chizo, however, betrays no anxiety about the occasion, asking only my advice on how to dress.

"Dress African," I say.

I want to tell her also not to speak about Jesus during the evening, but I fear any such advice will only ensure that she does speak of her Savior.

On the night of the dinner, she wears an elaborate outfit: flowing white robes made of Nigerian lace, a beaded necklace, earrings made from animal bones and a green head scarf, stiff from starch, that is folded elaborately and makes her look a foot taller. The construction of the scarf required the assistance of an Igbo neighbor.

My outfit is what locals call a "political suit," a five-button, light brown shirt made of lightweight cotton and a matching pair of slacks. My regular tailor has a flair for making these suits, and he accents his designs by placing alluring embroidery on the cuffs of the sleeves and pants as well as on the breast pocket.

Before going to the house of the IMF director, I stop at the Good News Barbershop, where Richard, my regular guy, works. In Accra, Richard is the closest we have to a haircutter to the stars. He cuts and buffs the heads of the wealthiest men in town—for the princely sum of $1.75, or about triple the cost of an ordinary cut.

Richard's appeal lies in more than his unerring sense of style. Invariably, he looks great, a twenty-something man immaculately dressed and manicured, a wide smile always on his face—he exudes charm and confidence and expresses an unshakable faith that a man's hair is his best advertisement. I see Richard every week because he has converted me to his first principle of hair care: always look like you don't need a haircut.

Richard does not rely on style alone, however. He hews to the highest sanitary standards possible in Accra. He sterilizes his scissors and shears before every haircut, and wraps safety paper around his customers' necks. After each cut, he applies alcohol to the head, then buffs the skin with brilliant-smelling powder.

Alas, Richard doesn't take appointments—does anyone in Accra?—so I never know how long I must wait for his chair to come open. Stephen drives Chizo and me to the barbershop and waits outside in his tiny Honda. I enter and find Richard's chair is empty. I exchange an elaborate handshake with him, ending with both of us snapping our fingers. Then Chizo greets him warmly and the two of them discuss stylistic options. After a brief debate, they choose an ultrashort cut that Richard calls a "fade," because the cut gives the illusion of a dark shadow enveloping my skull.

Richard performs his usual magic, and when he finishes, Chizo makes him smile by calling me "Sunshine."

When we enter Stephen's car and I tell him where I am going, he says softly, "I know the place."

It is 6:30, early evening. The streets are dark now, and I am reminded of why I prize Stephen's services. He can find anything and he never gives up until he does.

I sit in the backseat with Chizo, her Nigerian lace falling onto my lap.

"Why the need for ten men?" she asks. "Don't women count?"

"They don't count," I say. "Not for the purposes of holding a service."

"Is that fair? I thought you whites were fair? The whites are always telling us about women's rights."

I squeeze her hand. "Jewish tradition considers men to be more important when it comes to prayer," I explain. "Or the Orthodox Jews do. They are one tradition within Judaism. The Orthodox don't count the women; other traditions do."

"I don't understand," Chizo says.

Before I can explain, Stephen's car jerks forward, hurling Chizo against the front seat.

Stephen kills the engine and gets out, leaving the car sitting lopsided in a large pothole. We get out too. One rear wheel dangles in the air. Stephen surveys the situation. We are on a residential street in a better part of Accra. The car has blown a front tire. We go stand under a tree, along the side of the road, while Stephen replaces the blown tire with a spare.

I've seen Stephen do this before. His Fante sense of well-being permits him to address the task without rancor. "We are blessed," he shouts into the darkness. "My spare tire is very good."

Chizo teases him. "One touch," she says, referring to the speed with which Stephen gathers a gang of young men to help him lift the car out of the pothole and push it to the side of the road. Working without the aid of light, Stephen then removes the bad tire.

When he applies the spare, Chizo shouts approvingly, "All weather, Stephen, all weather."

She's telling him he can handle himself in any situation.

All weather or not, his progress is slowed by the darkness, and his periodic moans of disappointment worry me. I fear the dinner party is waiting for us to arrive before starting, and I check the time on my cell phone. I am relieved to see that we are not late—yet.

"Can't you hurry up, Stephen?" I ask, my frustration erupting at last.

I turn to Chizo and tell her that our usual roles will be reversed soon. Often I am the only white at gatherings. Tonight she may be the only black.

"Excellent, wonderful, very fine," she says. "Black is the color of your Jewish prophet, Jesus, isn't it?"

Her tone is mocking. She then reminds me of my frequent claim that the historical Jesus was black and that some Jews in ancient times were black too.

"I should be welcome, eh?"

She laughs, scornfully. "Your black Jesus is a giant lie," she says. "I will ask them all: Was Jesus black or white, Jewish or Christian?"

Her threat worries me. I plead with her not to ask such questions.

"I am making crack of joke," she says, laughing.

I sigh and ask hopefully, "At the dinner, can you avoid talking about Jesus?"

She smiles, mischievously, and doesn't answer. We stand quietly, watching Stephen tighten the final wheel nut. I again ask Chizo to avoid any Jesus talk at the dinner

Finally, she promises to behave, sort of. "I won't talk about Jesus," she says, "if there are no black Jews at dinner."

When we enter the house of the IMF director, he escorts us into his dining room. He cheerfully helps Chizo to her seat and points to mine, which is diagonally across from hers. The long, wide table is surrounded by about a dozen people. I immediately notice that Chizo and I are the lone interracial couple in the room. There is a black man at the table. He must be African, I surmise, though since he wears a yarmulke on his head I can't be sure.

Is he Jewish? What will Chizo say?

I find myself hoping he isn't Jewish.

Before we eat, there are prayers. The IMF director hands me a yarmulke, which I place firmly on my head. All the men are wearing them. Chizo, sitting across the table from me, smiles approvingly. Then the Hebrew starts. Prayers of various sorts that I have forgotten roll forth and I feel transported back in time to my youth on Long Island. The two men from Brooklyn do most of the talking. Then each of the men at the table is asked to say a prayer and

I gather from their accents that several are from Israel. My turn comes and I dredge up a Hebrew litany from the recesses of my memory banks. When I falter, one of the Brooklyn guys hands me a script and I carry on, stumbling on an unfamiliar Hebrew word and pausing. My embarrassment is relieved when the men from Brooklyn break into song and the rest of us join in, only Chizo silent, nodding her head, keeping time to the song with her body. The room is full of voices and I am suddenly aware of an odd sensation. My head turns and I know why I feel odd. The black man is now squarely in my gaze.

He is singing in Hebrew.

When the singing stops, food is served. The arrival of a plate of potato pancakes—and a side dish of applesauce—delights me. Next comes another personal favorite, matzoh ball soup, which I devour quickly and then request a second serving. The tall Hasid, sitting next to me, chides me for overfeeding on soup.

I shake my head. "You probably get this all the time," I say, spooning another matzoh ball into my mouth. "For me, it's been a while. I am savoring the moment."

The tall man smiles and then says, "You've been spending too much time with the *schvartzahs*. Come back to your people. You'll be swimming in matzoh ball soup."

He is smiling when he says this, as if he thinks he's helping me out.

A big piece of matzoh ball falls out of my mouth and into my bowl. The soup splashes into the air.

"Did you say *schvartzah*?" I ask.

"Yes. You don't know the word? It means 'black person.'"

I retrieve my errant piece of the matzoh ball and eat it absently. My grandmother spoke fluent Yiddish and I certainly know that *schvartzah* means "black person." I don't consider *schvartzah* to be a term of endearment but rather closer to an outright racial slur; for Jews, it is akin to invoking the N-word.

I tell the tall Hasid that he must not say *schvartzah* again. I tell him I consider the word to be a slur against black people. My voice is steady and I am trying to pretend that he doesn't know any better.

"There's nothing wrong with *schvartzah*," he says. "The precise meaning of the word is 'black.'"

"It is a negative word, taken by some as a slur," I answer. Then I add impatiently, "Look, I grew up in New York. I heard the word used many times. Few mean it as a literal description. It is trash talk, a term of disrespect."

He shakes his head in disagreement and repeats the S-word three times fast, as if we are schoolboys verbally jousting in the playground.

After the third *schvartzah,* my appetite for matzoh ball soup is gone. I am even thinking of tossing the soup in his face. I gather myself, remembering why I am here. I decide I must save the Hasid from himself—whether he wants me to or not.

I tap my fork hard on my water glass and prepare to take an extraordinary action. I make eye contact with most of the people around the table, raise my voice and then explain in slow, deliberate words that I have a dispute over semantics with the tall Hasid. I politely ask everyone in the room for their opinion of the word *schvartzah,* and for the appropriateness of the word in an African country where we are all guests.

The short Hasid jumps into the fray, siding with his fellow traveler. He says *schvartzah* so loudly, though, that our host, the IMF guy, looks alarmed.

Then the black man speaks, and from his first syllables his accent plainly marks him as originally from a French-speaking part of West Africa. "I have never heard the word before," he says, parsing his words with the care of a diplomat.

Before the Hasid can invoke the man's neutrality as a part of their defense, our host declares, "I have heard the word, and I don't want it spoken again in my house. Understood?"

The two Hasidim nod and smile and say they meant no offense. Israel declares loudly, "Welcome to Ghana!"

* * *

When the meal ends and Israel's wife serves coffee and tea, I grab the arm of the black man. Chizo reaches him at the same instant. I am on his left, she is on his right. His name is Jean-Claude and he is from Cameroon. He's some international adviser to the government. Before he can describe what he does, Chizo pops a question.

"Are you Jewish?"

The man laughs and laughs and laughs and laughs some more. When he stops laughing, he says, "How did you know?"

"I could tell you were Jewish," Chizo says excitedly.

The man laughs even louder now. "From my nose?" he says. "From the way I look? From how much I love matzoh?"

Now I laugh and Chizo grows quiet. "What's matzoh?" she asks.

Jean-Claude has confused her.

"Please explain," I say.

He looks Chizo in the eyes, taking her hand into his hand. "I was not born a Jew," he says. "I converted to Judaism when I married my wife. She is French, white and Jewish. When we divorced, I stayed Jewish."

Chizo stands openmouthed, astonished. She backs away from him now as if he is an alien.

He laughs again. "Why not?" he says. "I like Jews. And I don't find much difference between an African adopting Christianity or Judaism. Either religion can coexist with our traditional beliefs."

I nod in agreement and he smiles, running his hand down the middle of his shirt. "In my case, converting to Judaism was easy," he says. "I come from a tribe where the boys are always circumcised! So my conversion was less painful than for some others."

We both laugh and clasp hands.

"Jews and juju go together," I say.

"That's right."

Chizo stares at me. "Ask him," she says. "You ask him."

"Ask him what?"

"About Jesus."

"Can't you ask him?"

Jean-Claude grabs Chizo's arm and now the three of us are linked. "Ask me what?" he says in his deep voice.

Chizo draws closer to him. "Was Jesus black?" she whispers. "Was he really Jewish?"

Jean-Claude laughs louder now and turns toward me, our eyes meeting. "I suppose you have explained all this to her," he says.

"I've tried. I know I can't depend on the good Catholic fathers or the friendly evangelicals to tell her that Jesus was probably black."

"Amen," Jean-Claude says. Then he turns to Chizo and says, "Yes, the skin of Jesus was as black as mine."

Chizo pulls back from him and starts to pout. Their eyes meet, there is a long silence and then she asks, "Who cares if his skin is white or black?"

Jean-Claude beats me to the answer. "If Jesus is black, then God is too!" he says.

Chizo laughs and Jean-Claude calls her my "African queen."

Back at our house on Kuku Hill, after dinner, Chizo and I lie in bed, listening to the birds that gather late at night in the baobab tree outside our window. I ask Chizo whether she would ever consider converting to Judaism. She is silent. I don't think she is asleep, so I ask again.

"Would you consider becoming Jewish?"

Now she raises her head from the bed. The night birds are singing, and I take her in my arms. She kisses my lips and the warmth of her body soothes me.

I ask her again, and still no answer. I feel sleep snatching me away, when I hear her ask, "Why don't you become Christian?"

I can't. My mother was Jewish and her parents and the parents of her parents. Judaism has some hold on me, though I can't identify the source. I no longer follow any Jewish religious practices and I have violated, at one time or another, all of the social norms of Judaism. I find no contradiction between my marrying an

African, for instance, and my peculiar loyalty to Jewishness. Even the discovery of my "inner African," during these many months in Accra, poses no conflict since I have no doubt that in ancient times the border between black Africa and the Jews of Egypt and Palestine was porous. If Jesus was not actually black, then his whiteness was merely an accident of birth, because surely many Jews and early Christians were black.

When I attend the Rosh Hashanah service the next day, I am the necessary tenth man. I plan to perform the same role for Yom Kippur, the Jewish Day of Atonement, but the two Hasidim, very serious, say that I cannot do so unless I begin fasting the night before and fast through the entire day. The afternoon before, they call without warning and insist they must visit me in my home just as night falls. I thank them for the warning, and steel myself for their visit. Chizo, who believes that fasting refines spiritual ardor, celebrates my decision to fast. The two Hasidim forge common ground with Chizo, sitting in our living room, listening to some Igbo music and sharing small tales of long fasts from their pasts. "Talk brings talk," Chizo says. They explain to her that tomorrow all Jews have the opportunity to atone for their sins. The activity reminds Chizo of the Catholic practice of confession, but the greater frequency of forgiveness-seeking behavior in her faith impedes her comprehension of the Jewish approach. Indeed, she resists the idea that God can bestow forgiveness only once a year. "You Jewish are harsh," she says. "We Africans are not so good that we can wait a whole year to receive forgiveness." She says I must ask God's forgiveness on Yom Kippur, if only because if I fail to do so tomorrow, I won't get another chance for 365 days. I promise I will.

The next day, I go to a fancy hotel on Labadi Beach, not far from our house. A small banquet room has been converted into a synagogue for the day. Because of the heat, the chosen people of Accra can drink water, but nothing else. I nurse a bottle that I keep beneath my chair. The service is long and to break the tedium one of the ex–Mossad agents talks with me about the challenges of building roads in Ghana. The heat and the dust remind him of Israel, he says, but not the people.

I sit silently for long stretches and find my mind drifting to memories of mistakes I have committed in my life. I would not call them sins, though I suppose others might. Should I ask God for forgiveness? I remind myself that I am merely in attendance. I am only the tenth man. I am not, strictly speaking, worshiping. I am a body, the uses of which I am allowing others to decide, at least for the remainder of the day.

I never ask God for forgiveness. Chizo will be angry with me when I tell her. I know she will want to know whether I sought atonement, and I cannot lie, even if lying will spare me her criticisms. When the service ends, a sense of remorse comes over me, and I am sad. I am tempted to ask the Hasidim if I can seek forgiveness now, but I decide it is too late.

The ex–Mossad agent interrupts my thoughts, introducing me to his wife and two small children. I ask his wife how she manages, and she says she misses Israel, the country and its people. She does not need to tell me why. I say I am sometimes lonely here too. Our eyes meet, and she smiles. I look away and, when I return my gaze, she is talking to her daughter. I feel like a stranger and suddenly I miss Chizo intensely. But I cannot telephone her during Yom Kippur. The Hasidim are vigilant and I have been warned to keep my phone switched off.

An hour later, along with the other Jewish men of Accra, and their wives and children, we break the fast. Chewing on soft bread and slices of fresh pineapple, I telephone Chizo. My day of atonement is over.

achievement because, as a matter of fact, many applications for fiancé visas are rejected on the grounds that the applicants are neither in love nor plan to consummate a "real" marriage. Chizo and I now had a letter that said we were not trying to defraud the U.S. government and that, at least in principle, I could exercise my constitutional right to the pursuit of happiness through, in this instance, marriage to a foreigner.

I was in Accra at the time I received this declaration, and I celebrated with Chizo at Blue Gate restaurant. We feasted on piles of spicy tilapia, roasted vegetables, plantains and rice. We even downed a cheap bottle of Spanish sparkling wine and, after dinner, knocked back shots of local whiskey. Then we heard nothing from the U.S. government for the rest of the summer. I was about to complain anew to my lawyer when his e-mail arrived in early October, informing me that I could visit the U.S. embassy in Ghana to receive an appointment for Chizo to be interviewed by visa officials. This interview—and a battery of medical tests—was all that stood between her and a plane bound for London and then another to San Francisco.

In his note, my lawyer warned me to take the interview seriously. Employees at the embassy have broad discretion to reject applicants, even accuse them of fraud. I was to join Chizo for the interview and inform him immediately if anything went awry.

The chances of something going wrong seemed high because the embassy was a fortress and hundreds of Ghanaians gathered outside the visa building every day, hoping for the opportunity to enter and plead their causes. The United States turned down most of them, so there was a fatalistic feeling around those gathered. Just passing through security was difficult. The guards were locals, and even with my U.S. passport, my documents were closely examined and I was subjected to searches and X-rays and frustrating questions about why I needed to enter the embassy.

One hot morning, after running the embassy gauntlet, I stood face-to-face with a man, obviously from Ghana, who assisted visa applicants. I gave him my case number and asked if he had Chizo's file. According to my lawyer, her thick file—hundreds of pages of paper—had been shipped from the United States to Ghana.

The man stepped away from the other side of the counter and vanished. He returned five minutes later wearing a smile. He had the file.

I asked when Chizo could come for her interview.

"Come back with her in a month."

"A month!" I shouted.

The man made a nasty face. I apologized for raising my voice and explained that I had a British Airways ticket that would jet me away from Ghana in precisely twenty-four days. I wanted Chizo on the plane with me. The two jobs that had kept me occupied in Ghana for the past six months were both ending. I wanted out of the country, and I didn't want to return, certainly not to collect Chizo.

I begged the man to see Chizo sooner. He refused.

He told me I should feel lucky to get an appointment in a month.

I didn't feel lucky. I went back to Kuku Hill, nursing my disappointment.

At home, Chizo made pancakes for breakfast and I explained the problem. I had gotten her an appointment some thirty days from now. At this rate, she might spend another two months in Ghana.

"Go back to the embassy tomorrow," she said. "Ask again for an appointment."

I scoffed at her suggestion and not for the last time did I tell her she had a lot to learn about America. "Our country has rules," I said. "I'll just waste my time."

She insisted I return and I did. The next morning I ran the gauntlet at the embassy once more, my American passport trumping the elaborate procedures to keep out non-Americans with little or no chance of ever getting a visa. I passed through the search and screening procedures and finally, drenched in sweat, reached the same counter I'd stood at the day before. Today a smiling attractive woman greeted me. She even gave her name: Ama.

I explained to her that I had a plane ticket to leave Ghana in three weeks and I wanted Chizo to join me on the plane. I showed her a picture of the two of us.

"Your fiancée is beautiful," she said. "She has the face of Africa."

I smiled and gave her my case number. She walked away and quickly returned, cheerfully informing me that the file was on a desk nearby.

"You're ready to go," Ama said. "We can see Chizo next Monday. Come at ten."

I blinked in disbelief. "Yesterday a man told me she couldn't come for an interview for an entire month."

"Who?" she asked. I described him and she laughed. "He's not serious," she said. "Forget him. I'll take care of your wife."

I wondered whether she was playing with me. She gave me a form that would make entering the embassy easier in the future. Then she gave me two sets of instructions, each on a single piece of paper bearing the embassy's stamp. The first told me where Chizo needed to take her medical exam and the schedule of vaccinations she must receive. The other form was for the police to fill out, attesting that Chizo had never been arrested.

"Usually we wait until the interview to give out these forms, but I want you to get moving," Ama said. "I can see from your file you've waited a long time. I also know that if you've gone to the trouble of living and working in Ghana, you deserve to leave with Chizo on the date you want."

Ama's helpfulness was finally sinking in. I looked at her across the counter and started to cry. "You're the first person in this whole process that's acknowledged we are two people with feelings," I said. "Thank you so much. I am grateful."

Ama smiled. "I should be thanking you," she said. "Thanking you for marrying one of my sisters."

Ama kept her word. We saw her the following Monday. She conducted the interview easily, complimenting Chizo on her African outfit and me on my good taste in women. When I showed her the portion of my will that referred to Chizo's benefits, she stopped and looked at Chizo with alarm. "Where's your will?" she asked and then broke into laughter.

Chizo cleared the interview minutes later. Ama gave way to an American, a woman from Texas who was clearly in charge. She asked Chizo to identify herself by name and then to identify me by my full name. She asked Chizo to declare under oath that she was truthful in her declarations. Chizo repeated the declaration word for word. Then the

Texan took Chizo's police clearance form and her Nigerian passport and said farewell.

All that remained was for Chizo's medical tests to reach the U.S. embassy. We kept after the authorized clinic, and even met with the chief doctor, pleading with him to move quickly. Her test results were all negative and the doctor sent them directly to the embassy. A full week before my planned departure, Chizo and I returned to the embassy, ran the gauntlet once more, gained entry and saw Ama a final time. She handed Chizo her passport. Inside the document, pasted on a full page, was her entry visa into the United States.

On the afternoon of Halloween, we arrived in San Francisco, weary but excited. An immigration officer brought Chizo into a special room reserved for people coming to live permanently in the United States. I followed her. The man examined her papers. He found them in order and permitted her to pass through to American soil. Finally she and I were together in my country.

The joy we felt lasted a long time. Yet alongside our joy grew a sense of longing for what we'd left behind.

Even in our longing for Africa, however, our desires were not the same. Even as the ghosts of Africa came to haunt us, we found that some of our ghosts were not the same. They were different, and we couldn't escape them.

Chapter Twelve

Hotel Africa

One night out together, about a year after Chizo moved to Berkeley, I begin to realize I am not African enough for her, and yet I am too African for my own good.

Chizo and I are in a club in San Francisco. We've brought along her closest friend, Odette, a gorgeous yet brooding woman from central Africa. Odette is tall, lean and striking; approaching forty, she still looks like a fashion model. She has dark luminous skin, fine facial features and textbook posture. In Paris, where she lives with her husband, a French economist, Odette does a small business supplying her own African-themed designs to boutiques.

Tonight Chizo wears one of Odette's gowns, which drapes nearly to the floor but shows off her elegant neck and lovely arms. Odette, who is fluent in French, speaks little English and only tightens her face, flummoxed by my words, when I ask whether she is giving Chizo the gown as a gift. Chizo doesn't know either. Odette and Chizo attend the same English-as-a-second-language class at the Berkeley Adult School. They are the only African women in the class, and they form a natural alliance: both attractive, stylish, outspoken and English-challenged.

Odette's husband, who is spending the year at the University of California, is inexplicably averse to dancing in clubs, so Chizo invites Odette to join us for a night of live African music. I drive across the bay, Chizo sitting to my right and Odette in the ample backseat. We reach the small club well before the start of the show and take excellent chairs set against a wall to the left of the stage. While the band sets up, I talk excitedly about tonight's performer, Thomas Mapfumo, one of Africa's greatest bandleaders. Mapfumo sings mainly in the language of the Shona people and is Zimbabwe's most lyrical singer. His voice is gruff and soulful and the beat of his band is hypnotic. Zimbabwe is the home of the *mbira,* a sophisticated if small finger piano whose metal keys create utterly unique sounds, over which Mapfumo expertly sings.

When he steps onto the stage, Mapfumo seems ageless, his long dreadlocks swinging alongside his shoulders. The beat of the music gets me swaying in my seat. As I tap my feet, Odette and Chizo leap up and dance together, close to the band. They hold hands, sway, spin, gyrate, then break apart, approaching one another again, then spinning away. I watch Mapfumo taking the measure of these two women, each of whom dances as well as his own onstage dancers. As I ponder whether to join Chizo and Odette on the dance floor, a woman seated three chairs to my left calls out to me. I instantly know she's been watching me.

"Who are the African women with you?" she asks.

She has long blond hair and a pretty face: blue eyes, a turned-up nose and full lips. I slide across the open chairs to the seat nearest to her. Up close, she looks even better, and now I see she is with a friend, another white woman.

I introduce myself, and the blonde does the same. Her name is Marianne and she lives in San Francisco.

I tell Marianne that I am married to one of the African women—the shorter one—and that the other one is from Burundi though she lives in Paris and speaks French.

"Your wife is beautiful," Marianne says. "Where is she from?"

When I tell her she is from Nigeria, from the Igbo group, she jumps out of her seat and grabs my hands.

I am startled and even a little afraid, actually, until she sits back down. I look over at Chizo, absorbed in her dancing, swaying to the *mbira* alongside Odette. I study the two of them as they swirl, approach one another, hold hands, move apart, then connect again.

I turn back to Marianne and liberate my hands from her grasp. She looks me right in the eyes and I shiver. Then a weird sensation comes over me. I suddenly feel like I am the most important person in Marianne's world.

"Where did you meet your wife?" she asks.

When I say Accra—and I say it loudly, so she surely hears me despite the music—she abruptly turns to her friend. "Sweet Jesus," she shouts. "Did you hear that! He met her in Accra!"

She turns back to me, breathless, and grabs my hands again. I look into her eyes and see tears forming around the edges.

I am now completely terrified, certain I have met a mad person, of which there are surprisingly many in San Francisco, well known among its denizens as a magnet for misfits.

When I try to liberate my hands from Marianne this time, I cannot. Her grip overpowers me.

There is a lull in the music and Marianne's voice suddenly seems very loud. "I am engaged to an Igbo man," she shouts. "He lives in Accra."

I look at her friend, my eyes wide open.

Her friend says she's speaking the truth.

The man's name is Ike. "I've filed for a fiancé visa for him," Marianne says. "We plan to get married in California."

I am of course noting the parallels with my own life, pondering the odds of meeting Marianne here, or anywhere, and toying with the idea that, improbably, a sea change in romantic behavior is occurring in America, with some unaccounted for number of people seeking to mate with highly mobile Nigerians.

Marianne, interrupting my reverie, taps me on the shoulder and asks my wife's name.

I tell her and she says the name aloud, smiles and says it again.

"I love her name."

"Chizo means 'God's grace,'" I say.

"I love it."

Her words make me feel good. I relax, getting comfortable with her now.

"When were you last in Accra?" I ask. "What a fabulous city. An undiscovered gem. The beaches are wonderful, the people are fascinating and I feel safer in Accra than I do in California."

I am beaming, the memories rushing back. But then Marianne says something that erases the smile from my face. "I've never been to Accra," she says. "I'd like to go. I just can't spare the time or expense to travel over."

Her words shake me. She's never been to Accra? Is she crazy? I consider fleeing, joining Chizo on the dance floor. I can't pull myself away, paralyzed by Marianne's confusing story. Yet her earnest demeanor and personal warmth stop me from dismissing her outright. She wants to talk. I brace myself, ready to hear the rest of her story.

"I met Ike on the Internet," she says. "We e-mail a lot."

I purse my lips and become aware, for the first time, that I am a good deal older than Marianne. I adopt a fatherly voice, and do not hide my alarm.

"You met a Nigerian over the Internet," I say. "Is that wise?"

"I'm born-again," she says. "I met him on a Christian site. He's also born-again."

I roll my eyes. "Are you the last to know that Nigerians specialize in Internet fraud? Even Christian sites aren't off-limits to scammers."

I fear I've gone too far, but my warning makes Marianne smile. Obviously, she's heard this before.

"I'm glad you're honest," she says. "I believe what Ike tells me because he's a vegetarian. Vegetarians don't lie."

Really? Perhaps Ike only says he is a vegetarian in order to please Marianne. I bite my tongue, let the music dominate while I take the measure of this strange tale. I have met hundreds of Nigerian men in recent years and every one has eaten meat.

Marianne's friend tugs at my arm and shouts into my ear: "I'm concerned that Marianne not get hurt. Can you advise her?"

Her eyes search mine. I know what she is looking for. She wants assurances that her friend isn't being set up for a fall, or utterly mad to contemplate marriage to an unknown African.

"Meet the man in person," I tell Marianne. "See him on his own turf." And because Accra is such fun, I add, "You must visit. Go soon."

My advice seems banal, sensible beyond question. The friend cheers me, but Marianne disagrees. She wants to meet Ike for the first time in America.

"We e-mail, we talk on the phone, we send each other photos," she says. "We're intimate."

Her description suggests the illusions of intimacy—and plenty of space for fantasy to reign. I take Marianne by the hand, look into her eyes and search for the appropriate words. "Let me introduce you to my wife," I say. "When she takes a break from dancing, she can say plenty about the charms of Accra and the ways of her people."

I promise to return, then drift over to Chizo on the dance floor. For a long time, Odette, Chizo and I dance together. Then Odette drops out, and Chizo and I keep moving, Chizo doing her breathtaking thing while I look like a confused chicken, trying to follow Chizo's prime dance-floor directive: move as little as possible. My feet inch forward and back. My arms swing ever so slightly. My shoulders rise and fall imperceptibly.

Chizo gives me a thumbs-up and I experience a surge of pride over my dancing.

I've got the beat—barely!

When Chizo and I stop dancing, I tell her she must meet someone. "You'll never guess who," I say. We find Odette in her seat but no Marianne or her friend. They're gone. Perhaps they moved to a different part of the club or just left. We stay until after midnight, leaving during Mapfumo's encore. On our way out, there's still no sign of Marianne or her friend. On the drive back to Berkeley, I tell Chizo about her and describe Ike, Marianne's boyfriend, as best I can.

When I'm finished, Chizo says, "I know the guy." Nothing more. Nonchalant, as if she meets an American with an Igbo mate every other day.

"One hundred twenty million Nigerians and you say you know the guy," I snarl.

"Not surprising. Her boyfriend is Igbo. He lives in Accra. Even you met most of the Igbo in Accra."

She's right. I met hundreds of them; I even know some by name. Nigerians have settled in Ghana for decades, and Igbo are especially quick to relocate. Tired of the pressure of Nigeria's jam-packed, crime-ridden and electricity-starved cities, footloose Igbo—like Chizo—foresaw an easier life in Accra, moved there and stayed.

"You even met him," Chizo says of Ike.

"I did?"

"He's the boyfriend of the Igbo woman with the fancy restaurant. The one who held the *mapouka* dance contests once a month. One night, we met Ike there."

"Marianne says Ike is a vegetarian."

Chizo snorts. "We watched him eating goat kebabs that night," she says. "He's no vegetarian."

While I don't recall Ike or his eating habits, I can't deny Chizo's logic. The idea of a Nigerian man eschewing meat as a matter of principle is absurd.

"Can't we help Marianne?" I ask.

Chizo shakes her head. "You whites are so stupid. How can two people fall in love never having met one another? And the woman bringing him to America, getting his visa, paying his ticket, marrying him—and never meeting him in the flesh? Would you have married me that way?"

I don't answer, because we both know I would not have married Chizo sight unseen. I suddenly notice a police car following me. I am driving on the Bay Bridge, heading east to Berkeley, and I'm in the middle lane. It is nearly one in the morning, and the bridge is empty. The cop car is easy to spot, about a hundred feet behind me.

I check my speed. I'm doing sixty. Nothing wrong with that.

I change lanes, and the cop car changes lanes.

I slow down, the cop car slows down.

When I clear the bridge, the cop car, still about a hundred feet behind me, speeds up, gaining on me. I instinctively slow down and then hear the police siren go off. Damn! I'm being pulled over. I breathe deeply, tell myself to relax. No problem. I can handle this. I am sober, after all, having been so keen on Mapfumo's music that I drank only a couple of beers the entire evening, the second hours ago.

I steer my Volvo into the right lane and start to pull over. The cops don't want me to. Over the megaphone, one cop orders me to take the next exit. Then I'm told to make a right turn. I make the turn and pull into a parking lot, rolling to a stop, the cop car on my tail.

I cut the engine, take my driver's license out of my wallet and find my car registration in the glove box. I wait, clutching my documents, expecting to hear a tap on my window any second.

Nothing.

I wait and wait. Finally I get out of the car, license and registration in hand. I see two white cops standing in front of their car, watching me. One of them holds a big flashlight.

"Is there a problem, Officers? You followed me for a long time."

The flashlight cop asks, "Are you okay?"

I say yes, and he says, "The two women in the car, are they bothering you, causing you any trouble?"

I smile. "No. One is my wife and the other is a friend."

The cop doesn't smile back. "We're just making sure you're not in any trouble."

Trouble? I feel the urge to tease the officers—to inquire whether I have broken some unwritten rule against having two black women in a car driven by a white man. But it is late and I don't joke with cops.

"Can I go?" I simply ask.

The flashlight cop grunts, giving me permission to leave. I get back into the car. Behind the wheel, I fumble my keys and suddenly feel exhausted. I sigh. Odette talks rapidly in French, no doubt confused. I turn on the engine and Chizo asks me what the cops wanted.

I don't know, I tell her, and drive off. I check behind me, four or five times, making sure the cops aren't trailing me again.

They aren't.

I return to the freeway and take the university exit, the one nearest to our cottage. Odette lives around the corner from us. We drop her home and watch her get inside. A few minutes later we are inside our own place. I shower. The warm water relaxes me. The cops made me very nervous, actually. There's no easy explanation for their behavior. After a long time, I shut off the water, dry myself, brush my teeth and get into bed. Chizo is asleep. I look at her sleeping. I listen to her breathing. I kiss her on the lips. She doesn't stir. I touch her cheek. She doesn't move. I hold her. Still, nothing. I finally accept that I must face my inability to sleep on my own.

I sit up in bed. My mind races through scenes at the club. I remember Mapfumo's voice. I hear the *mbira*. I think about Marianne and the Igbo man she's never met but intends to marry. I study Chizo's reactions. And then I confront the unsettling notion that's troubled me since meeting Marianne: *Perhaps I am more like her than I care to admit.*

Sure, I went to Africa. I lived in Accra with Chizo, sharing the ups and downs of ordinary life. Yet maybe I'm no wiser than Marianne. Maybe she shrewdly avoids visiting Accra because a visit would spoil her fantasy of the perfect African? Maybe illusions trump reality, at least in romance? Maybe Marianne will love Ike more in America because she avoided meeting him in Africa.

Is ignorance bliss?

I lie back down, curl against Chizo and enjoy the warmth of her body. I try to sleep and can't. Memories besiege me. I remember courting Chizo in Accra, then sharing a house with her and letting "Africa" seep into my bones and ultimately "discovering" my inner

African. What if my experiences were nothing more than an elaborate smoke screen, obscuring the ultimate reality that Chizo and I are so different that she can never truly comprehend me and my world and that I can never grasp her or her world?

Maybe we are condemned to be intimate strangers, immersed in each other's lives yet always staring at each other across an unbridgeable gulf.

Wide awake, I contemplate the folly of my rational, orderly approach to encountering Mother Africa, and marrying one of her daughters. Perhaps I can never know Chizo and her world well enough to make a rational decision about whether to spend a life with her. Could Marianne have the right idea, after all, surrendering to the mystery of one stranger confronting another, then groping together in the dark, hoping for the best, letting the Lord be their shepherd? Maybe I am the naïve one, believing that I've actually protected myself against disappointment by doing everything possible—or at least everything I can imagine—to learn about Chizo and her world?

As I survey these difficult questions, images from my Accra days dance across my ebbing consciousness. I suddenly feel bereft. In the middle of the night, I miss Africa. I miss the vitality, the routine surprises, the humbling vulnerability pervading ordinary life. How I admire the courage of Africans to stand up daily to banal uncertainties and ruthless deprivation. In America, life is cloaked in a heavy garment of fear, anxiety and the relentless drive for self-protection. In Africa, outer armor is stripped away, and people are permitted—dare I say entitled?—to experience the rawness of their own solitary human predicament. For reasons I cannot comprehend, in Africa I feel more human than in America. I yearn to return for another dose of . . . me?

I think about Marianne the next morning and for days after. I hold silent conversations with her. I want to tell her everything. For her benefit—and my own?—I want to pour out the whole story of my marriage to an African. Chizo gets tired of my incessant talk of Marianne and accuses me of harboring a crush on her. I scold her: "You, Chizo Okon, jealous of a white woman," I say. "You have nothing to worry about. I am all for you."

Chizo is charmed. She knows well my tastes in women, and art. She puts down some unpeeled plantains that she is sizing up for cooking and walks to the opposite end of the cottage, where some of my smaller statues occupy the top of a bookcase. She picks up my cherished *blolo,* the red statue of the big-chested woman that I purchased in Ivory Coast. I am attached to this statue partly because I bought it right before we were robbed at gunpoint with the European couple. The statue is also a favorite because, according to Baule tribal lore, I have adopted her as my "otherworldly" lover.

Chizo lifts the *blolo* off the shelf and comes over to me. I take the *blolo* and cradle her against my chest, making a big show of kissing her big nipples. Though most of the statue is red, the nipples are black, the same color as the hair and eyebrows. I kiss the nipples a second time, moaning as I let my lips linger on them. Chizo grabs the statue from me and waves it in the air. I fear my *blolo* will suffer harm. We wrestle for control of the statue until Chizo gives up and allows me to return it to the shelf where it ordinarily rests.

I give the *blolo* a farewell kiss. "By kissing my *blolo* so passionately," I declare, "I am pledging allegiance to my African woman. No chance for Marianne."

"You are African on the inside," Chizo says, laughing.

Our joking makes me feel I can resume talking about Marianne. I complain that I'll never see her again. I failed to get her phone number and didn't give her mine. I regret my unusual lapse. I invariably collect essential information. While Chizo slices and then fries two plantains, I mourn Marianne's passing from my life, imagining that we are soul mates separated by circumstances beyond our control. Perhaps Marianne's spirit inhabits my red *blolo.* Perhaps she is my lover from another world and Chizo's jealousy is justified.

Snacking on hot plantains laced with pepper, I accept the loss of Marianne and convince myself that our chance encounter is best left unimproved, a dangling commentary on our parallel lives.

Time passes and I forget about Marianne. Then one Sunday—a Mother's Day—Chizo and I attend a special Catholic mass in San Francisco. The mass, held monthly, is performed in the Igbo language. The Igbo number about one thousand in Northern California and include at least a few priests. Most Igbo are Catholic, having been visited in their Nigerian homeland by waves of missionary priests, chiefly from Ireland, beginning about one hundred years ago. The church remains a center of Igbo life, both back at home and in America, and in the Vatican, one of the highest-ranking cardinals is Igbo, a source of pride among not only the ethnic group but all Nigerians.

Today two Igbo priests preside over the mass, which is already under way when we arrive and, as usual, well attended. There is a festive atmosphere, underscored by the fervent singing of the all-Igbo choir. In the pews, women wear colorful dresses and flamboyant head wraps, twisted into shapes that reflect traditional aesthetics. A few men wear suits; most sport flowing robes, some of Nigerian lace of the sort I wore on my wedding day. These are members of an Igbo association of Northern California, of which I am an honorary member by virtue of my marriage.

When we get settled in a middle row, I look around and spot a white woman seated in one of the first rows. I catch a glimpse of her face and only later realize it is Marianne.

I fidget through the rest of the mass, impatient to greet her. When the mass ends, I tell Chizo that now is our chance to warn Marianne.

"Can't you at least tell her you've seen Ike eat meat?"

Chizo refuses.

"Can't you warn her?"

"No."

"Why not?"

"I want to wicked you small."

"Chizo! Be serious."

"Ike could take revenge on my family," she says gravely. "He could find my parents and hurt them. He could hire a juju doctor and poison me."

"From eight thousand miles away. How would he even know your name?"

"Marianne could tell him. Tell him I said he lied about eating meat—and who knows what else. He might accuse me of spoiling his hustle."

Chizo's fears seem ridiculous. I think she doesn't want to help Marianne and wants an excuse. Chizo confesses. "I won't stop an Igbo from getting ahead," she says. "Maybe Ike has one chance to come to America, and Marianne is it."

"So you'd lie to help him get ahead," I say. "You'd hurt an innocent person."

Chizo shrugs. "Even good people lie. No one is above mistake."

My rejoinder is interrupted by the arrival of Marianne herself. She is coming toward us at high speed, smiling.

"So we meet again," I say. "I feared I'd never see you again."

"What an occasion," she says. "Mother's Day, Jesus, and all these strong, stylish African women. Life doesn't get any better than this."

"Amen," Chizo says.

I introduce Marianne to her. They hug and exchange kisses.

"So you found the Igbo mass, good for you," Chizo says. "My husband told me about your boyfriend, Ike. When he comes to America, he'll be happy you made connections with the Igbo."

"He's already happy," Marianne says. "He's always telling me how much he loves his people and how proud of me he is for finding them on my own."

She reaches into her pocketbook and removes a few photos of an African man wearing his hair in cornrows.

"This is Ike."

"He's handsome," Chizo says. She studies the pictures closely and says she knows him.

"You do?" Marianne says.

"For sure."

"Can you tell me about him?"

"I only saw him around Accra. I never spoke to him."

"Is there anything you can tell me about him? Anything?"

Chizo won't say any more, so I cut in. "Can't you tell her even a little?"

"Are you trying to make me talk by force? I don't remember. Ike is past tense."

Chizo glares at me, and I change the subject. I ask Chizo if Marianne should visit Accra.

"You should," Chizo says. "If you do, please meet Jimmy, my chimpanzee. I miss him. Say hello for me."

Marianne wants an explanation.

Chizo describes her job at the zoo and how she became the surrogate mother of an orphaned chimpanzee and took care of him, for more than a year. The chimp was barely a year old when they met, and she watched him grow and mature.

"Wow!" Marianne says. "What an experience. You're lucky."

Chizo confesses she didn't always feel lucky, especially when Jimmy bit her. "I taught him to stop biting," she says. "I loved him. He was smarter than most children, and certainly stronger. I got giant muscles from lifting him."

A melancholy look creeps onto Chizo's face. She stops talking. Our eyes meet and my thoughts turn to Jimmy. I miss him too. There is no chimpanzee refuge in Accra, or anywhere in Ghana actually, so Jimmy lives behind bars. He's still in his cage at the zoo. How sad. We used to wager whether Chizo would get to leave Ghana before Jimmy did. I bet on the chimp. For a while the zoo seemed prepared to fly him to a terrific sanctuary in Zambia. The chimps at the sanctuary, nearly all orphans, ran free over a wide area of jungle, protected by a roof composed of nets and a tall, electrified perimeter fence. The protection was more aimed at keeping other animals—and especially wild chimps—out and not the orphans in. Jimmy was all set to go, the money for the transport was raised—and then the deal collapsed. In one of those sad but predictable Africa mishaps, Jimmy's case got mired in bureaucratic limbo and, in time, his plight was completely forgotten. In a country where humans might not get released from prison when their sentences expire because of bureaucratic ineptitude, how could I expect the system to liberate a chimp?

When the U.S. embassy issued Chizo her visa, she joked that she would not leave until Jimmy got his freedom too. I went nuts and Chizo stopped joking, but we both felt bad about leaving Jimmy behind. Indeed, at the final stage, the visa process went so quickly that her farewell to Jimmy seemed botched. We went together to the zoo for the final time and I watched Chizo painfully act out a departure scene: packing her bags, driving to the airport, getting on a plane, flying away, landing in faraway America. I doubt Jimmy understood anything. How could he? When she left him that October day, he seemed plenty happy, sated on peanuts and chocolate ice cream that I secretly fed him—breaking the rules for a good cause, I thought, the possibility that he would remember me for ages.

In California, Chizo grieved over leaving Jimmy and even now nourishes some sadness over his continued captivity. While she cavorts freely in America, he remains in a small cage, which is getting relatively smaller all the time because he is growing larger. Plans for his return to a jungle setting are on indefinite hold. He is getting too old to adapt to a big change, and it looks likely he will never leave the Accra Zoo.

"There are many other reasons to visit Accra," Chizo says. "The beaches, the music, the people. But Jimmy is a special attraction. Please visit him and say hello from me."

"I will try," Marianne says. "I will. Really, I will."

Marianne never visits Accra. Chizo and I stop attending the Igbo mass in San Francisco, switching instead to a church near Berkeley

attended by many immigrant Catholics. One of the priests is a
Nigerian from the Delta region named Father Ray. He is a member of the Ijaw group. The Ijaw aren't exactly cousins of the Igbo
but Ray shares many of Chizo's customs, speaks her language and
(especially) enjoys her favorite dishes: pounded yam, coconut rice,
spiced tilapia and pepper soup. Father Ray preaches weekly, and
though he does so in English, a few Igbo families reliably turn out.

We never see Marianne at this church because she lives on the
other side of the bay. Years pass and we don't see her. Then one day
I get curious. I dig up Marianne's e-mail and write her, asking
about Ike and whether she's visited Accra yet.

The next day she writes back.

Ike came six months ago. They are married, living together in
San Francisco. He is looking for a job, and she is happy to have
him, in the flesh. She still hasn't gone to Accra, or anywhere else
in Africa.

I guess she doesn't know what she is missing.

I do.

Chapter Thirteen

Barbecuing My Big Nkisi

Holding her nasty Henckels cleaver high in the air, Chizo is scaring the wits out of me. Chasing me at high speed, her Henckels in her right hand, she explains that I should not be afraid. She doesn't intend to carve me up; she's merely imitating a favorite character in a popular Nigerian movie: the loving but knife-wielding wife given to acting out mock attacks on her husband. "I'm funning you," she says. "Wives in Nigerian movies always funny their husbands by chasing them with knives."

I am twenty feet away from Chizo, separated from her by the width of a quiet street, wondering whether to believe her words while at the same time imagining what the neighbors think of an overweight white man, wearing only a bathing suit and sandals, being menaced by a wiry black woman in dreadlocks who can run so fast with a large knife in a raised hand—as if she's had plenty of practice.

"What if someone calls the police?" I shout. "Can you imagine the report. 'Skinny black woman with giant knife chasing heavy-set white man up and down Francisco Street'!"

I pause to let my words sink in. Sometimes, Chizo is open to persuasion. Maybe this is one of those times.

I watch her carefully for clues that she may choose to relent.

This is not one of those times when my words turn the tide.

Chizo charges toward me, shouting "Four-eyes" (a reference to my eyeglasses) and swinging her cleaver above her head. She lets out a long battle cry. I gather myself and breathe deeply, weighing where I should run to next. I decide to turn tail and race up the front steps of a neighbor's house.

When I reach the landing, the neighbor's door covering my back, I turn and watch Chizo race after me, stopping at the base of the steps. She plants herself, the cleaver in her right hand dangling below her waist.

I am cornered. I am trapped. My final humiliation is near at hand.

I start to cry.

"Don't funny me now," Chizo says. "You know I'll never hurt you."

I raise my head and our eyes meet. "Please put down the knife," I say. "Lay it on the ground, and step back."

I try to sound like a hard-bitten cop, a Mafia hit man, or at least somebody who is no longer playing around with the woman he loves. My tough talk gets nothing. She won't put down the knife.

I begin to plead. I know in my heart that Chizo is funning me. I know she enjoys scaring her husband. I even believe she got the idea from watching Nigerian movies. I know all this, or do I?

I am still afraid. I cry louder.

"The knife scares me," I say.

I bought the Henckels cleaver from Macy's, and I know its power. I was tired of seeing Chizo destroy serviceable chopping knives on goat bones. The Henckels is a match for any bone Chizo wants to chop.

"Can we please go back to the cottage?" I ask. "You are making a fool of me in front of the neighbors. At least in the cottage, you can make a fool of me in private."

Chizo prefers a public drama. "Let one of the neighbors call the police," she says. "The police will laugh at you. Big giant of America, afraid of kitchen knife and your tiny African wife."

I shake my head, tears rolling down my cheeks. I try to remember how we reached this point. Fear has robbed me of my thoughts.

Oh, that's right. Chizo was cooking. The usual: pounded yam, cassava, plantains, fried goat, coconut rice. I made an innocent comment about the type of oil she was using: big, thick, fattening palm oil, imported from Nigeria and bought for an exorbitant price at the Igbo grocery story in central Oakland. I merely said I'd prefer she fry the plantains with canola oil.

Maybe because she'd heard my advice many times before, and always ignored it, at least when cooking plantains, she dismissed me with a wave of a hand and the warning, "Don't step on my shoe."

I already have, so my effusive apology is lost on her. She is angry. Lately, I have stepped too often on her shoe.

A few weeks later, we are packing our belongings. At long last we are moving out of the cottage in the backyard of my ex-wife's property and into our own house a few miles away.

The move is an opportunity for Chizo to fix a long-festering problem—and that's not her relationship with my ex-wife.

I need to give a bit of background in order to explain the problem, which has to do with my collection of tribal art: wood statues and masks from Africa. I began collecting African art even before I met Chizo, on my very first visit to the continent (a trip to Burundi for *The Wall Street Journal*). I stored my collection in the cottage. When I bought statues in West Africa, I would not keep them in our Accra house but rather would carry them to Berkeley, on my periodic trips back to the United States.

In this manner the cottage became filled with statues. I placed them on ledges and shelves, on top of dressers and tables. I hung masks on the walls above the kitchen and bathroom sinks. In short, there was no position in the cottage from which at least a few statues were not plainly visible.

In Accra, I warned Chizo about how I'd filled the cottage with statues. Because she agreed to live in the cottage, she worried about the growing number of pieces. She believes these statues contain spirits, some good, some bad, some neutral. While I worried about Chizo and me living in Berkeley within one hundred feet of my ex-wife, Chizo worried about living with my African art collection.

Her first night in the cottage, after two tiring ten-hour flights and a couple of hours of trick-or-treating, she ignored the statues and slept well. But the next morning, after rising from bed, she took me by the hand and we inspected statue after statue. Chizo talked about each one, saying whether she thought this particular statue carried good powers or bad. When she found the red *blolo,* she acted as if greeting an old friend, petting the statue on the head. To those pieces she considered bad, for whatever reason, she mumbled words in Igbo—words she said were intended to rob the statues of evil, or at least keep the evil at a safe distance.

When she came to the largest statue in my collection, she stood mute. The statue is four feet tall and weighs eighty pounds. The head is enormous, with large eyes set under glass, a wide-open mouth and teeth nearly the size of real human choppers. The statue's body is riddled with large nails. Each nail, to the Kongo tribe member who made the statue, represents a promise. Every contract, deal or promise made within the confines of a certain village in the Congo was consecrated by driving a nail into the statue. In the Kongo language, the statue is an *nkisi,* or "nail figure."

My *nkisi* is the centerpiece of my collection: the most striking piece, and the most valuable. I purchased it from an African art dealer, a Gambian Muslim named Musa, who arranges for a buying agent to scour West and central Africa, acquiring a container load of pieces once or twice a year. The agent told Musa that this *nkisi* came from a Kongo village overrun by rebel armies in the late 1990s. Routinely soldiers looted villages and their booty often included artwork, which they knew could be sold to collectors in Europe and the United States (elite Africans, meanwhile, usually steer clear of such work).

Musa's story of the *nkisi* carried a whiff of truth. Besides, my statue is simply too big and beautiful to have been a cheap copy prepared hurriedly by local artists in the hopes of hoodwinking a tourist. One hundred years ago, German and Belgian explorers of Africa had carried off many *nkisis,* bringing them to Europe. Dozens now sit in museums in Germany, Belgium and Portugal. Only a few months before meeting Chizo in Accra for the first time, I visited a Berlin museum that contains a handsome collection of *nkisis.* The museum's curator gave me a private tour, and we lingered at the section devoted to the *nkisi* statues, marveling at their combination of beauty, size and elegance.

The *nkisi* in my cottage is no equal of these museum pieces, yet the statue is authentic and I more than admired it. I could not imagine giving it up. So when Chizo stood before it, her body shaking with fear, I grew concerned.

"Leave this statue behind," she said. "Don't bring danger into our new house."

I protested and she cut me off. "Okay. Bring the statue, leave it outside. In the backyard. There is a place, protected from the rain, near the hot tub. Leave it there."

I said nothing and the debate ceased. We moved our belongings over a period of weeks, until the new house was ready to go and the cottage was empty of all but the *nkisi.* The statue seemed majestic in the center of the room, as if inhabiting its own house. One afternoon, at the last possible moment, when my ex-wife stands hovering outside, waiting expectantly for my final exit, I come and embrace my *nkisi.* I face a strange choice—between my wife and my most valued statue. For a long time I consider telephoning Musa, asking him to buy back the *nkisi.* Even at a substantial cost to myself, its return to a responsible dealer, who would find the statue a good home, makes sense. Why upset Chizo? She had compromised, after all, in moving the rest of my collection into the new house. Why not let go of the *nkisi*—for her sake?

I don't call Musa. I stand near my statue, which suddenly seems like my little brother. "You are part of my African family," I say aloud. "You are part of my connection to the motherland!"

Then my declarations are interrupted by the sound of the cottage door swinging open. My ex-wife, Nora, ducks her head inside.

"What gives with the statue?" she says.

I sigh and try to speak, but no words come out.

"I'm sending Liam in here to help you get it out. You're supposed to be out by noon."

I check my watch. I'm an hour over her limit.

"I can't decide about the statue," I say, but Nora is already gone. A minute later my son arrives. I take the head of the statue and he holds the base. We lift it, put it into my Volvo and drive to my new home.

All is fine at first. Then one afternoon I find myself part of a drama conceived, produced and acted out by Chizo.

Act one begins innocently enough, with Chizo asking me to sit down on the upholstered swivel chair I keep in my study.

When I sit, she pulls my arms behind the chair and slaps handcuffs on me.

"Where did you get these cuffs?" I ask. "They're comfortable."

These are not police issue but rather leather cuffs.

"Only the best for you," Chizo says.

I nod, pleased.

Instead of asking how much the cuffs cost, which is what I do, I should be rising from the chair and running out of the house. While I wait for Chizo to answer, she's cuffing my ankle to the bottom of the chair. When I try to escape, I fall back into the chair.

Chizo steps toward me and laughs. "The cuffs are strong," she says. "They are reigning. Give in."

"I am at your mercy," I reply. "Please be kind."

Chizo casts her eyes to the ceiling. "Oh Lord, give me the strength to help my husband find the path of righteous. Give me the strength to expel the devil who threatens to terrify me and turn him into a fake husband."

Fake husband?

"What's this about?" I ask.

She pushes the swivel chair into the living room and then to the front door. Directly across from the door stands the *nkisi,* placed strategically so that visitors must confront the statue and, while we are asleep, it can guard the door against unwanted intruders.

"Oh no," I say. "No."

"I asked you to keep the statue somewhere else," Chizo says. "You ignored me. You brought the statue into our new house. I pretended to go along. No longer. Now I am protecting myself because if I don't, the devil will rule."

Chizo's voice is calm and clear. She is not funning me and I am growing very nervous.

"Release me, darling, and I will see that the *nkisi* gets a new location."

She smiles and says, "Allow me."

From out of nowhere comes a can of lighter fluid, the stuff used to jump-start barbecues. I try to leap from the chair, forgetting my predicament, and come crashing back down.

I moan loudly, feeling pain and seeing clearly Chizo's next move.

"No," I yell. "No, no, no!"

She is squirting lighter fluid on the statue. The liquid drips from the *nkisi*'s ears and mouth and chest.

Now she holds a lighter and snaps it. A flame shoots into the air. Chizo brings the flame near my nose, then swings the lighter to the *nkisi*'s chin. Flame meets wood and I hear a sizzling sound.

"Are you setting my statue on fire!" I scream. "In the house! You could burn down the whole place."

Chizo snaps off the lighter. "You're right. Let's go outside."

She picks up the statue by the head and carries it through the front door. Then she wheels me out into the bright sunshine and I see the statue sitting in an empty driveway, ready for setting on fire.

"I'm so glad you're thinking about safety," I say sarcastically.

She comes over and kisses me, a long kiss that makes me think she's having a change of heart and may remove the handcuffs.

"I'm barbecuing your big *nkisi*—for your own good!" she whispers defiantly.

Alarmed, I once more try to liberate myself. I can't. I fall back into the chair and then watch helplessly as the flame of her lighter meets the statue at four or five places. My body sags. I shake and squirm and jiggle. Then I topple the chair onto its side and roll down the driveway, moaning in pain.

Chizo catches my chair, puts me upright and brushes the dirt off my face. She kisses my forehead while I breathe heavily.

"Please stop," I say.

"Honey, I want you to watch me barbecue your *nkisi*."

I shake my head and watch. The statue is smoldering now. For some reason the fire won't catch, perhaps because the statue is made of tropical hardwood. Chizo sprays more lighter fluid onto the *nkisi* and then runs the lighter over it again. Still, no flames. She grabs a pile of discarded newspapers, layers them onto the statue and sets the papers alight. This time the fire ignites. Flames engulf the body of the statue, though thankfully the enormous, beautiful head won't catch fire.

I feel I am watching a medieval witch burning. At the very instant that I conclude the statue won't possibly survive my wife's attack, Chizo grabs a garden hose and douses the statue with long blasts of water. She keeps inundating it long after I yell for her to stop. Having feared fire damage, I now fear water damage. My pleading goes unanswered. Chizo drowns my *nkisi* with impunity. I slump into my chair, defeated.

"Uncuff me, and I'll dry the statue," I say sometime later. "Water can be worse than fire with old wood."

Chizo decides to dry the statue herself. I watch from the chair, occasionally giving instructions. She deftly scoops out water from the mouth and ears and dries down the body vigorously. She carefully rubs the glass eyes, and the glass box, fixed to the *nkisi*'s waist, where shamans likely kept their potions and herbs.

When she's done drying the statue, she uncuffs me. I rise from the chair, slowly. I groan. I feel stiff and sore. I stand motionless and erect, a few feet from the statue. I am afraid to touch it. My eyes meet Chizo's and for a long time we stare at each other without speaking.

She finally breaks the silence.

"Bring your big *nkisi* back into the house," she says. "I've killed the evil spirit now. Or chased it away. The danger is gone. You can keep the statue in the house now."

I blink furiously, letting the words sink in. Then I pull Chizo toward me, holding her tight. I break free and touch the statue. Then I hold Chizo again. Our bodies intertwined, I try to make sense of what's happened. I cannot. Instead I let go of my questions and accept the cuffing, the fire, the water—and all the rest of Chizo's improvised exorcism.

She puts her arm around me and draws me close again, while I relish my instant amnesia. Psychologically, I have moved on. I smell her hair, I feel her skin against mine, I look into her eyes.

"I feel safe again," she says.

Me too.

I savor the moment. Unexpectedly, I have triumphed. My statue survives, Chizo is relieved and once more we are happily married.

PART SIX

Delray Beach and Berkeley
2006

*W*hen I told my mother I intended to marry Chizo and live happily ever after in America, she asked, "Why can't you marry Maya Angelou?"

We were in my parents' New York house, in their small living room. My dad was out, probably shopping at dollar stores, which had become a hobby of his. Alone with Mom, I took the opportunity to declare my intention to marry an African. I considered Mom the more reasonable of my two parents, and I expected her to greet my news, if not warmly, then with less detachment than my father might show. Instead I faced her question about Maya Angelou, the great African-American writer who had famously read a poem at Bill Clinton's first inauguration as president.

When I said nothing, my mother repeated, "Why can't you marry Maya Angelou?"

Her question caught me off guard and I scrambled to change the subject, saying I'd enjoyed reading Angelou's memoir of her years in Ghana, All God's Children Need Traveling Shoes.

"I'm delighted to hear about the book," my mother said. "Now I know you have something in common with Maya Angelou. So why not marry her?"

Her sarcasm made me hold my breath. My mother was not happy, and I began to think I should have told my dad first.

My mother was waiting for an answer, so I gave her one.

"Maya Angelou isn't looking for a husband," I said.

"She isn't? Have you checked?"

"I'm surprised you even know her name, Mom. Did you learn about her from Oprah?"

My mother winced. "Enough already with Maya what's-her-name," she said. "I've got another idea. Why not marry Halle Berry?"

"Halle Berry," I said. "You want me to marry her."

My mother looked away. "We aren't talking about Halle Berry."

"What are we talking about? Tell me what you mean."

"Fine," Mom huffed. "There are so many talented, successful black women in the world and you have to marry a woman who works in a zoo? In Africa?"

"You'd prefer what?" I asked, my disappointment showing. I resented her implication that for her son to cross the color line in romance, he must have an exceptional opportunity. Like the chance to mate with Halle Berry.

"Chizo is actually great at caring for chimpanzees," I said. "You should see her with Jimmy. She's breathtaking. You should see her in action."

My mother tightened her lips. "Don't start again. We're not going to Africa."

I'd invited my mother to visit me in Ghana but she said she and my father were too old to visit Africa, even easygoing Accra. "We won't even travel to California anymore," she said.

"You'll meet Chizo in America someday," I said quietly. "You'll like her."

"My feelings don't matter," my mother replied. "Whatever makes you happy . . ."

She looked away and closed her eyes. Then she said, "Wait until your father hears this."

Chapter Fourteen

Jew Meets Juju

My mother is a long story, and Chizo is a long story, so writing about their adventures together intimidates me, even though I know that this chapter has a happy ending. At times, I approach my mother and my wife with trepidation—and that's when I'm encountering them individually. When I contemplate them together, the combination of fear and caution brings me to the edge of abject terror. I naturally worry about documenting the encounters between these two forceful women, if only because of the recriminations that might result. They do read, after all. Yet I cannot avoid addressing how the two most important women in my life get along.

I have a less selfish reason for telling tales about a seventy-something Jewish woman and a thirty-something African female. Chizo's encounters with my mother rank among her greatest triumphs in America (and, to me, the most unexpected). From the very start, Chizo aims to charm my mother. I am skeptical, but she proves me wrong. She succeeds in charming my mom, becoming the only woman in my life ever to do so.

Why did I expect my mother to escape Chizo's charms? Perhaps because I share some of the shortsightedness most sons display toward their mothers. I see my mother through the prism of my own life. From my limited perspective, her steady jabs at me—viewed by her as good-humored "motivational" techniques or admirable displays of candor—can overwhelm. She was a grade-school teacher for many years, after all. The logic of the classroom, where the teacher sets the rules, informs her dealings with the world. She's strict. She's constantly grading people. She dislikes pranks. She's invariably sober to the point of appearing puritanical, her Jewish heritage notwithstanding. To suggestions that she's not always a bighearted lover of humanity, her constant refrain is "What! Me hostile!"

Before she met my mother, Chizo heard she didn't do well with the women in my life. After Chizo met my mother and saw this problem up close, she concluded that I am to blame.

"You argue too much with your mother, and she takes it out on us," she says.

She advises me to surrender to my mother's will to power, wholly endorse her every opinion and speedily attempt to satisfy her every whim without complaint.

"Agree with everything she says and say yes to everything she asks for," Chizo advises.

"Everything?" I reply. "Are you serious? If there was a Nuremberg trial for Jewish mothers, mine would need a very good lawyer."

Chizo punches me in the shoulder. "I don't know what trial you're talking about but that's just the kind of stupid comment that will upset your mother. Stop saying things like that."

"Okay. I will. I promise."

"And ignore her harsh remarks. Keep quiet."

"How might I do that?"

"Stay cool. Follow my step."

"I'm not cool."

"I'm teaching you to be cool. The first principle of coolness is to say nothing. Silence. The coolest people say nothing at all."

Silence is golden? Indeed, Chizo's ability to go silent for long periods is possibly the secret to her surefire method of ignoring the slights—unconscious and premeditated—flowing from my mother.

"Is silence a form of juju?" I ask her.

"No, it is a form of Christianity."

When facing my mother, Chizo vows that she will maintain a

Christ-like resolve to turn the other cheek. Whenever difficulties arise, she will appeal to a higher power for strength. She plans to respect my mother in the manner that God probably wishes Job to display toward Him: respect without conditions or hope of rewards and in the face of exacting trials too horrible to comprehend.

Chizo's resolve is put to the test after my father dies following a long illness. My mother is spending the winter alone in her Florida house, and Chizo and I want to visit her. I tell my mother in a phone call and she says yes, Chizo and I can visit, so long as we don't stay in her house.

"We can't stay in your house," I say. "Did I hear you right?"

"You heard me right. I can't have the neighbors finding out you married a black woman. I'd never hear the end of it. These people can be pretty nasty."

"Are you serious?"

"You don't know what these people are like. They never stop. They just pick away at a person's wounds."

"Wounds? They would object to your son marrying an African? They don't even know me. Why would they care?"

"You really live in a bubble, son. In a dreamworld. In the real world, people care."

Her people, she means. Her Florida neighbors. These neighbors are not, actually, secretly members of the Ku Klux Klan. They are not clandestine supporters of a white-supremacy group either. Nor do they privately advocate "ethnic cleansing." In fact, my mother's neighbors are old Jewish people, mostly from New York, mostly born in the 1920s and 1930s. This particular bunch—Mom's gang—live in a gated community of about eight hundred ranch-style homes close to the pretty town of Delray Beach. The gated community was built not long ago by an Israeli, a fact that seems to enhance the value of the houses in the minds of some of the owners. According to my mother, who claims to be privy to some sort of census data, 792 of the 800 homes are occupied by Jews.

My mother doesn't say whether only the Jewish residents will be upset by Chizo's visit, or whether the eight non-Jewish families also will be angry.

Two of these eight families are black, my mom insists. On the premise that Chizo will get a free pass with these families, my mother expects to receive "endless grief" from 798 families.

All over my wife's skin color?

I tell my mother I have a clever solution to her problem.

She says nothing.

"Do you want to hear my plan or not?" I ask.

"No, I don't. My mind is made up. Stay in a hotel. I'll pay for it."

I ignore her and say, "Okay. Here's the plan, ready or not. Tell your neighbors that Chizo is your cleaning lady."

I laugh nervously, though I am not joking. I know the neighbors would believe my mother. I know my plan can work. Besides, I think staying in a hotel is stupid and insulting.

"I vote for the cleaning-lady story," I say cheerfully. "A definite winner."

My mother huffs. "I'm not telling *that* to anybody," she says. "I don't even want people to ask me who she is."

I think of Chizo's general advice on my mother, but I am not ready to surrender. I try a new approach, ditching my sarcasm and impatience, adopting the tone of a sympathetic friend. "I'm disappointed in you, Mother," I say soothingly. "You were never like this when I grew up."

I hark back to the 1960s and the civil rights movement, when my parents, if not out marching, voted Democratic and deplored mistreatment of African-Americans. They even sent me to an "integrated" school on Long Island. In junior high, I played basketball—starting center, actually—on an otherwise all-black team. My mother had two black women, sisters from South Carolina, live with us for several years. Sure, they were housekeepers, but they ate at the same table with us, and when they moved on to study nursing and work in Queens, my mother stayed in touch.

"Why fear your neighbors, Mom? You taught me to respect

black people and to root for them to overcome adversity. You taught me to reject prejudices."

I begin to remind her how we all sat in front of the TV watching Martin Luther King orating. I remember how his words brought my parents, as well as me, to tears.

"Marriage is different," my mother says.

"Mom, please."

My voice sags and I suddenly feel helpless. She says nothing, and I can't shut up.

"You can't make us stay in a hotel. You can't."

A long silence and my mother says, "If you can't stay in a hotel, don't come."

I feel defeated. I have nothing left to say. I promise to call my mother back and hang up. I put down the phone and cry. When I find Chizo, she asks me why I am crying. I give her the gist of my conversation with Mom and ask her what I should do.

"We can stay in a hotel," Chizo says without pausing to ponder the situation.

Her rapid reply angers me. "Aren't you insulted?" I ask.

She stays cool and silent, reacting only by raising one eyebrow.

"Well, I'm insulted," I say.

"If this is what your mother wants, let's go along," she says. "We promised we would do what she wants."

"There are limits."

"No, there aren't," Chizo says. "Do what she wants."

"Please. Stop. This is my country. We can't accept this."

"You're not listening. I am not offended. I don't care. Your mother is from olden times."

"That's not an excuse."

Chizo pushes back her dreadlocks from her face and looks away. "Do you think this is news to me that some whites don't like to be around black?" she says. "I know some whites don't want to be around us. If one of these whites is your mother, I can deal with it."

"My mother likes black people," I say. "The problem is her neighbors don't."

"The neighbors?"

"Old Jewish people like her."

Chizo laughs out loud. "I don't care," she says. "Leave the old Jewish people alone. We stay in a hotel, we see your mother, we don't shove our marriage in her face. You do your duty. Promise."

Chizo holds out her arms. She wants to hug me, seal the promise. I let her pull me toward her. "You know I'm only doing this because my father died and she's alone," I say.

"Call her back," Chizo says. "Tell her we'll stay in a hotel."

I call my mother. I do what I'm told. I tell her we are coming—and to reserve us a no-smoking room.

Chapter Fifteen

The Queen of Shuffleboard

My mother collects us at the Fort Lauderdale airport in the last car my father bought her. Some aging blue convertible made by General Motors that runs only because my mother hardly drives it. We toss our small bags into the trunk of the car, which my mom reminds me is an Oldsmobile Cutlass. Impatient to leave the curbside area, Mom hustles us into our seats. I sit next to her in the front, while Chizo positions herself behind me in the backseat.

Mom pulls away from the curb. She wears a purple cape, and a little white hat sits atop her mountain of hair. She's a redhead, and strikingly attractive, even now, when she's a bit heavier and slower-moving than in her prime. Her skin, wrinkled and fairly buried under makeup, remains fair and soft and slightly reddish in color.

"You look different," my mother says, studying Chizo in the rearview mirror.

Chizo's prized dreadlocks are today covered by a long, silky hair extension.

"Is that your real hair?" Mom asks.

"No, Mom. An extension. I weave it onto my hair."

My mom grips the steering wheel tightly and says only, "I need to pay attention to driving."

Before my dad died, she stopped driving entirely and now she's highly anxious behind the wheel. We leave her alone. After some thirty minutes, we exit the freeway and take city streets to the center of Delray. Mom parks and we stop for coffee, then walk to the beach. It is February, barely 8:00 A.M., breezy and balmy. Chizo wears a light blue Nike tracksuit, an Adidas T-shirt and Puma shoes. The temperature is about the same as what we left in Northern California, yet still Chizo shivers. Standing next to Chizo, my mother seems shorter than I remember. Has she shrunk with age? As I snap a picture of them, my mother looks up, grimacing.

"Don't photograph me," she commands.

Too late. I already have.

We approach a drawbridge that spans a canal. Large boats pass through here. Chizo has never seen a drawbridge and we wait for a large boat to pass. I explain to her how the center of the bridge can be raised. We greet the man who operates the bridge. He sits inside a small booth. We wait for some time on the pedestrian walkway and then a large boat comes and we watch the bridge rise and the boat goes through and then we watch the bridge come down.

"America, America, land of moving bridges," Chizo says. "In Africa bridges never move. They fall down."

She turns to my mother. "Thank you for showing me."

We cross the bridge and reach the beach. My mother waits for us while we walk along the surf. The water is chilly and the wind blows sand in our faces. We're both tired. The last time we slept together on a plane was during our eight-thousand-mile journey from Africa to America. I'm stiff, and Chizo is sleepy.

Back in the car, Chizo dozes. My mom concentrates on driving. I'm quiet. As we approach the entrance to my mother's gated community, I rouse Chizo. Visitors must stop at the security hut and identify themselves as guests of a certain owner. My mother has an electronic tag on her car, and she drives through the gateless entrance.

She winds her way to her street and pulls into the driveway of a bright ranch-style home. She opens her garage door with a remote. Her car slides in. We get out and enter the house through a door in the rear of the garage. Only when I am seated in my mother's kitchen, sipping an orange juice and noshing on a bagel, do I compliment Mom on getting Chizo and me inside without any neighbors seeing us.

We're sipping weak coffee when Chizo asks Mom whether she misses having sex. Before she can answer—or rather before I can intervene and change the subject—Chizo asks my mother whether she fancies any particular man.

My mother, without hesitation, admits to having sexual desires. But she explains that my father, Mike, was very handsome and that many of the available men she meets now are not. They are ugly, actually.

"I don't like ugly either," Chizo says approvingly.

Mom smiles and says, "Besides, I'm not going to chase a man, and at my age, most women have to."

I am speechless. I haven't heard any of this from my mother even though, since my dad died, I call her nearly every day that I'm not traveling outside of the States.

While I ponder my mother's answers, Chizo launches into a fresh line of inquiry. "If you could take any man to bed," she asks, "who would you pick?"

My mother purses her lips and runs her hands through her hair as if contemplating one of the universe's deep riddles. Seconds pass. I get up from the table and look out the kitchen window at the man-made canal behind my mother's house and the row of houses beyond the canal. My head turns when I hear my mother tell Chizo that she'd like to romance the movie star George Clooney.

"Good choice," Chizo says, then asks me, "Is he the one married to Angelina?"

"You mean Brad Pitt," I say. "Clooney is better looking. And he might be single."

I smile and ask my mother to consider another proposition: buying a new car.

"Can we talk about cars some other time?" Mom says. "Cars aggravate me."

"Sure," I say.

The gap in the conversation gives Chizo another opening.

She asks my mother whether she's had sex since my father died.

I sit down, stare out the window and bury my face in my hands. I stop breathing and for a moment consider leaving the room.

Before I can, my mother says, "I haven't had sex since Mike died, but I'd like to."

"You should have sex," Chizo says. "You are not a stick or a piece of wood. Just make sure the man uses a condom."

Chizo then asks me whether I might buy a box of condoms for my mother.

A box? A whole box. Might a three-pack suffice?

"Do I get her condoms for Mother's Day?" I ask.

My eyes meet Chizo's and she smiles. "Oh, darling, poor you, I am so sorry." She apologizes for asking too much of me. Reaching across the kitchen table, she takes my mother's hand and says, "I'll buy you the condoms, Mom."

My mother smiles and Chizo smiles back. Then my mother says she appreciates Chizo's concern—but she can buy her own condoms, thank you!

Chizo and I want to take a nap. My mother insists we sleep in her bedroom—for our whole visit. Chizo smiles; my face is drawn. I do not interpret my mother's invitation as a sign of reconciliation; rather I worry that she can now cite one more sacrifice made to accommodate her son and his African lover.

My cynical thoughts vanish when I collapse onto my mom's king-size bed. "The room is so big," Chizo says excitedly. She stands at a wall-length window looking out onto the man-made canal. Then she discovers the walk-in closets, which seem enormous to her. There are two of them; one remains clogged with my father's clothes. And there is an enormous bathroom with a large shower that can comfortably fit two adults.

Chizo undresses and goes into the shower. I follow her in. Afterward, we return to the bed. Within minutes, Chizo is asleep. I wriggle free from her, leave the bed and begin pacing the room. I'm glad the visit seems to be going well, but I worry that Chizo carries her concern for my mother too far. At times, I feel like crying out, "Enough already! You're being too nice to my mother. You're being too helpful."

I know I can't stop Chizo's charm offensive. She lavishes patience and respect on every senior she meets. My mom is only a particular beneficiary of her general outlook. "I am not like you whites, worshiping children and ignoring the people of olden times," Chizo says. "They like to talk. They want people to listen to them. I listen. You speak with two tongues about your mother. I speak with one."

As a child in Nigeria, Chizo learned to appreciate older people. For many years, she lived with her maternal grandmother in the university town of Owerri, which remains the intellectual heart of "Igboland," the section of southeast Nigeria that is dominated by her ethnic group. While she calls Owerri "a village near the bush," it is actually a medium-size city of a few hundred thousand people. Yet Owerri feels like an overgrown village and is more orderly, sane and forgiving than Port Harcourt, which serves as the hub of Nigeria's rich oil industry and is home to her parents. Chizo spent her earliest years in Port Harcourt, which has a population of at least one million people and counts among Africa's busiest and most expensive cities.

When Chizo was ten years old she went to visit her grandmother in Owerri and never returned to Port Harcourt. Grandma, her own children grown and gone, was lonely and little Chizo made her happy. She treated her like a princess, giving Chizo a very large room of her own in a spacious, clean house. Chizo shared the house only with Grandma and Grandpa, a quiet, dignified man who walked with the assistance of a mahogany cane. One of Chizo's earliest memories was making mischief: hiding Grandpa's long, dark walking stick, then enduring his playful taunts before returning it to him.

Grandma took care of both her husband and Chizo with an intensity that belied her own easygoing nature. Chizo finished high school and moved into young adulthood within the bosom of her grandmother's home. While Chizo's parents and siblings shared a small room on a dense and noisy Port Harcourt street, Chizo lived in a quiet, bucolic section of Owerri. A river ran near her house, and there were some thick woods nearby. She often wandered alone into the bush, gathered fruits and roots and swam in the river. In a Nigeria falling apart from misrule, Chizo's childhood seemed Eden-esque.

While Chizo sleeps, I wander through my father's closet, running my hands over his old clothes, hung neatly on two long rows as if awaiting his return. I select a blue jacket and am surprised that it fits. My father always seemed so much larger than me. I look at myself in the mirror and don't like the color.

I put the jacket back on the rack and I recall the only time my father met Chizo. It was a week or so after she came to America for the first time. Mike was in the hospital. He had a baroque history of heart problems and my mother kept close watch on his treatment. Chizo and I were making a quick swing through the Northeast. A professor at Johns Hopkins had asked me to visit, so we traveled across the country to Baltimore and then went by train to Brooklyn, stopping for a night before traveling to Long Island and my parents'.

When we entered the hospital room, my father looked weary, his once-silvery hair turned white and his good looks faded, though hardly absent. Stretched out in a hospital bed, hooked up to tubes and marooned in plain clothing, Mike still could muster some pizzazz. He greeted Chizo with a smile and a twinkle in his eye. He tended to charm women. In his heyday he wore flamboyant clothing and doused himself with strong colognes. Chizo instantly liked him. Even nearly dead, Dad exuded cool. He was mysterious. He preferred short, vapid, funny quips to anything truly revealing and coherent. He rarely disclosed his personal opinions on serious matters, or more precisely, he appeared to harbor no such opinions. He was aloof, which was part of his attractiveness. Of course, in his studied distance from others, he was typical of men of his generation. Born before the Depression and yet too young to serve in World War II, he was drafted into the army during the early 1950s and served in Germany as a medic. He mainly treated sexually transmitted diseases and ever after presented himself as an expert on the subject. Back in civilian life, he married my mother, became a salesman and stayed one for the rest of his life. Imagine a better-looking, carefree Willy Loman, and there is one version of my dad.

The afternoon they met, Chizo helped my father leave the hospital. In the corridor, on the way to the parking lot, she held on to his arm as if he were an ailing president of some obscure country. In the car, he insisted on driving, and he drove us home flawlessly. He specialized in long-distance driving: three thousand miles in four days, or Long Island to Florida in forty-eight hours. He could seem listless, even comatose behind the wheel, yet mobilize with alacrity at the first sign of road trouble. He took enormous pride in his driving and delighted in talking about automobiles. Except for his weakness for American-made cars, his judgments on car culture were unerring.

We spent a quiet couple of days together on Long Island, sitting around my parents' small house, saying little and eating much. Mike loved food, sometimes even more than people, and his Italian heritage—both his parents came from southern Italy, from the city of Bari on the Adriatic Sea—endowed him with a vast appetite for pasta, meatballs and other regional delicacies. Curiously, he never drank much wine and on this visit I shocked him by drinking large quantities of Chianti and Cabernet. He was accustomed to drinking cheap wines from screw-top bottles, so that when I bought corked wines, he acted as if I had gone overboard. My mom abstained, but Chizo joined us. In Africa, I'd introduced her to middling Spanish and French wines (all we could afford or obtain). While she much preferred the sweet West African variant of Guinness beer, by the time she moved to the United States she could consume a half bottle of red on her own.

Perhaps the wine helped ease the tension. My father and mother didn't plan to attend our wedding, which we would hold in San Francisco in a few weeks, but my father at least toasted us with a glass of wine at his lips. My mother, sober as always and firm in her unwillingness to travel to see me ("We don't fly!"), joined in with declarations on our behalf.

Alas, Chizo never saw my father again. In the summer of 2004, his long contest with heart disease came to a rapid end. To the shock of my mother, the insertion of a new, improved pacemaker undid his fragile health, dooming him. My mother was so distraught I thought the wisest course was for Chizo to remain in California while I flew to New York to be by his bedside. Chizo did not object. Though I felt her absence, especially at my father's small funeral, I also knew my mother appreciated my sacrifice in enduring the experience alone.

There was no doubt Chizo would face my mother again, somewhere. Seeing her now, asleep in my parents' bed, I suddenly feel elated. In my father's closet I spot his fine Western bolo ties hanging on a metal hook. There are maybe twenty of them, acquired on his cross-country road trips.

Out of the cluster, I select a half dozen bolos I like best. A brown boot with a stone in it. A heavy silver ornament studded with turquoise. A small black stone set in a silver base. A thin copper plate that depicts a bemused Indian dancing.

I carry them over to the bed and rouse Chizo. "Look at these," I say excitedly. I put the heavy silver one around my neck and tighten the leather strings, which feel rough on my hands.

"Wow," Chizo says, now wide awake. "You are photocopy of your father."

*   *   *

For dinner, my mother takes us to an "early-bird" special at the Golden Corral, an all-you-can-eat restaurant that serves hearty food at the level of a good, traditional diner. Turkey from the bone. Roast beef. Baked fish with an overdose of sauce. Various corn dishes and piles of corn bread. A medley of potatoes. Pizza, pasta and meatball lasagna. An ample salad bar that few visit. A mammoth dessert section with a dozen different pies and cakes, brownies, a wall of ice cream and such exotic desserts as peach cobbler and bread pudding.

The Golden Corral has room for about five hundred people and at peak times there are no empty seats. The place shares a parking lot with a Wal-Mart and there is a decidedly red-state feel to it. I am stocky, and yet I seem svelte at the Golden Corral. The customers are big. Chizo seems emaciated by comparison, like someone rescued from a famine.

When we enter, my mother silences me. "We're here for eating," she says. "No comments about the customers. Save your energy for eating."

Indeed, there is a deceptively complex process of negotiating the Golden Corral, which seems to have learned crowd control from the folks at Disneyland. Prices vary by time of day, though there is no limit to how long you can remain. The most vexing question involves the choice of a drink. The drink costs extra and Mom reflects mightily on which to choose. As a senior, she gets a discount on her own meal and on her drink. She insists that Chizo take her discounted drink and that she go without one in order, I suppose, to keep the bill under an imaginary ceiling she maintains for dinners of this type.

Mom gravely instructs us to follow her lead, suggesting she will levy a stiff penalty on anyone who interferes in her dealings with the cashier. She pays first and, because we're here at four-thirty, we get an extra discount.

"Nice," my mother says.

She insists on paying and she gives our drink order (two sodas; there's no alcohol here) to the cashier. While we wait for the cashier, who is an African-American, to calculate our bill, my mother introduces Chizo as a Nigerian married to her son. And then she introduces me.

Chizo and I are standing far enough away from the cashier that we simply wave in her direction and smile. The cashier waves back.

My mother moves on. After all, there is major eating to be done, in all the food groups. My mother has a strategy, and I have a strategy and we must get to work. My strategy, not that it matters, is to assemble three different dinners, in succession, and to make an honest attempt at eating each. First, I want a tray of turkey, corn, corn bread, roasted potatoes and a side dish of clam chowder. Next, I want baked halibut, mashed potatoes, green beans, a side of lentil soup and more corn bread. Then for the last round, I'll get chicken, pasta, ravioli and anything delicious on offer that I've missed on the first two rounds.

Chizo has never been to a place like this before, and on her first venture from the table—when I'm gathering my turkey dinner—she stumbles around, glassy-eyed, staring at the piles of food, hesitant, being elbowed aside by customers with a greater sense of purpose. I discover her, disoriented and woozy, in front of a bank of baked beans, sliced onions, french fries, hamburgers and chicken tenders. Her tray is empty, and she seems paralyzed.

I take her by the hand and return her to our table. I put down my tray of food and tell her to sit and relax. "I'll come back with burger and sides," I say. "Round one."

When I return with Chizo's meal, I find my mother talking excitedly to a waitress, another African-American woman. My mom seems to be telling her Chizo's life story and after a minute or so introduces me as Chizo's husband. The waitress greets me politely. She's in charge of bringing drinks to diners, so I tell her I want Diet Sprite and she nods. Mom keeps talking, though, describing how Chizo and I met.

The waitress appears to be listening intently, lingering at our table even at the risk of receiving a reprimand for ignoring her other customers. A light goes off in my mind. My mom is using Chizo to ingratiate herself with the black staff at the Golden Corral. She's not just some old Jewish lady from New York, some wrinkled snowbird who can be easily ignored. She's soulful. She's hip. She's so connected to black people she even has one in her own family.

I might be embarrassed for this thirty-something waitress, with a short Afro and a weary smile, except that I imagine her regular customers never take any interest in her. I am proud of my mom for treating this low-paid, routinely ignored black woman as an individual. My mom has a gift of making a stranger feel like the center of attention—as if somehow she and the stranger are discovering together a blinding truth about human existence through their chance encounter. I relax. I listen to their banter. I squeeze Chizo's hand.

"My mom is a big talker," I finally say to the waitress.

"She's very friendly," she says.

"I bet she's told you all about me."

"Yes. And about your beautiful wife too." She asks Chizo, "Were you really the surrogate mother of a chimpanzee? How interesting!"

The waitress smiles, then leaves.

I take a breath and ask Mom to please stop telling every black person she meets that her son is married to an African. "If you're not confessing this curious fact to white strangers, then you're not doing it for the right reason," I say.

I brace myself for a storm.

"There's nothing wrong with me saying it," Mom says. "You are married to an African. And black people are happy to hear it. Don't you think so, Chizo?"

"Yes, Mom. They are. You're right."

I glance at Chizo and frown. There's no way to win an argument with my mom when my wife is around. I try once more anyway.

"Mom, the black people are being polite."

"No, they aren't. They like hearing about Africa."

"Mom, they are so used to white people disrespecting them that they are relieved to be merely condescended to."

"You're wrong."

"I'd feel differently if you made the same confession to white strangers. You don't tell them your son is married to an African."

"I don't because they won't understand."

"You mean the whites would disapprove."

"Yes, that too."

When we leave the Golden Corral, we promise not to eat again until the next day. We waddle along a sidewalk that rims the parking lot. Chizo and I walk a few steps ahead of my mom. My arm is around Chizo's waist and, as we walk, I kiss her a few times. I notice my mother signaling for me to look behind her. I do, and I see two young white men bent over at the waist, pretending to vomit. Chizo keeps walking. When the men see me looking at them, they stop pretending to vomit and straighten up. I turn my back on them and catch up with Chizo. The white men veer off and she never notices them.

Inside the car, my mother grabs the wheel, starts the engine and leans toward me. "You see how they are down here," she says.

"Maybe those guys ate too much," I say.

"Come on. They were pretending to throw up at the sight of a white man and a black woman together."

"That's too sick to be true," I say.

Mom says nothing and pulls away from the parking lot. We drive back to her house in silence. Or rather I am silent. Chizo and my mom talk about food while I am lost in thought, wondering whether my mom is right. Maybe Florida is a kind of racial nuthouse. Living in Berkeley, Chizo and I are spared the sort of odd-ball scrutiny that would be normal in less sophisticated parts of America.

Back in the gated community, my mom rests, while Chizo and I go for a walk. We roam the neat sidewalks of the community, passing identical homes whose exteriors are ruled by a master plan that permits scant deviations. We visit the shuffleboard court, and I introduce Chizo to this unfamiliar game. She quickly displays a deft stroke and a talent for pushing my disk out of valuable slots. I once excelled at shuffleboard; no longer. I have lost my touch. With the zeal of a novice, Chizo wins three games straight. She wants to begin playing for money, five dollars a game. I promise to resume the competition tomorrow, hoping that the delay will cool her off and maybe I will win a game.

Chizo isn't ready to quit. She watches two people playing on the other court. They are obviously husband and wife and just as obviously old enough to live in the community. We watch them quietly. The woman is better than the man, maybe because she wants to be.

"Why doesn't your mother play?" Chizo asks.

"She plays bridge."

"What's that?"

"A game where you sit in a chair. My mother likes to be seated."

The man and woman shout at each other over every play. The woman wins in the end. They sit on a bench, across from us, laughing. Chizo asks the woman, "Would you like to play a game?"

The woman looks at me. "She's new to the game," I say. "You can probably beat her."

The woman is skeptical. Her husband says, "Go ahead. Play one game."

The women line up their disks. "You visiting?" the husband asks me.

"From California."

He wants to know who I am visiting. "No one you know," I say.

He glances in Chizo's direction.

"My wife," I tell him. "Her first time in Florida."

He nods. "She likes shuffleboard?"

"I'm not sure."

We watch the two women play. I root for Chizo, knowing how she likes to win at games. The man's wife is skillful, though, choosing to play second and then knocking away Chizo's best placements. The game comes down to the final round. Chizo has a chance to win and puts her final shot in the center of the ten-point triangle. The woman follows and knocks away her puck. The game ends in a draw.

"You'll get better with practice," the woman says.

The couple drives off. We stroll to the clubhouse, about a half mile away. There is a coffee shop and an auditorium large enough to showcase some aging talents who played the Catskills resorts fifty years ago. I show Chizo the workout room. We walk on adjacent treadmills, keeping a leisurely pace. A bank of TVs hangs from the ceiling, the audio on mute. An old man lifts free weights in one corner. An old woman rides a stationary bike.

I am too full to really exercise, and I end up watching CNN, reading the news scroll at the bottom of the screen. When the man and woman leave, we are alone. Chizo collects a couple of hand weights and pretends to shadowbox with them. I snap photos of her in pugilistic pose.

Next we visit the library, where I check e-mails on one of two computers. We end up poolside, stretched out on lounge chairs before an expanse of open water. Chizo removes her loose cotton overalls to reveal a bikini. She puts her hair into a bun, exposing her long, graceful neck. I remove my shirt and shoes, leaving me dressed only in a pair of swim trunks. The sun is bright and the weather is warm enough for a dip. We jump into the pool, holding hands as we leave the edge. We bounce off the bottom and Chizo splashes me. As a defensive measure, I wrap myself around her. I look at the old people sitting poolside. No one seems to care who we are or why we are here.

Night is falling when we return to Mom's house. She opens the door and says, "I'm on the phone with Shirley."

Shirley is her older sister. She lives up the street. Her husband is still alive, though he suffers from advanced Alzheimer's. We sit down at the kitchen table.

Mom tells Shirley, "They're back," and hangs up.

She brings out drinks, juice and diet soda, and joins us at the table. Chizo describes her newfound prowess at shuffleboard.

"She's gifted," I say. "A natural."

"We can't wait to play again," she says.

Mom is surprised how far we walked.

I want to visit Shirley before it gets too late. Chizo and I shower and change our clothes. We emerge from Mom's bedroom to find her holding in one hand a silver ring with a large turquoise stone. In the other hand, she holds a set of earrings: silver leaves studded with matching stones.

"Mike bought me these," Mom says. "I want Chizo to have them."

She hands Chizo the ring and then the earrings.

"Thank you, Mom," Chizo says. She removes her own earrings, replacing them with the silver leaves. Then she puts the ring on the ring finger of her right hand.

The ring fits. Perfectly.

Chapter Sixteen

On the Road

I'm advising Chizo, who never drove a car in Africa, on the best way to bring my Volvo 940 station wagon to a halt at a stop sign. "Come to a complete stop," I say. "Don't roll."

"I'm not rolling," she answers from behind the wheel.

"You are. You rolled through the stop sign."

"I didn't."

"Don't deny it. You'll lose points on your road test for failing to stop properly."

"Enough," Chizo shouts. "Enough."

She jerks the Volvo to the right, sending me sideways. She pulls along the curb, bringing the car to an abrupt halt. She shuts off the engine. We sit in darkness, saying nothing, alone with our frustrations. The dashboard clock nears 10:15. I now regret giving Chizo a late-night driving lesson.

Breaking the silence, I say, "I'm only trying to help."

She's heard those words before and glares at me across the front seat. "You are not a good teacher," she says.

I'm probably not, I confess. But what are our options?

"You could let me drive the way I want," she says.

"You don't get to choose the rules of the road," I say. "You follow the rules that exist."

"You Americans and your lousy rules," she sneers. "I'm tired of this American law, please."

I shake my head. Things aren't going well. Chizo has failed the road test twice before and tomorrow she is scheduled for her third attempt. We are, you might say, cramming for the test. The stakes are high. If she fails a third time, she loses her learner's permit and can't drive, even with me by her side, until she passes the written test all over again. And she passed the written test only after five attempts.

"Let's get moving," I say.

We must persevere; we are condemned to face driving together.

She pulls away from the curb and picks up speed. She turns onto Ashby Avenue, one of Berkeley's main streets. The speed limit is twenty-five. She pushes the Volvo above thirty-five.

"Slow down," I say. "Slow down."

"Shut up," she says and kicks the gas, pushing the car faster.

"You're done," I say. "Pull over now."

"I'm not driving fast. I'm safe."

"The speed limit is twenty-five," I say. "You go this far over the speed limit during your test and you'll fail."

"Stop saying I'll fail. Your words are juju against me. Like you're wishing me I fail."

"You're not ready for the test," I say. "Please delay."

She keeps speeding. I finally put my left hand on the wheel and she pushes it away.

I tell her again to slow down.

She won't.

"Pull over," I shout.

She hits the brake and jerks the car to the side of the road.

"Hand over the key," I say.

She turns off the engine, while I get out of the Volvo, step onto the sidewalk and stretch my arms and legs. I'm stiff from serving as her legally required passenger. I'm reaching toward the sky, gazing at the stars, when I hear the engine roar.

I see my Volvo pulling away from the curb.

I grab the nearest door handle as if trying to stop the car from moving.

"What are you doing?" I shout at Chizo through the window.

My Volvo is rolling down the street now and I am running alongside it. I expect Chizo to slow, once she sees me trotting. I even smile, pathetically, and wave.

She guns the engine.

I run faster, shouting louder, straining to keep pace.

Hopeless. I let go of the door and stumble forward, fearful I will fall flat in the middle of the road. Desperate to stay upright, I steady myself, then watch my Volvo roar off into the night. All at once, I feel confused, embarrassed and angry. I feel sorry for myself, then realize I might get hit by a car. I limp to the safety of the sidewalk.

Peering into the darkness, I imagine Chizo will stop for me on the other side of the next intersection. I look down the road and for an instant I see a woman beckoning me toward her. Then she is gone. I stare into the darkness, and I conclude I've seen a mirage. There is no one out there. My Volvo and my wife are gone.

Alone in the night, I curse loudly, wondering how I will get home. I can't believe she's abandoned me. I call her cell phone and she doesn't pick up. I try again and then a third time. No answer. I get her voice mail and leave a message. Then I start walking in the opposite direction, toward the South Berkeley BART station. I take a train two stops, get near enough to my house and then I walk the rest of the way.

When I arrive home, I find my Volvo parked in the driveway and Chizo in bed, listening to her favorite Igbo band, the Oriental Brothers, on an iPod.

I tell her I was mugged on the walk home from BART. Three young men stripped me of my wallet, slapped me across the head and knocked me to the ground.

"You lie," she says. "I don't see any bruises."

"Okay. I wasn't robbed. I twisted my ankle. I limped all the way home."

"You speak with two tongues."

"What? How could you leave me?"

"I don't like people who speak with two tongues."

She won't apologize and I pout. We are still not talking when, after undressing quietly, I slide into bed next to her. She kisses me and says, "I won't take the test tomorrow. I will cancel."

I pull her toward me and try to forget her road rage. She's more mature now. She's getting sensible. I smile at her and she smiles back. We kiss and make up.

She says she's sorry. I apologize too. Our warmth deludes me into thinking I can ask her for her key to the Volvo.

"I'm keeping the key," she says.

"Why?"

"I need it for driving."

I pull away from her and look confused.

"You heard me. I'm driving. Without you."

I remind her she'll be breaking the law.

"I'm not the only one who drive without no license," she says. "The only thing is to watch out and be careful. To watch out and be careful for the police people. And don't hit somebody. Because if you hit somebody that will be the worst."

I stare at the ceiling for a long time and finally ask, "For how long?"

"Until I pass the test," she says.

"That could take months. You'll drive for months without a license. What if you get into an accident? We could lose all our money in a lawsuit."

"I won't hit somebody."

"You'd better not."

She puts her head on my chest and I feel her dreadlocks on my skin. I love her smell and her beautiful skin and the warmth of her body. I decide that the experience of lying in bed with her provokes in me a kind of temporary insanity, which explains why I seem to agree that she can drive without a license.

"Stay off the freeways," I say sternly. "Obey traffic rules. Drive slower."

She kisses my cheek and draws me closer. "I'll learn more quickly, driving on my own," she says softly.

The next morning, after she makes me blueberry pancakes and coffee, and while I eat, she slips out the door. I realize after a few bites that she's gone. I rush out the front door—just in time to watch her back out of the driveway, stamp on the accelerator and send the Volvo into reverse. The car hops the curb and jackknifes, climbing the side of the steep hill across the street backward. The tires squeal, and the car comes to a halt at a precarious angle. I feel my eyes pop out of my head and I lose my breath. For a moment I fear the car will flip over and come crashing down—four thousand pounds of metal and glass hurtling in my direction.

Gravity and the laws of physics somehow combine to hold the Volvo in place. Seconds go by. Chizo looks into the rearview mirror. She lets go of the wheel and runs her fingers over her lips. Then she nonchalantly guides the vehicle down the slope and onto the street. There is a thud when the bottom of the Volvo bangs against the curb. Fortunately, no car was parked in her path, and no pedestrian happened to be strolling along the sidewalk.

Chizo throws up her hands, acknowledging her close call. Then she drives off—this time going forward and on the street.

I go back into the house and try to finish my breakfast. I've lost my appetite. I sit at my desk and try to write. I can't. The possibility of Chizo getting stopped by the cops blots out all other thoughts. I keep imagining her in handcuffs, and my Volvo loaded onto a police tow truck. I see her in the local jail. I close my computer. I can't concentrate. My fears run amok. I am like a smoldering flame.

When she returns later, I explode. "You must stop," I say. "Give me the key."

She refuses.

"It all your fault, anyway," she says.

"Not that again," I say wearily.

"You're to blame. You are."

I suppose I am. I persuaded Chizo not to pay a bribe in an

exchange for a supposedly valid license. At the shop where Chizo braided hair some days, one of the braiders and her husband swore that a rogue employee at the DMV was accepting bribes for licenses. No tests, no waiting. For five hundred dollars in cash, all her troubles would be over.

I refused to allow Chizo to do it.

For a week, she tried to convince me to pay the bribe. I kept reminding her of a promise we made to each other before we came to America. We promised never to break any laws to gain an advantage. I told her that, unlike in Africa, where playing by the rules carries an enormous handicap and actually seems to be insane, in America honesty is the best policy and people who play fair are rewarded.

Back in the house, still shaking over Chizo's unplanned reverse maneuver, I listen to her insist, "If you'd only let me pay a bribe, I'd have my license now."

"It wouldn't work," I say. "You were being scammed. I saved you from losing five hundred dollars."

I want Chizo to spend the money on a driving instructor instead. The trouble is that she refuses to be taught by any Asians, and it turns out that, in Northern California, Chinese and Vietnamese immigrants seem to dominate the ranks of driving instructors. She says she will get a non-Asian. I tell her that no school will let her choose an instructor by race or ethnicity. "I don't believe you," she says. "In America, customer is king."

One morning she calls a few driving schools and each time she asks the school to give her a teacher who is a white American or an African-American. No school will make that promise. "Don't you have any black or white teachers?" I overhear Chizo say.

As she speaks, I sit nearby, squirming. Then I tell Chizo that the school is right to hang up on her.

"You sound ridiculous," I say. "Worse, you are insulting people."

"You are *mugu*," Chizo replies, invoking a Nigerian term for the innocent target of a costly scam. "The Chinese are owners of your country. You let them invade and take everything. You are *mugu*."

Her accusations silence me. Stymied in her hunt for a teacher, she decides to stop looking over the phone. Instead she settles on an African driving instructor recommended by one of her fellow hair braiders. He is a man from West Africa who teaches driving on his own. He has a car and charges by the hour.

I meet him before Chizo's first lesson. His English is poor but his car is clean and outfitted with a set of controls on the passenger's side. He even has a business card and claims to carry special liability insurance. I shake his hand and gently request that he bring my wife back in one piece. He laughs. Chizo sets off with him and two hours later they return, cheerful. Over the next month, she receives many lessons from him.

One weekend I take her driving and ask her to perform certain basic operations. After a half hour I conclude that her African teacher shares some of her own appetite for cowboy driving tactics.

"He hasn't taught you a three-point turn," I say incredulously.

Chizo hasn't even heard of the maneuver. Her manner of making a left turn, meanwhile, is a good imitation of a driver on the way home after an evening in a bar. She says her teacher approves of her swooping, loopy turns. Her teacher also approves of her way of checking her rearview mirror. She does so, slyly, seemingly without effort—and giving the impression that she cares more about her personal appearance than about who else might be sharing the road with her. Indeed, her whole performance behind the wheel is so cool and easy that I suspect an experienced driving tester will consider her oblivious to potential hazards. When I advise her to watch out for the other guy—and to anticipate the driving mistakes of others—she chastises me for expecting the worst and insists that she gains power from positive thinking.

She sticks with her African teacher and, after another two lessons, he tells her to schedule a road test. He takes her to the DMV in his car and she fails. Another lesson and he declares she's ready to try again. This time she drives the Volvo with me to the test and, while I wait in the office, she gets confused at an intersection near our house and doesn't make a left turn, even though the arrow is green. The DMV evaluator halts her test. Her abrupt return to the office dashes my hopes.

"My test was canceled," she says glumly.

I now have an opening to campaign against her African teacher. I suspect he simply reinforces Chizo's tendency to consider road rules as a kind of scam that good drivers learn to avoid in favor of their own distinctive style. Driving, in short, is a new way for Chizo to express herself. In general, I admire Chizo's desire to do things her own way—whether in dressing or dancing or cooking or even climbing a flight of steps. But doing her own thing while driving makes proving to a stranger her knowledge of the basics more difficult, maybe even impossible.

Her frustration over her repeated failures, however understandable, is much less than my own.

After tossing me out of my Volvo, Chizo becomes a full-time outlaw driver, blowing me off, unconcerned with the risks of a bad outcome. I worry a lot about bad outcomes, while she worries less. Every day that she avoids capture by the police, or a collision with a law-abiding driver, emboldens her further.

She drives for weeks in outlaw mode. And by then I am so dispirited I meekly ask her one night whether she has proved her point. Might she at least take the test again?

"Why bother?" she says.

I wince. I shake. I begin to weep.

"Crocodile tears," she says and laughs in my face.

I stop crying and tell her she must cease and desist from driving. Immediately! I am the commander of the Volvo, after all. She holds the key in the air. I jump for it and she pulls it away.

She dangles the key in front of me again and once more I can't grab it.

Then the key vanishes into her pocket. "Don't you order me anymore," she says. "You're not giving me a driving test."

I surrender to her will. I know I am no match for her. Then one night, she comes home in a tizzy and excitedly tells me a story. A Berkeley cop car trailed her for a half hour. She turned, he turned. She stopped, he stopped. She changed lanes, he did. The slow-motion chase went on like this until she was a few blocks from our house. Then the cop moved on, and she parked the Volvo safely in the driveway.

"He was targeting me for ticket but could find no fault," she says, relishing her triumph.

I won't celebrate with her, and though I share her relief, her story stiffens my resolve. I decide enough is enough. I will stop the madness!

The next day, I call my mother in Florida. I ask her to visit me, begging her to break her no-flying rule. I explain that only Aretha Franklin and John Madden are famous enough to get away without flying. I have an emergency and my mother must fly to California at her earliest opportunity.

"What's the problem?" she asks.

"Can I tell you when you get here?"

My mother wants to know now. She fears an illness in the family. When I explain the situation, she laughs.

"Stop laughing," I snap. "Chizo's laughing already. I need to be serious."

Serious is easy for my mom. She switches gears and says, "Let me make sure I understand. You want me to ride along with Chizo so she's no longer driving without a license."

"That's right. She goes where you go, you go where she goes."

My mom agrees to fly out, help with my kids and ride along with Chizo. The two of them are an odd couple, but they go everywhere together: the mall, the grocery store, the braiding shop. I'm happy, though I know my happiness carries an expiration date: the date on my mother's return ticket to Fort Lauderdale.

On the night before she leaves, she asks Chizo for a favor.

"Anything, Mom."

"Get another driving instructor. A good one. Even an Asian one."

I earnestly maintain a straight face, while inside I quietly scream, "Hooray, Mom!"

Chizo tightens her face and I wonder whether she will make my mother ask again. I hold my breath and hope for the best.

"Okay, Mom. For you, I'll take a Chinese teacher."

My mother isn't finished. She confidently announces that, after her departure, Chizo won't drive alone anymore. "You'll get a new teacher and obey the law."

Chizo swallows hard. "I accept," she says.

Mom seals the deal with a handshake. Chizo, showing no signs of remorse, says we should celebrate. I scour my wine rack for a bottle of champagne, shove it in the freezer and an hour later we are toasting my mom, Chizo's new instructor and our brave new world of following the rules.

The day after my mom's departure, I arrange for the venerable Berkeley Driving School to send over its best available teacher. A week later, a small, wiry man from Sri Lanka arrives at our house. His name is Jay and he speaks with a clipped, hard South Asian accent that forces Chizo to listen closely. I realize I am in the hands of a professional when Jay hands Chizo a sheaf of papers that contain illustrated driving tips. They are essentially cartoon versions of driving basics that he's created with his own hand.

"My intellectual property," he says. "I am a top driving teacher. Ten years. Many successes. Many good results." Then he turns to Chizo and says, "Follow my teaching and you will pass your test."

I am impressed, even if Chizo is not (yet). I explain a bit of her curious approach to driving and Jay informs me calmly that my worries are over. "I am in charge now," he says and places Chizo behind the wheel of his Toyota Corolla. When she settles into the driving seat, she puts on a pair of stylish sunglasses that certainly don't improve her vision. Jay orders her to lose the sunglasses. She complies, ending a practice that her African teacher tolerated and I long complained about (fruitlessly).

They take off, Chizo peering through the window with her naked eyes. I feel relieved. I play a Brenda Fassie CD and dance alone in my living room. Two hours later, Jay returns with my wife. He is businesslike, crisp and optimistic. He confidently predicts that Chizo needs three more lessons before tackling the road test again.

Jay sticks to his plan. After his fourth lesson, he clears Chizo for takeoff. One Sunday morning I go out on the road with her in order to test his conclusion. Within a half hour I duly confirm the dramatic changes in her driving patterns. She's no longer speeding. Her turns are sharp and angular. She's more relaxed, alert to the other drivers and willing to display caution even at the expense of her personal "style points." She checks the mirrors about as often as a new driver should.

When Chizo pulls the Volvo back into our driveway, she asks me whether she is ready and I end my studied silence. "Line up the test," I say. "You are ready to pass."

Wordlessly, I thank Jay for working a miracle.

The next Friday, I join Chizo at the DMV office nearest our house. The vibes are good. She is assigned Ramon as a tester. That we know his name, and even have held earnest conversations with him, is a sign of our plight. Since the start of her campaign to obtain a license, Chizo has taken the written test a total of nine times and the road test a total of four times. In the new-driver section of this DMV office, Chizo is approaching legendary status. Her journey on the path toward legal driving now exceeds fifteen months. I know Ramon, a genial and well-spoken African-American man, because one time, after Chizo failed a road test and we argued in front of him, he actually took my side and patiently told Chizo to consider her husband an ally. "He's got a license and you don't," Ramon said. "He must know something about driving that you don't."

Flushed with good feelings about Ramon, I leave him alone with Chizo. He asks her to review the basic operations of the car and slides into the passenger's seat. I watch her drive away, out of the DMV parking lot and into the streets. I am in a state of high anxiety, and I cannot keep still. I pace outside the office, waiting for the verdict. In my mind, I replay some of the past disasters. The longer I wait, the more excited I become, even hopeful.

When I see Chizo return, I'm so excited I can barely keep myself from charging after the Volvo. She pulls into a space reserved for drivers finishing the road test. She and Ramon both exit the Volvo. I creep along the driver's side and actually hear Ramon declare, "You've done well but you could've done better."

My heart sinks. Then he says, "You passed!"

Chizo screams and hugs Ramon and won't let him go. She screams louder and longer and squeezes Ramon closer. He finally wriggles free from her and lets me shake his hand. Then he gives me his work sheet on her test. Incredibly, she earned a perfect score.

We follow Ramon into the DMV office and over to the new-driver section. He glances at a computer screen and realizes that tomorrow is Chizo's birthday. "Is this your best birthday present ever?" he asks.

She smiles and he hands her a form and sends us to a colleague at the next window.

A small friendly white woman, seated in a swivel chair, takes the form from Chizo and warmly congratulates her. "That's it, done deal," she says.

I ask the friendly woman how she knows my wife. "She's famous, honey," she says. "Isn't that why you married her!"

Chizo drives us back home, her temporary license safely in the glove compartment. Inside our house, I jog into my office and make a photocopy of the paper. Chizo calls my mother to give her the news. Then we hug and kiss. It is lunchtime now and Chizo decides to prepare pepper soup for herself. She stands outside in the sun, her Henckels cleaver in her right hand, and chops the hard, bony stockfish imported from her homeland. She fills a big pot of water, and pours in various spices, including the awful-smelling one that resembles dirt. Then she introduces pieces of chopped stockfish and cups of ground dried shrimp into the mix. She stirs the soup with a long spoon, rests, then goes outside in the sun, and then returns and stirs the pot some more. The smells of her pepper soup are fierce and I start coughing and then open doors and windows to clear the air.

Chizo laughs. Her smile makes me happy. I start to cry, only now appreciating that our long ordeal is over. She thanks me for sticking with her through all the fights we had over her distinctive manner of learning to drive. I set aside my painful memories and praise her for persevering, for ultimately listening to others, changing and growing.

"Step by step, my dream comes true," she says as if talking to herself. "Just be patient. There's nothing like patience."

At the risk of undercutting our joyous moment, I tell her she must drive carefully in her first days and weeks as a licensed operator of a motor vehicle. Then I add, "You should take one or two more lessons from Jay, maybe to get more comfortable driving on the freeway. And also, practice parking."

Hearing her teacher's name, Chizo leaves the task of soup making and grabs her cell phone. She finds Jay's number and calls him and thanks him. He says some words to her that I don't hear and then she replies with a phrase that makes me think she's somehow fashioned a new home in America. Drifting over to the cooking range, holding her phone in one hand and stirring her pepper soup again with her other hand, she now admires Sri Lankans—or at least one of them. "You are a champion," she tells Jay.

PART SEVEN

New York City
January 2007

*C*hizo is a mother.

Long before I met Chizo, when she was living in Owerri with her grandmother, she had a child. The father was a professional soccer player. Chizo wanted to marry him but Samuel, her father, refused to let her. He disapproved of the man's tribe and occupation. Samuel also was angry that Chizo had gotten so entangled with the man without first seeking his permission.

In a hospital, with her grandmother by her side, Chizo gave birth to a girl. She named her Happiness.

In Nigeria, aspirational first names are common. My favorite is Goodnews (which Nigerians spell as one word). Prosperity is another popular moniker; so is Sunday. Names that contain "God," especially as a prefix or suffix, are highly prized. Godwin and Godfrey are winners, for instance. Such names reflect the optimism of a positive people. According to respected international opinion polls, Nigerians are the most optimistic people on the planet by a wide margin. Even though when Chizo gave birth to her daughter she was young, jobless and dependent on her grandmother for housing, she felt only optimism about her newborn's future (and her own). Even though Nigeria in 1992, at the time of Happiness's arrival, was sliding into a dictatorship and misery was spreading, Chizo chose an optimistic name for her daughter without any sense of irony. She presumed her daughter would actually experience much happiness, "which is what we Nigerians are looking for," she said.

Leaving her child for stretches of time seemed normal to Chizo. Many mothers in West Africa, even those with husbands and prosperous lives, leave their children for long periods, often because they find work far away or simply because older female relatives are willing to look after younger children, allowing footloose mothers to realize their aspirations.

Chizo first left her daughter when Happiness was about three years old. Chizo went to Lagos, the largest city in Africa, to work in the grocery store of a family friend. She would visit Happiness every few months. When Happiness was about six years old, and just starting school, Chizo moved to Accra, Ghana, about a twenty-hour car ride from Lagos on a road that hugs the Atlantic.

When I first met Chizo in Accra, she told me about her daughter. I was happy she had a child because my vasectomy meant I could not father more kids. I was not shocked to learn that Chizo had not seen or spoken to her daughter for years. I accepted and sympathized with her situation. Travel was expensive anyway. There was no way to telephone her grandmother. Even sending her mail was difficult. No one had ever written a letter to her grandmother, for instance, and her house had no address; her street had no name.

About five months after I met Chizo—as Christmas 2001 approached— she traveled to Nigeria to see her daughter for the first time in a long time. In Owerri, she found her grandmother's house empty and dark. Neighbors told her that her grandmother was dead. Chizo was shocked. She cried and cried and cursed herself for failing to visit her grandmother sooner. She decided that God had punished her for vanishing for so long.

Without resting, Chizo boarded a bus for Port Harcourt and went to her parents' home. There she found her daughter. Samuel and Edith were happy to see her. They had assumed Chizo was dead. They celebrated her return, even slaughtering a goat in her honor. They thanked her for returning home and understood that her failure to call or write was entirely normal. They forgave her for missing her grandmother's funeral for the same reason. Chizo felt relieved and no longer cursed herself.

She stayed a month in Nigeria and then returned to Accra without her daughter. Her parents were glad to keep the girl. About six months later, Chizo and I got our house together. We set up a children's room, and Hap-

piness visited twice, once when my own children came to Accra for more than a month. The second time Happiness came with Edith. By the time of her second visit, I had applied for Chizo's visa to enter the United States. We agreed that Chizo should come to America first and get settled and that Happiness would join us later. In the meantime, she would live with Chizo's parents and, at our expense, she would attend a private school and have a daily tutor.

Because we wanted Happiness to live permanently with us in America, the U.S. government was a party in our plans. I became the girl's legal guardian and sponsored her visa application. Supposedly, my doing so made the wheels of government turn faster. After a complicated bureaucratic process, filled with confusion and frustration, my application was approved. An employee of the American government, posted in West Africa, stamped an entry visa into Happiness's passport a few days before Christmas 2006. She was good to go.

We gave Happiness a couple of weeks over the holidays to pack and say her good-byes. I arranged for her to take a long, direct flight from Accra to New York City. Accra was then the only city in the region from which she could fly directly to the United States. Because she was a child of fourteen who had never flown before, I felt she was too young and inexperienced to change planes in a European airport. We also chose Accra because our old friend and driver Stephen would bring her to the airport and ensure she actually got on the plane. I harbored a fear that Happiness might be kidnapped and I urged her to tell no one outside her family that her transit to America was assured. For that same reason she told only her closest family and friends of her impending departure.

When I called Stephen to explain that I had a delicate assignment for him, he was delighted to hear that, at long last, Happiness would join us in America. To make sure she reached her Delta flight on time, I asked Happiness to travel by road to Accra more than two full days before her scheduled air departure. She arrived on schedule. Stephen collected her at the main border crossing with Togo and drove her to his own home for safekeeping. She was not to leave his house; those were my instructions. He has two daughters of his own, and they were glad to have a new girl around.

On the morning of the flight, Stephen rose early to accompany Happiness to the airport. By special arrangement, he had received permission to move with her beyond the ticket area and to the final point of exit from Ghana—where immigration officials stood behind a row of kiosks and stamped the passports of people leaving their country. When a person stamped Happiness's passport and she officially left Ghana for the Delta boarding area, Stephen would telephone us. Because in California we are eight hours behind Accra time, we expected to hear from him around midnight.

His morning was our night.

Chapter Seventeen

The Pursuit of Happiness

Chizo sits by the cast-iron stove in our living room, warming herself, her flannel pajamas clinging to her body. I fiddle with a pile of CDs, removing a Coltrane disc and dropping it into the disc tray. The clock approaches 11:00 P.M. We must fly across country tomorrow morning, departing around dawn, but we cannot go to bed until we know that Happiness is flying to America.

We await a signal from our man in Accra.

Coltrane is midway through "Alabama" when my phone rings. I let it ring a second time and then the ring dies.

Chizo stands up, reacting to the signal from Stephen. I put Coltrane on pause. Chizo hands me a calling card. I dial an 800 number, type in the code on the card, then type in Stephen's cell phone number: first the country code for Ghana and then his personal number.

On the third ring, Stephen answers.

"Where is Happiness?" I say, not letting him speak. "Is she with you? Any problem with the ticket?"

"Good morning, G," says Stephen, ever the genial Fante.

"Good morning," I reply. "I'm grateful for your help."

I am more than grateful, in fact. I have actually hired Stephen to help with Happiness's departure. He's getting a nice payday for his services.

"I'm with Happiness," he says. She has her boarding pass, and she is early for her flight. He then explains that he must go beyond the call of duty in order to get her on the plane.

"The immigration officer won't let her pass to the boarding area," he says. "He won't stamp her passport."

"What!" I say and ask Stephen to repeat himself.

Stephen speaks English well, and he says, even more clearly this time, that the immigration officer refuses to let Happiness exit Ghana.

"He wants money," Stephen says.

"How much?"

"One hundred and fifty dollars."

"That's a lot."

"He wanted two hundred and fifty. I bargained him down."

Stephen has no time for explanations. He must leave Happiness standing at the immigration counter, rush into the city to gather more money and then return. He keeps a stash of cash in his house and must go and get it.

"The worst part," he says, "is that the government man is right. She is missing the stamp. When she passed into Ghana from Togo, she didn't get stamped. We searched her passport and the stamp is not there. He is imposing the fine on her."

I can't speak, I am so angry and worried. I feel helpless. Somehow words come out of my mouth and I ask Stephen angrily whether he has protested and Stephen says he has and that the government man is ignoring his complaints.

"He promises if I bring the money, he will let Happiness pass," Stephen says.

There's nothing for me to do except to trust Stephen. I ask him to remind Happiness to stay exactly where she is until he returns. "Tell her not to move," I say. He agrees.

I hang up and start screaming, "Those bastards, those bastards. She may miss her plane."

I tell Chizo the story, shouting the whole way. When I'm done, she stuns me by speculating that Stephen is concocting the entire drama as a way of getting more money from us.

I ponder the possibility, and the effort at least offers me a respite from screaming. "He could just ask me for more money," I say. "I would not deny him."

"Well, anyway," Chizo says, "Happiness will tell us what happened."

"That's if she gets on the plane."

"Be positive."

Chizo stabs the log in the stove with a poker. Smoke drifts toward her. I push a button on the CD player and Coltrane comes back. Her body stiffens.

"Don't wicked with me your jazz," she says.

I hit the pause button, go to my shelves of African music and select a Lagbaja album, *We Before Me.* Lagbaja is a Fela-inspired Afrobeat singing group whose songs are about the grim realities of life in Nigeria.

Chizo listens to the music, closing her eyes. I have nothing to say to her. I satisfy myself by shouting, and after a few minutes of shouting I feel spent and go silent. Against my outrage over the bribery demand is my own self-loathing over not anticipating the problem with the stamp. My fears of Happiness getting kidnapped have been realized after all, for the immigration officer is essentially holding the girl hostage, knowing that she must have a sponsor somewhere in America who surely will pay to gain her freedom. One hundred and fifty dollars is surely at least one month's salary for this officer. He must be delighted, I think, to have discovered such an easy path to a windfall.

Worse than the money of course is that Happiness may miss the plane. Delta doesn't fly again from Accra to New York for another few days, and the ticket is nonrefundable, putting another fifteen hundred dollars at risk. I pace back and forth nervously, then surrender to the rumbling beats of Lagbaja, momentarily distracted by the group's mesmerizing horn section and the song "Nothing for You," whose lyrics testify to how in Africa disappointment can loom around every seductive corner.

I resume screaming and Chizo tells me to relax. "We've been through worse," she says.

So true. There was the weird saga of the philandering English teacher at Happiness's private school. He carried on an intimate friendship with one of her classmates and, when exposed, at first received only a mild suspension. When the classmate admitted to having sexual relations with the teacher, he was fired. Only then did Happiness declare that the teacher had once tried to rape her too.

Overwhelmed by these memories, I collapse on the couch and suddenly feel that if we can only get Happiness out of Africa, these trials will seem insignificant, even humorous.

"If getting her out of Africa is this hard, is the worst yet to come?" I ask, laughing nervously.

My attempt at humor falls flat. No answer from Chizo. She faces the fire, and won't turn around to look at me. I slide off the couch onto the wood floor, groaning again. My brief moment of sanity has been chased away by my many fears. I worry that Happiness won't be ready for school and that, as a fourteen-year-old girl in urban America, she will suffer social problems. I fear her English won't be understood and she may be homesick for Africa. And that Chizo, who has not seen Happiness for three years and two months, will not even recognize her daughter, much less bond with her. I wonder how my own children—my son two years older and my daughter a year younger than Happiness—will welcome her. Perhaps most shamefully of all, I worry about the loss of intimacy between Chizo and me. Or rather more selfishly, I fear I no longer will be the center of her attention. As much as I look forward with some pride to reuniting mother and child, I also expect that the reunion will carry an emotional price that neither Chizo nor I appreciates.

I sit down next to Chizo and our hands intertwine. I feel her hair on my face. Her closeness calms me and I shut my eyes and listen to her breathing. I lose track of time. A loud ringing stirs me from a kind of sleep and, dreamily, I try to answer my phone. Too late, the ringing stops. I missed the call. My awareness returns and I think of Stephen. I dial his number and he answers.

"She's onboard," he says. "She flies in minutes. I'll stay until the plane leaves the ground."

"Oh, Stephen," I say, then can't find any more words. Handing the phone to Chizo, I go to bed. I close my eyes and feel awake. When Chizo joins me, she reminds me to shut off my cell phone. She does the same. We have only cell phones in the house and when they are switched off, she says, "No more disturbances."

The next morning is a race. We must catch an early flight from Oakland to New York. We drive about twenty minutes in the dark and arrive at the airport well before sunrise. We park in a lot outside the airport, take a van to terminal one and then join a short line. We check in. Boarding passes in hand, we pause and I telephone Stephen. I retrieve the phone card from my wallet, punch in the long list of numbers and he answers. It is night in Ghana now and he is home and happy that I am pleased with him. I promise to send him money (a larger amount now) in a few days, when I finish with the business of collecting Happiness. He wishes me well and I hang up. Then, carrying only small bags, Chizo and I pass through security and board a nonstop JetBlue flight to JFK in New York. The flight leaves thirty minutes late. I fret over the delay. Chizo has her own concerns: How much bigger is her daughter now? What will her braids look like? Will she be happy or sad? Skinny or heavy?

Our aim is to arrive before the Delta flight winging Happiness to New York. We reach JFK a few minutes behind schedule. Alarmed, we speed-walk onto a shuttle that brings us from the domestic to the international terminal. Now that we are on the move, our excitement is mixed with anxiety. Is Happiness standing around somewhere, bereft? Has the Delta stewardess, who is supposed to remain with her through the entire entry process—

immigration, baggage claim and even the customs clearance—abandoned Happiness? Is the girl even now talking to a strange American and unwittingly risking harm? These are not my questions alone. Chizo is nearly jumping out of her skin, striding step by step with me.

When we arrive at the place where international passengers pass through customs with their luggage, we are relieved. The Delta plane from Ghana is still in the air, minutes from touchdown, according to the overhead monitor.

The Africans, milling around, murmur among themselves. Clusters of older men and women pace the linoleum floor. A few children wander to and fro. Chizo takes an open seat in a corner near a window, while I search for an electrical outlet. My cell phone is nearly out of juice and, aware that Delta may call me with news of Happiness, I want my phone to stay on. I find an outlet down a long hallway, behind a small kiosk. I kneel, duck behind the kiosk and feel against the wall, inserting the plug. Standing near my charging phone, I strain to see Chizo. I feel strange alone and I want to join her.

I leave the phone, tucked safely behind the kiosk, and I find Chizo talking with a man from Ghana. His daughters and a son are on the plane. The son is older than our Happiness and his daughters are younger. The man lives in Brooklyn and his children are coming to live in America. He doesn't say whether they are making their first visit and I don't want to interject any questions and make him self-conscious. I am glad merely to bond with him in a small way. His presence calms me because I realize someone else is going through the same experience as I am. I am elated to learn of other children on the plane. There's strength in numbers. They may have met Happiness and drawn succor from one another. I tell the man that Chizo and I met in Accra, and his face comes alive. He smiles and tells me, his face falling, that he actually hasn't been in Ghana for many years.

I don't ask why and dash away in order to visit my phone. I grab it and check the screen. No missed calls. Good. I let the charging go on and saunter back to Chizo. She's joking with a man from Ghana, and his laughter relaxes me. He isn't worried about his children getting held up by immigration officials. That's my biggest fear: some bureaucrat may object to her papers or simply refuse her entry on a whim. No laws protect Happiness on the other side of the border, only once she's here. When I tell the man from Ghana about my nightmare scenario, he looks mystified. "You're in America," he reminds me. "The government treats people fairly. Workers follow rules. No one will bother your daughter for no reason."

Chizo agrees. "Rules here wicked me small, but Americans are fair," she says.

The man says he wishes Africa could embrace the American way of fairness. "Even American time," he says. "We are too slow in Africa and the big men do whatever they want, no matter who suffers."

"Macho men," Chizo says.

"I'm glad to be gone. Ghana is no place for my children to grow up."

"There's no fun in America, though. Only work."

"My son will study hard, get a good job here."

"He can always visit Ghana."

"And stay in my house in Accra," he says. "No hotels for my kids."

I listen to their back-and-forth in amazement. Maybe I know too much about my own government, which seems increasingly incompetent, irrelevant and even dangerous to its citizens. Yet competence is relative. To these Africans, the U.S. government seems like a model of fairness and effectiveness. And their faith in the potential for hardworking people to ascend the ladder of American wealth and status seems naïve, but who can argue against the power of such a belief? Immigrants! I shake my head and then remember I must visit my phone.

I find the phone where I left it. There is one bar on the battery life now, and I unplug the phone, pocket the charger and race back to Chizo. The plane has landed, and now the drama—if there will be any—should begin. I imagine Happiness leaving the plane with her escort and waiting in the special line for new immigrants. Technically, she's not visiting the United States but rather "naturalizing," so her entry today is the first stage in a rather well-defined process of gaining her "green card," or permanent residency. She should be carrying, in addition to her passport, a fat envelope, stuffed with official papers. I reminded her and Stephen, again and again, to make sure she kept these papers on her person, and not checked with her luggage. Chizo, meanwhile, coached her on answering simple questions that an immigration officer might ask: What is your full name? Where will you live in America? What is your date of birth?

It is dark outside now, past six in the evening. I'm tired and yet our long day seems only on the verge of beginning. Members of the Delta flight crew stroll past. Then some of the passengers, and then more of them and more and more. I expect Happiness to be among the last. I notice the Ghanaian stands now, his eyes searching the entrance for more arrivals. He edges toward the other end of the hall, moving in small circles, then holding position, moving again, gradually growing closer to the opening until he seems to be greeting the arriving passengers.

Chizo remains in her seat. I wave to her. The Ghanaian's kids are here. She rushes over to me and watches the children surround him, the son nearly as tall as the father and the two girls keeping a respectful distance, their hair neatly braided, African cotton wrapped tightly around their backsides. The father moves and the children follow and then they are gone.

I drift toward the entrance. Chizo hangs behind, cool, still in her seat. I look back and she is not looking at me. I can't make eye contact with her. I accept that we each will greet her daughter in our way. Separating seems fine now. In the end, Chizo and I have our own realities, we are alone together and nothing in this long-awaited rendezvous will narrow the gulf between us.

I edge closer to the entrance, straining to see the last of the arriving passengers, the stragglers, the people from the end of the line, men and women exhausted from a long trip and yet enlivened by taking their first steps on American soil. As I watch them, I fear that Happiness's arrival may highlight my differences with Chizo more than bring us together.

In another time, in another place, I might feel melancholy over my conclusion, but not here, not now, not as I stand on the edge of one chapter in my life and at the outset of another. I turn back and see Chizo still seated, distant. Once more, our eyes do not meet. I let my gaze linger and I know even more clearly than before that Chizo wants to experience the reunion with her daughter in her own way.

I turn and stare at the entrance. Nothing. Then suddenly I see her, fresh braids swinging on her shoulders, shiny brown beads stitched into her hair extensions. Next to her is a smart-looking Delta escort, a young white woman walking close to a bedraggled teenager dressed in black sports shoes with blushing red laces, blue jeans and a black jacket.

Happiness does not see me, and I rush toward her, calling her name. She turns and sees me, her mouth open wide. The Delta woman looks surprised to see a white man and one who is crying. I say nothing and suddenly feel Chizo right behind me, literally breathing on the back of my thick neck, and the escort recognizes us now, yes we are the people meeting Happiness, we are present and accounted for, so her job is done. Then Chizo and I thank the escort in unison. She peels away, leaving Happiness with us, looking astonished, openmouthed and weary.

Chizo grabs her daughter and holds her close.

I step back, giving them space, and Chizo says, "You're here at last. Thank God." She slips a thick purple coat around her daughter's shoulders and sets the furry hood around her hair. Happiness's coat—actually Chizo's own first winter coat—hangs open at her waist. She struggles with the zipper, and Chizo takes over, finishing the job. Then outside we go—into the cold New York night.

Chapter Eighteen

Avenue H

The Q subway line runs all the way through Brooklyn, passing the Flatbush neighborhood where I was born. The line ends at Coney Island, home to Nathan's hot dogs, a venerable amusement park and the Brooklyn Cyclones minor league baseball team.

We slept at my friend's house last night. This morning we go to Manhattan. Near Times Square, I visit the office of one editor and then lunch with an editor at *The New York Times.* Before these meetings, I stand inside the official team store of the New York Yankees, where Chizo, Happiness and I are finding refuge from the cold. When I depart, I remind Chizo that, while I'm away, she must stay close to her daughter. "Walk behind her," I insist and rather emphatically, because in Africa a respectful child will often walk well behind a parent. In New York a trailing child could vanish before his or her parent turns around to register the untimely disappearance.

"What is the need?" Chizo replies.

"Can't you follow my advice on trust?" I say. "Keep Happiness in front of you. Hold on to her. Take her arm in yours. You don't want to lose her on her first day—and especially not in New York."

Chizo makes a face that suggests I am unjustifiably cautious. Lose her kid? "You are nut," she says. I repeat myself. Maybe she isn't hearing me. She is tired from yesterday's long plane flight, and she had a poor night's sleep on a convertible couch in my friend's house. Wearily, she delivers a bemused look, as if losing her daughter is the longest of long shots, the most improbable scenario in a universe of improbabilities.

I smile and then emit a rumbling belly laugh. My satisfaction over helping to engineer this mother-and-child reunion has me a tad delirious. Bucking the odds, I offer my advice once more and, when Chizo again says nothing, I tell her I must leave now for my meetings and demand that she repeat my advice about Happiness.

"I'll tell her to stay in front of me," she finally says.

I leave and after lunch return to the Yankees store at a preset time of fifteen minutes past two o'clock. From the store entrance, I see Chizo and Happiness drifting through the section devoted to replica uniforms. I stroll over and wonder whether I should buy a Derek Jeter jersey. When I get near Chizo, though, I forget about the jersey and kiss her cold cheek. "So far so good," I whisper.

Happiness wants to know what baseball is. "A game," I say. The answer satisfies her. She shows me a photograph of her and Chizo, surrounded by life-size fantasy characters. The photo, which bears the date, January 17, in bold letters, was taken in a toy store a few blocks away. The two of them are seated at opposite ends of a colorful wagon, about as far away from each other as possible. Each wears a startled expression as if they are strangers who are only just realizing that a photographer has taken their picture together— and now he wants to make them pay for it.

"Souvenir," Chizo says. "Ten dollars."

Happiness slides the photo, which is wedged into a colorful cardboard frame, into her backpack.

I check my watch. We must go. Chizo helps zip up Happiness and then she arranges her clothes, draping a scarf around her neck and jiggling her earmuffs.

Outside, the sun is bright and there is a chill in the air. Chizo and Happiness shiver and hunch their shoulders. I want to get these frozen Africans underground. There is no time to waste. My eyes search the street corners as we walk along Forty-second Street. I identify an entrance to the Q line heading downtown. We descend a stairway, follow signs and position ourselves on a platform in between two train lines.

In a few minutes, we board a local train, which will stop at every station along the way to Coney Island.

We spread out in the car. It is midafternoon, a weekday, and the car is not yet filled with commuters. Aside from a couple of old women, we are alone. Chizo and Happiness sit across from me, still cloaked in hats, scarves and heavy coats. We have at least thirty minutes on the Q line, maybe longer. I savor the time to myself, listening to Miles Davis on my iPod and thinking about Brooklyn, which I've come to enjoy so much because of its vast ethnic and racial diversity, its unpretentious revival and the surprising ease with which one can move from one neighborhood to another.

Collecting Happiness has come off without hitch. The meetings with my editors went well. Chizo is glowing with love and contentment, despite the cold and the time pressure. I regret the brevity of our visit. I wish we could visit Coney Island, where we would eat Nathan's fried crabs, brave the wintry weather to ride a historic Ferris wheel and stroll along the beach. Instead we must obey the JetBlue schedule. Before going to JFK, we have to return to a large, rambling three-story house in Flatbush, where a close friend of mine lives a short walk from the Newkirk station. We left our luggage there. After a brief rest, we will be joined by a driver from a car service that runs out of an office in the shopping arcade above the subway station. The driver will take us to JFK for forty dollars. Then we fly directly to California, where Happiness's new life will really begin. New York is only prelude, a small opening into the vast mystery that awaits Happiness, Chizo and me.

Brooklyn tugs on me nonetheless. I spent the first two years of my life near here—too short to form definite ties, of course, but because of my parents, Brooklyn shaped me. Both of them were born and raised in Brooklyn, and they carried the lessons of life in the borough wherever they went. Returning here to collect Chizo's daughter seems no coincidence but rather part of the arc of my own life. Suddenly feeling self-possessed, as if realizing my life has a logic of its own after all, I marvel at how I am recapitulating my entire history in a single visit to Brooklyn. My parents took me out of Brooklyn when I was two years old in order to escape the changing complexion of the borough—in particular the growing presence of African-Americans, who in the 1950s and 1960s began to dominate many neighborhoods that were once home mainly to white ethnics. My parents fled to a colorless suburb on the south shore of Long Island. They had more children (I am the oldest), and the entire family came to Brooklyn only to visit my grandmother, who for many years continued to live in a small apartment in Flatbush. When she died, we stopped going to Brooklyn altogether.

This visit feels totally different from any other. I am here for the first time with my African wife—and her daughter straight from the motherland. As we move through one of the most polyglot places on the planet, I feel like we are a transatlantic rainbow coalition—and that I have somehow repudiated the sins of my father. My parents abandoned Brooklyn in pursuit of whiter neighbors; now in my maturity I am part of a project to construct a very different kind of African-American family. In my own variety of racial reconciliation, I emphasize the African in African-American. My parents ran from black people; I run toward them. Might I be settling old scores today on the Q line? Might I be ending this story back at the beginning?

I don't claim to know for sure. Even reconsidering my words makes them seem to fade and vanish. There are no certainties in marriage, across racial and geographic lines or within them. What I know is that my heart has its own logic, and my heart belongs to Chizo. I used to ask myself why I fell in love with Chizo and the reasons always eluded me. Chizo says she first fell in love with the gap between my front teeth and then God told her that her love for me was good and so she kept loving me. That's her story and she's sticking to it. I love the way Chizo moves, how she talks, the touch of her skin and the lines of her neck. I love how she finds surprise and merriment in the most unexpected situations. I adore her quiet dignity. In repose, she stands as a beacon of class and self-possession in a world of confusion and contradiction. Her unquenchable thirst for living in the moment balances my own peculiar obsession with the past and future.

I cherish our laughter together. I remember often a line I read somewhere about the wisdom of sticking with the lover who makes you laugh. "You are funny and I am sexy," Chizo told me once. And then when I repeated her words, she said no, "I am funny and you are sexy."

I no longer wonder why we ended up together and how we persevered. My own marriage is a mystery to me, beyond my mere reason to comprehend. How does the bosom of another person become home? How did I reach the point where my most private longing is to die in Chizo's arms? I have even come to believe that a higher power—call him God as Chizo does—protects and sustains our marriage.

I hear the rumble of the Q train and look across the car and see Chizo and her daughter in repose, the flickering light running across their faces. Hurtling toward Coney Island, I actually don't know where Chizo and I are going. In the end, we have only this moment in time. Gazing at my beloved, I abide in the moment. I forget about my parents' dubious decision to leave Brooklyn and what might have been had they stayed. I forget about the trivial coincidence of bringing Happiness to Brooklyn for her first encounter with America. With the slightest alteration in airline schedules, her first steps might have come in Atlanta or Washington, D.C., cities where I have no personal history. I forget about the riddle of my romance with Chizo, the never-ending mystery of our engagement. I forget about race and religion, the secular and the divine. I gaze at Chizo and blow her a kiss.

She is looking at Happiness and doesn't see me.

"I'm sending my love vibes your way," I shout.

My love vibes arrive. She hears my voice and grabs at the air, collecting piles and piles of my love. Then she waves her arms and shouts, "Here come mine!"

I grab the air and press my hands against my chest. I close my eyes, put away my iPod and enjoy the waves of contentment running through my mind and body.

For a long time I have no thoughts. Joy envelops me. I feel warm all over. Then I hear the screech of the train coming to a grinding halt. I open my eyes and look to see where we are. The sign on the platform says "Cortelyou Road." We must get off at the next stop, Newkirk Avenue.

I tell Chizo, "Next stop. We get off."

When the train slows in advance of the next stop, I rise and move across the car to the door. The Newkirk station was built one hundred years before and sits aboveground on a surface stretch of the Q line. The door opens and I turn and see that Chizo and Happiness remain seated. "This is our stop," I shout and go through the door.

Chizo leaps to her feet and races through the door. She's so quick she's on my heels even as I step onto the platform. I turn and smile. She smiles back. Our love vibes are shooting back and forth between us.

The door on the subway car closes and the finality of the thud alarms me. "Where's Happiness?" I shout.

She is still seated on the train. I can see her face through the window. Our eyes meet for an instant.

Chizo sees her too and hurls herself at the car. She tries to pry open the door with her hands. The door won't come open and the train starts to move. She pulls harder and the door stubbornly remains stuck. She is yelling now and the train is moving faster. She is moving too, her fingers trying to grasp the rubber seam in the door. She tries to work her fingers into the seam but she cannot. The seam won't come open even a fraction of an inch. And the train goes faster now, gaining speed with every instant. Chizo stumbles and cries and then staggers forward, the train racing away, leaving her behind and taking Happiness somewhere far away.

Chizo turns and chases the train, running full speed ahead on the platform. In this part of Brooklyn, the track runs aboveground and the next station is dimly visible in the distance. Chizo runs to the end of the platform and I pursue her, though trailing a good

distance behind. Even in the best of times Chizo outruns me easily. Now I am unprepared for a race and run too slowly. I am frightened that she will jump off the platform and onto the track and
keep running. The image of her running on the track and maybe
getting hit by a speeding train fills me with dread.

Hearing my screams, Chizo stays at the edge of the platform. I
plead for her to wait. The train is long gone now. What's the point
of her running after it?

She backs away from the edge, turns in my direction, her face
terror-stricken.

"We have no time to waste," I shout. "Hurry! Follow me."

I start running back to the center of the platform and ask
myself, What's the drill when you lose a child on the New York
City subway?

Simple.

Find a cop.

Chizo catches up to me. I grab her by the hand and we rush up
a stairway, frightened and holding hands even though I slow her
down. We ascend two flights of steps and emerge into the main
lobby of the station. As if by divine intervention, two police officers are standing there, ready for action. I stare at the officers, a
black woman and a white man, making sure they are not a mirage.
Then I approach them and extravagantly announce that we have
lost a teenage girl on the Q line heading toward Coney Island.

"The girl just arrived in America yesterday from West Africa," I
say. "She's wearing a cap with a red pom-pom." I explain how we left
the train and the girl didn't follow. "She doesn't live in New York,"
I say. "I'm not even sure she knows what part of America she's in. She
has no one to call, and doesn't even know our cell phone numbers."

"I'm her mother," Chizo says. "I am to blame."

I expect the officers to treat us like two delinquent parents,
shake their heads in disgust and send us away to our miserable fate.

Instead the white officer shrugs. "This happens all the time,"
he says. The woman cop is already on her radio, calling the next
station, reporting a missing kid, mentioning the red pom-pom.

"Hold the girl there," she says. Then she turns to Chizo. "Her name?"

"Happiness," Chizo says.

"Is that her name?"

"Yes. Happiness."

The woman grins. "Let's hope she's lucky too."

Out of nowhere, a third cop appears and says he's going to the next station and that we should come with him.

"I'm so sorry," Chizo says.

The woman cop says, "They know at Avenue H to hold on to your daughter. That's if she gets off. . . ."

Her voice breaks off. Her concern is my fear. What if Happiness stays on the train, goes all the way to Coney Island and then gets off? Sooner or later we will find her, but by the time we do who knows what might have happened to her? And then there is the nuisance and expense of having missed our plane and gone practically mad with worry.

No time to fret or thank the first two cops. The third cop is leaving, and we must follow him down to the trains. Chizo reaches him first. He peers in one direction, looking for signs of the next train. She settles alongside him and is telling him something when I approach. "My husband told me to stay close to her," she says. "I didn't listen."

We wait for the next train. I can't stand still. Chizo looks absently in the direction of Avenue H, the next stop. The cop is on the radio, telling someone he's on his way. Then he tells us, "People lose kids all the time."

Like this? I want to tell the officer that we spent more than a year getting this girl out of Africa. We spent countless hours discussing her future and making arrangements for her arrival. We even prepared painstakingly for our reunion in New York. Now in less than twenty-four hours we have lost the girl in the most embarrassing manner. I bet the other parents who lose kids at least have held on to them longer than we did.

The cop keeps talking, trying to calm us. "At this time of day, there are two officers at every station," he says. "Since 9/11, the subways are actually the safest place in the city. If you have to lose a kid, this is the place to do it."

The cop winks at me.

I feel stupid and wonder why the cop is nice, why he is trying to make us feel better. I take Chizo's hand and draw her toward me. "Do you feel lucky?" I ask her.

We hear the rumble of a train in the distance and shuffle our feet in anticipation. The train screeches to a halt.

She's there. Bundled up in Chizo's winter coat, the scarf around her neck and the dark wool cap with the red pom-pom. Inside the Avenue H station, a young black woman is with her and a police officer. I remember the woman from the train. She sat near us. The cop is smiling.

Happiness looks relieved. "Good job getting off at the next stop," I say. "You're smart."

Chizo holds her tight and speaks Igbo to her. I thank the young woman for helping her off the train.

The cops move on, and the woman leaves.

Chizo and I are alone with Happiness. Mother and daughter are still speaking Igbo. I wonder what to do next.

In another time, in another place, we might celebrate our second reunion with Happiness in as many days by going to Coney Island, devouring Nathan's finest, walking the beach and peering out across the endless horizon trying to glimpse the shores of West Africa so very far away and yet so near.

But we must hurry to catch a plane.

We must go to the other side of the tracks and wait for a train in the other direction.

American time rules us.

We get into position, and I call the airport driver. He is parked in front of my friend's house, impatient, wondering why we are late.

"Wait for us," I say. "We are coming."

Acknowledgments

Chizo inspired me to write this book, and I'm grateful for her patience and determination, her sense of humor and her energy. Even when I feared I might never finish, she exuded hope and optimism. She sustained me.

Thanks to Chizo's parents for bringing her into the world and for loving their daughter from a distance. Thanks to all the members of her family, especially her aunt Ngozi and her late aunt Patience.

Thanks to our friends in Accra, Ghana, especially Stephen Kobina, Mark Davies, Kofi Coomson, Remel Moore, Daniel Morris, Guido Sohne, Chichi and Bala, Constance, Julia, Eric Osakwan, and Jimmy.

Thanks to Mary and her sister Adele, Fatou and the other indomitable hair braiders in the African Tradition shop in Berkeley, California. Thanks to Ken, Robert Mbama, Father Ray, Sister Franca, Comfort and all the African immigrants who welcomed Chizo in America. Special thanks to Regina; to Peter Hubbard, Chizo's first English teacher; to Honorah Curran; and to Tom Higgins, the dear friend who married us.

Thanks to Liam, Oona and Happiness. Our marriage is inconceivable without these three mysterious teenagers.

The task of writing fell to me alone, and the shortcomings of this book are solely mine. Credit an extraordinary editor, Lisa Drew, for this book's merits. Lisa embraced me as a writer and taught me much about telling stories from my own experience. She steadfastly supported me, sharing her wealth of experiences and sending me in one fruitful direction after another. I am forever in her debt. My only regret is that Lisa claims to have retired as an editor. May she stage a comeback—starting with my next book!

My literary agents, Jane Dystel and Miriam Goderich, deserve special thanks. Without their tireless advocacy and patient guidance, I would have written this book, but no one would ever have gotten to read it. They were indispensable, every step of the way.

I'm also grateful to Corey Dubin, Alex Gronke, Harry Gruenert, Jane Harris, Betsy Laganis, Wendy Lustbader, Paul Maritz, John Markoff, Eric Tosky and Mark Zusman. I thank Ellen Moore for her gift of the title.

My mother endured with equanimity and cheerfulness the prospect of being one of my characters. She did not read a word of the book in advance. Chizo and I are grateful for her support.

Some months after I decided to write this book, my father died. Michael Zachary told stories endlessly and combined a madcap sense of humor with some strange notions about the world and his place in it. He lives on inside me—and in the photos of him that Chizo has hung up around our house.

About the Author

G. PASCAL ZACHARY is a writer, author and teacher. He consults on African affairs for foundations and is a former foreign correspondent for *The Wall Street Journal.* He teaches reporting and writing at Stanford University, publishes widely on African affairs and is the author of *The Diversity Advantage: Multicultural Identity in the New World Economy.* He met Chizo Okon in Accra, Ghana, in 2001, and two years later they were married in San Francisco.